THE SOONERS

A Story of Oklahoma Football

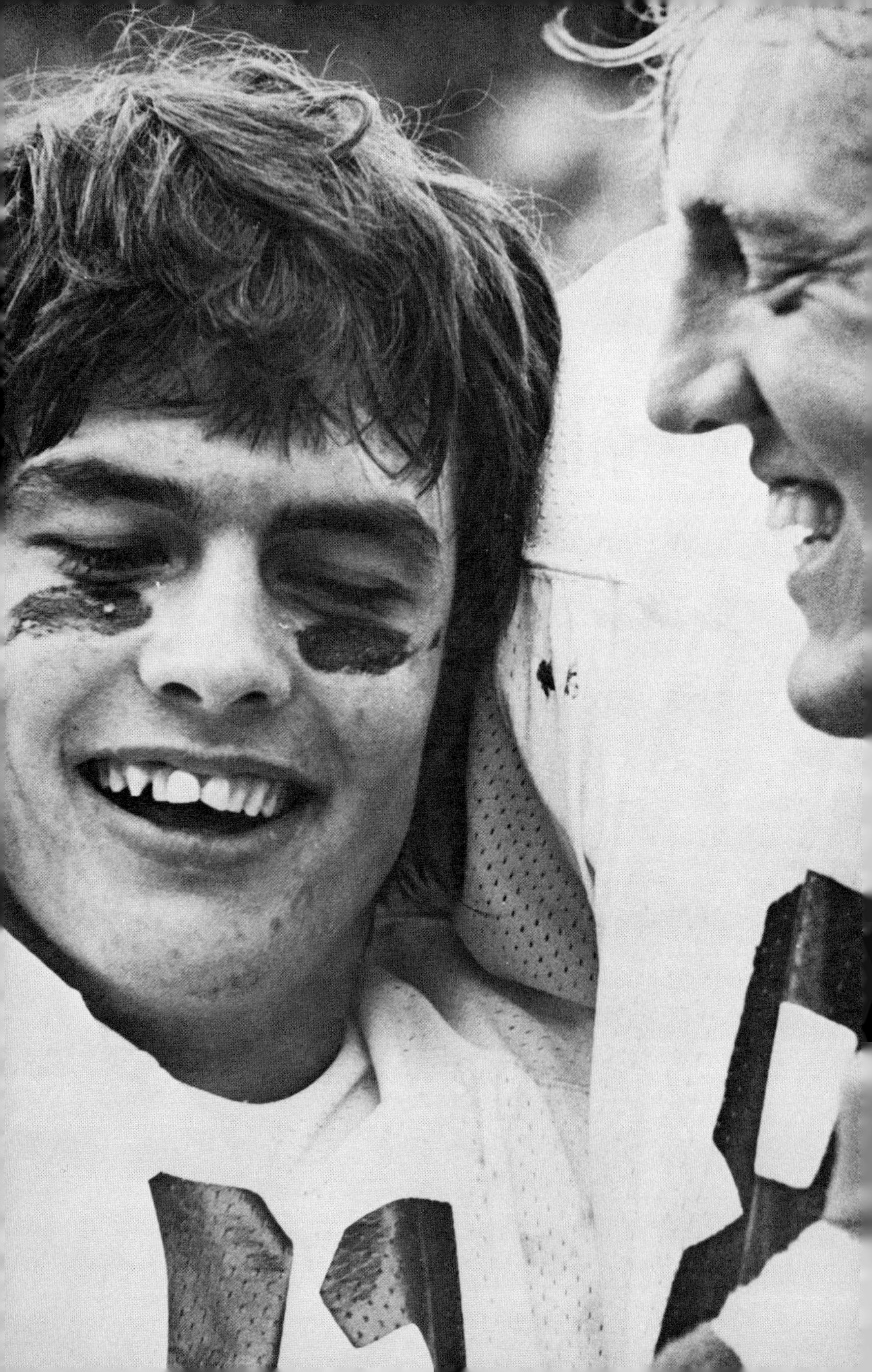

THE SOONERS

A Story of Oklahoma Football

by
Jim Weeks

THE STRODE PUBLISHERS
HUNTSVILLE, ALABAMA 35802

Photographs Courtesy Of The University
Of Oklahoma Sports Information Department
And Tom Blevins Of The *Norman Transcript.*

Contents

Foreword

I am proud of the football tradition at the University of Oklahoma and grateful for my opportunity to continue this great heritage.

We who have been closely associated with football at OU do not have to be reminded of its successes, immortal players, challenging opponents, and exciting games because we live with these aspects day to day. We frequently are reminded of the funny stories, sad stories, and inspiring stories that have become a part of our lives.

This book will help you share all of these experiences with us. That is why I'm so enthusiastic about this book. I trust it will help you feel the same as I do: That OU football is the best in the nation. And I hope that when you read it, you will enjoy it as much as I did.

Barry Switzer
Head Football Coach
University of Oklahoma

To My Daughter Debbie
The Most Loyal OU Football Fan I Know

Future Big Reds

It appeared to be one of those ordinary sunny but cold December days in the small eastern Oklahoma community of Eufaula.

Actually, it was far from an ordinary day. It was the day the townspeople of Eufaula were honoring one of their own as only a community of 4,000 can. They had a parade, speeches, and awards, and just about everyone in the town was there to honor a college football player.

Among the participants in the parade were two youngsters in oversized, red and white football uniforms and heavy helmets. They proudly carried a banner that said: "Future Ironheads and Big Reds."

The word "Oklahoma" may mean many things to many people.

It may mean cowboys and Indians and cattle drives and land runs.

It may mean Will Rogers, the cowboy philosopher of the 1930s; or Sequoyah, the Cherokee Indian historian of the early 1800s; or even Mickey Mantle of more recent fame as a baseball star for the New York Yankees.

It may mean the popular musical by Oscar Hammerstein and Richard Rodgers.

It may mean the dust bowl or red clay buffeted by never failing winds, raked by tornadoes, yet yielding vast reserves of oil.

It may mean sparkling lakes and green, wooded hills.

And to millions of people it also may mean football at the University of Oklahoma.

This is a story of that aspect of Oklahoma's history. Actually it is the story of youngsters who carry banners and dream of being Sooner football players and of some of the men who help them realize that ambition.

Football Comes To The Territory

John A. Harts had no way of knowing what he had started at the University of Oklahoma in the fall of 1895. The 20-year-old Harts came to the new university on the prairie in Oklahoma Territory to study and teach some classes. He had played some on the football team at Winfield College in Kansas and arrived with the idea of starting a team at the new university.

There is evidence that there may have been a form of intramural football played at Oklahoma the two preceding years. It was organized, if that is the word, by Edwin DeBarr, a professor of chemistry and physics and one of the university's four original faculty members. DeBarr had played halfback while attending the University of Michigan.

One day in September of 1895 at Bud Risinger's barber shop on the north side of Norman's Main Street, Harts brought up the idea of forming a university team. He became its captain and coach.

The university had only 148 students at the time, and 121 of them were taking high school preparatory work. Harts recruited some friends and likely candidates and introduced them to the new American game of football.

The members of that first team at Oklahoma were John P. Evans of Pond Creek, Bert Long of Norman, Horace Simmons of Fort Sill, Ed Barrow of the Chickasha Nation, Fred Bean of Oklahoma City, ·Bernard Reuter of Fort Reno, Newt Medlock of Noble, Bert Dunn of Lexington, and Will Short, Japer

Clapham, and Joe Merkle. They made their own uniforms.

The idea of having a university team quickly became a popular one on the campus. May Overstreet, the only woman faculty member, and students Ray Hume and Ruth House were named to a committee to decide on the school colors. They selected crimson and cream, the official colors today.

The only game of that first season was scheduled against a team from Oklahoma City. The visiting team included players from the Oklahoma City high school and a Methodist college. The game was played on a makeshift field just northwest of where Holmberg Hall presently is located on the university campus.

Unfortunately, Harts, Oklahoma's only experienced player, suffered a knee injury before the game. But he recruited Risinger and Fred Perry, who had played some football at the University of Kansas six years earlier, although neither was enrolled as a student.

It made little difference. The Oklahoma City team not only won, 34-0, but did not allow the university team a first down. The game also was much rougher than the inexperienced university players had expected, and the Oklahoma City team loaned OU some of its substitutes late in the contest.

It was the only game that OU scheduled that year. But the University of Oklahoma had its first football team 25 years after the game was started in the United States, five years after the opening of the university, and 12 years before Oklahoma was admitted as a state.

Harts left at the end of the school term to prospect in the Arctic, never knowing that he had started football at a college that would hold a unique place in the history of the game in this country.

Second Fiddle To Oratory

The game of football continued to progress in caliber and popularity at the University of Oklahoma in the next nine years. During that period Oklahoma had four coaches bringing varying experiences to the development of the university team.

Although John A. Harts, who promoted and coached the first Oklahoma team, had left, the university played two games in 1896 but with no designated coach. OU won both games against Norman High School.

Oklahoma's football program got a boost in 1897 when Vernon Parrington was hired to head the newly formed English department. Parrington had played football at Emporia College in Kansas and was a substitute at Harvard University, one of the early powers in the college game in the United States.

Parrington's teams employed the Harvard style of play with cross blocking in the line and had big linemen and small backs. Columbus C. "Lum" Roberts of Medford was captain of all four Oklahoma teams coached by Parrington. No other Oklahoma player has ever achieved such an honor.

In 1897 each player was responsible for his own home-made uniform. Leather cleats were nailed to the shoes. And some players were even ahead of their time. Many allowed their hair to grow longer than the style of the day in hopes of protecting their heads.

Oklahoma played only two games each during the 1897 and 1898 seasons and won all four. The university avenged its first loss in a football game by defeating Oklahoma City, 16-0,

Vernon L. Parrington, OU coach from 1897 through 1900.

in 1897 in Parrington's first game as coach.

Also in 1897 Oklahoma played its first game against another college team, meeting Kingfisher College at Guthrie, then the capital of the territory. Oklahoma's team took the train from Norman to Guthrie and that prompted a discussion between the conductor and brakeman, who were undecided as to what type of team they were transporting. In his book, *Oklahoma Kickoff,* Harold Keith reports that the conductor concluded:

"If they look like they will fight at the drop of a hat, they are football players. If they look like they will run at the drop of a hat, they are baseball players. These are football players."

Actually the game, which also was the first away from the Norman campus, received less publicity at the time than the Territorial Intercollegiate Oratorical Contest in Guthrie. This despite the fact that the game between Oklahoma and Kingfisher was interrupted during the second half by the sheriff of Logan County. The sheriff had never seen a football game and mistook the activity for a drunken brawl. However he allowed the game to continue after college officials explained what was happening.

The games in 1898 provided two firsts in Oklahoma football. Oklahoma played the town team of Arkansas City, Kansas, in the first game outside Oklahoma Territory. And Oklahoma met Fort Worth University in its first game against another university team on the Norman campus.

The schedule was increased to three games in 1899 with OU's first meeting with the University of Arkansas. In the final game of that season Oklahoma bowed to the Arkansas City town team, 17-11, its first loss in seven games with Parrington as coach.

Oklahoma probably had the best player of this very early era in 1899. Fred Roberts, a stocky, strong, and fast youngster from Mayfield, Kansas, was a rugged tackler and elusive runner. In fact Roberts was such an outstanding player that he was recruited by Washburn College of Topeka, Kansas, for the 1900 season. Oklahoma was not actively involved in recruiting yet.

Oklahoma played its first game against the University of Texas in the opening contest of the 1900 season. Texas had been playing football for two years longer than Oklahoma and won the game at Austin, Texas, 28-2. But Oklahoma recovered to win three of its four remaining games and tie Kingfisher College, 0-0, in the other contest that season.

Parrington, assigned additional academic duties in 1901, asked to be relieved of his duties as football coach. So Roberts was hired as player-coach for the 1901 season.

Oklahoma opened the 1901 season against Texas again and lost, 12-6, at Austin. To help finance the trip Oklahoma met

Baylor University at Waco, Texas, two days later and won its first meeting with the Bears, 17-0.

Roberts brought a much-needed new concept to Oklahoma football in 1901. More students were encouraged to participate in the game, giving the squad a full second team and improved practices.

Oklahoma won its next two games, then bowed to Texas, 11-0, in a rematch at Norman. But the latter showed that playing a team of prestige gained attention and could make money.

Following the season Roberts resigned as coach to spend full time on his farm. However Oklahoma officials hoped to lure Roberts back into coaching once the season was underway and left the position open.

The university played its first three games of 1902 without a coach. The third game was against the Dallas Athletic Club of Texas, made up of former college players working for the Texas and Pacific Railroad, and marked Oklahoma's first appearance at the Texas State Fair.

Oklahoma lost the game, 11-6, and decided to hire one of the players from the Dallas team as the OU coach. So Mark McMahan, captain and tackle on the 1901 team of the University of Texas, became Oklahoma's fourth football coach.

McMahan was hired for $250 for the season and on the promise that he would provide some trick plays to what had been a power-oriented Oklahoma attack. Later in the season Oklahoma did score on its first possession on a trick play in its first game against the University of Missouri but lost, 22-5.

McMahan expanded the schedule, playing nine games in 1902 and twelve in 1903. Five games had been the maximum for Oklahoma teams until then. McMahan also recruited players and practiced with the team. Perhaps he was best known for his rough manner.

The 1903 season was an eventful one for Oklahoma football. The university tied Texas, 6-6, the first time Oklahoma had not lost to the Longhorns in five tries. And Oklahoma played its first game against Texas A&M, winning, 6-0.

Oklahoma also met the University of Kansas for the first time during the 1903 season. McMahan was sold on training, not even allowing his players to drink coffee. However two of

Oklahoma's players convinced the coach to allow them to drink coffee instead of the usual milk served at the meal the evening before the game at Lawrence, Kansas. They were the only two players who did not become ill that night. Oddly enough Oklahoma would face a similar incident 56 years later.

Oklahoma lost that 1903 game against Kansas, 17-5, with its only points coming on an 18-yard field goal by Dan Short. It was the first field goal in OU history.

The university also met Bethany College of Lindsborg, Kansas, in 1903. Oklahoma bowed, 12-10, against a team that enployed such new maneuvers as cutbacks, an unbalanced line, and a direct pass to the quarterback. The coach of that team was Bennie Owen who later would play a much more significant role in the history of football at the University of Oklahoma.

The university hired 22-year-old Fred "Buck" Ewing as its football coach in 1904. Ewing had been a tackle and captain of the Knox College team in Galesburg, Illinois, that had beaten

Mark McMahan, OU coach in 1902 and 1903.

such Midwestern powers as the University of Notre Dame, Northwestern University, and Kansas, and lost by only one touchdown each to the University of Nebraska and the University of Chicago, coached by the legendary Amos Alonzo Stagg. So it was not surprising that Ewing was disappointed in his Oklahoma team, which he compared to the second team at Knox College.

But Ewing did bring some new ideas to the territorial university. As coach he did not participate in practice or games. And he used only students who were scholastically eligible.

The 1904 season had two significant games.

Oklahoma met Oklahoma A&M for the first time in history at Guthrie, the territorial capital that was approximately halfway between the two schools. Oklahoma won the game 75-0, but the contest probably is best remembered for what remains the most unusual play in OU's football history. On the fourth play of the game the Aggies' B. O. Callahan punted from the Oklahoma A&M end zone. He had to rush the kick, and the ball went almost straight up. Boosted by a strong wind on the chilly day, the ball went behind Callahan and bounced beyond the playing field.

In those days a loose ball off the playing field could be recovered by either team. So when the ball bounced into Cottonwood Creek, rimmed on the banks by ice, it was followed by players from both teams.

Oklahoma A&M's Baird was the first to reach the creek and attempted to retrieve the ball with a stick. But Oklahoma's T. Becker Matthews knocked Baird into the chilling water of the creek. Oklahoma's Ed Cook finally recovered the ball, returned to the bank, and touched the ball to the ground for a touchdown. The teams played the remainder of the first half in their water-soaked uniforms but exchanged garb with substitutes for the second half.

In its final game of the 1904 season Oklahoma lost to Bethany, 36-9, thus calling more attention to the coaching skills of Bennie Owen who had beaten the university the year before. Following the season Ewing resigned to return to the University of Chicago medical school. Thus the door was opened to one of the great eras in the history of football at the University of Oklahoma.

Owen For Oklahoma

When he came to the University of Oklahoma as its head football coach in 1905, 30-year-old Benjamin Gilbert Owen had all the characteristics necessary for success. Bennie Owen had an impressive background as a player, had proved himself as a coach, and had the ability to gain the respect and support of his players.

Owen was OU's football coach for 22 years, adding a stability that Oklahoma football had not had to that time. And his teams established Oklahoma as one of the powers in this section of the nation. He made major contributions to Oklahoma's athletic programs before he resigned as athletic director in 1935.

Owen had been the quarterback of the only University of Kansas team coached by the famed Fielding H. "Hurry Up" Yost. He led the Jayhawks of 1899 to a 10-0 record. Next he had coached at Washburn College in Topeka, Kansas, and then went to the University of Michigan as an assistant coach of Yost in 1901. That Wolverine team won all 11 of its games and out-scored its opponents, 550-0.

But Owen attracted Oklahoma's attention as the coach of the "Terrible Swedes" of Bethany College in Lindsborg, Kansas. Owen's teams at Bethany had a 22-2-2 record that included those defeats of Oklahoma in 1903 and 1904.

Owen was the first exponent of fast, wide-open play in the Missouri Valley area. And his teams were the first in this section of the nation to adopt the direct snap from center to a back four or five yards behind the line. His teams also used the forward pass much more than perhaps any team of its era.

From Yost, Owen learned to teach the quarterback kick, a play on which the quarterback would place a kick over the unsuspecting defense in hopes his pre-warned backs could recover the ball for a gain. It served as the forward pass of early football. He also emphasized sportsmanship and off-the-field manners. Because of this, he was credited with attempting to change the image of frontier Oklahoma from a rough, uncultured territory.

Coach Owen had an unusual way of establishing his authority, often laughing at any player who opposed him and leaving it to the other players to straighten out the situation.

Owen made one of his contributions to football at Oklahoma even before the opening of the 1905 season. He helped lay out OU's new football field, Boyd Field, and track and baseball fields in the same area. The grandstand accommodated 500 spectators. Boyd Field was located on land now west of the present OU Field House and where the University Press building is on the main campus.

Owen's first team at OU was an immediate success. The 1905 team won seven of nine games.

In the second game of the 1905 season Oklahoma met the famed Haskell College Indians of Lawrence, Kansas. Haskell had beaten Kansas and Missouri each of the previous four years, had defeated Nebraska in 1904, and had beaten Texas, 17-0, a few days before the 1905 game at Norman.

Oklahoma had never beaten Kansas, Missouri, or Texas, and Nebraska was too much of a football power to even consider scheduling an unknown such as OU. In a game marred by several fights Clarence Reeds of Norman, a substitute who played in only the final three minutes, scored a touchdown on a 15-yard run for Oklahoma's 18-12 victory over Haskell.

The next week Oklahoma was brought back to earth when it suffered a 34-0 loss to Kansas, Owen's alma mater. But then, playing its fourth game in two weeks, Oklahoma surprised Texas, 2-0, in a game played in Oklahoma City in the university's first triumph over the Longhorns in eight tries. Oklahoma center Bob Severin of Guthrie tackled Texas' halfback and captain Don Robinson in the end zone in the final minute for the safety that provided the winning margin.

In the same year Arthur M. Adlen, a student of history and physiology whose father was a jeweler in Norman, wrote the lyrics for "Boomer Sooner," using the tune of Yale's "Boola, Boola." "Boomer Sooner" remains an OU fight song today.

Owen was not richly compensated financially for the success of his team that first season at Oklahoma. The OU Athletic Association, which had hired Owen, still owed portions of the salaries promised McMahan and Ewing, the two preceding coaches. So for the first three years that he was OU's football coach, Owen accepted IOU's from the athletic association and operated a restaurant in Arkansas City, Kansas, in the offseason.

Reeds, Geyer, And Victories

In 1906 some major changes were made in the college game of football, primarily because of the public outcry that the game was too brutal. Changes in the rules eliminated many of the brawling aspects of the game, limited the design of formations, and put more emphasis on eligibility rules.

The year of 1907 was significant for the State of Oklahoma, Coach Bennie Owen, and the University of Oklahoma. Oklahoma was admitted as a state into the United States of America. Owen lost his right arm as a result of a hunting accident. And the first governor of the state, Charles N. Haskell, discharged the OU president, David Ross Boyd, and several other faculty in an effort to exert more political control at the state institution.

But the state, Owen, and the university survived. And surviving also has been the nickname Sooners, which too began officially in 1908. Until then OU's football team had no official nickname although it had been known as the Rough Riders and Boomers.

The OU nickname was a carryover from the name Sooners that originated during the earlier land runs in various territories that soon would become Oklahoma. Those Sooners who pre-dated OU were individuals who entered the territories and made claims before the designated starting time. Individuals who entered the territories and made claims before the designated periods were clearly entitled to the Sooner nickname.

Bennie Owen was OU coach from 1905 through 1926.

In fact Owen himself had taken part in a run from Kansas into the Cherokee Outlet, but at 17 years old he was not old enough to legally claim any land.

Owen's 1911 Oklahoma team won each of its eight games and was the Sooners' first unbeaten, untied squad since 1898 when OU played only two games. Characteristic of most of Owen's teams, it was boosted by the speed and quickness of its players and allowed its opponents a total of only 15 points, a record that stands today for an OU team playing as many as eight games.

The 1911 team opened the season with a 104-0 triumph over Kingfisher College. But it made its real mark of the campaign by defeating Missouri, 14-6, at Columbia, Missouri, for Oklahoma's first victory ever over the Tigers. However Missouri won only two games that season, suffering its first losing season in seven years.

Oklahoma also scored its first triumph over Kansas, winning, 3-0, at Lawrence, Kansas. It was one of only two losses for the Jayhawks, although they also had two ties. Hubert Ambrister of Norman kicked a field goal in the first three minutes for the winning points.

Those early victories over Missouri and Kansas also were significant because the two schools then decided to play Oklahoma on a home-and-home basis.

Oklahoma ended the 1911 season with a 6-3 victory over Texas at Austin, Texas, handing the Longhorns one of only two losses in seven games that season. OU captain Fred Capshaw of Norman scored a touchdown to bring the Sooners from behind in the first half, and the second half was scoreless.

One of the outstanding players on the all-victorious 1911 team was sophomore fullback Claude Reeds of Norman. Many historians of Oklahoma football rank Reeds among OU's all-time great players.

Reeds, the last of four brothers to play for the Sooners, attended the university preparatory school instead of Norman High and was well versed in the fundamentals of football when he entered OU. He was known as a superb blocker, vicious tackler, excellent punter, and for his running skills into the line and in open field.

Accounts differ as to the exact distance, but Reeds is

credited with a punt of 107 yards against Texas in 1910. Some of his other feats were passing 75 yards to tackle Billie Clark of Comanche for a touchdown against Nebraska in 1912 and scoring the winning touchdown to defeat Colorado's previously unbeaten Rocky Mountain champions of 1913 in his final collegiate game.

Some consider Reeds to be Oklahoma's first all-America selection, although he was not named on the most accepted all-America team of his day named by the famed Walter Camp. But at that time, Camp, known as "the Dean of American sports," had little appreciation for the college game outside the East. During the four years of Reeds' college career, 1910 through 1913, Camp's team honored only seven players outside the eastern United States.

Reeds was selected on the *Outing* magazine honor roll of college players in 1913. He was one of six fullbacks on the honor roll, thus the claim by some that he was an all-America selection. He was inducted into the National Football Hall of Fame in 1961, being the first former OU player to receive that honor.

In 1912 Owen decided to use the forward pass more in the Oklahoma offense. The forward pass had been originated in 1906 by Coach Eddie Cochems of St. Louis University in St. Louis, Missouri. Reeds was a fine passer, but his substitute at fullback in his final two seasons would become the most famous passer in the early days of Oklahoma football. Forest Park Geyer of Norman was nicknamed "Spot" because of his passing accuracy. And Geyer played a key role in the undefeated 1915 season.

Geyer's skills at throwing the football had been ably demonstrated earlier. When OU met Missouri at Columbia, Missouri, in 1913, Reeds was not allowed to play. Missouri Valley Conference teams did not allow their opponents to use players who had completed three seasons, and Reeds was in his fourth year. So Geyer, then an inexperienced sophomore, was substituted for Reeds at fullback, and Neil Johnson of Norman replaced Ambrister at quarterback for the same reason.

Neither Geyer nor Johnson had played in such a significant game. Missouri won, 20-17, but not before Geyer nearly led Oklahoma to what would have been a stunning upset.

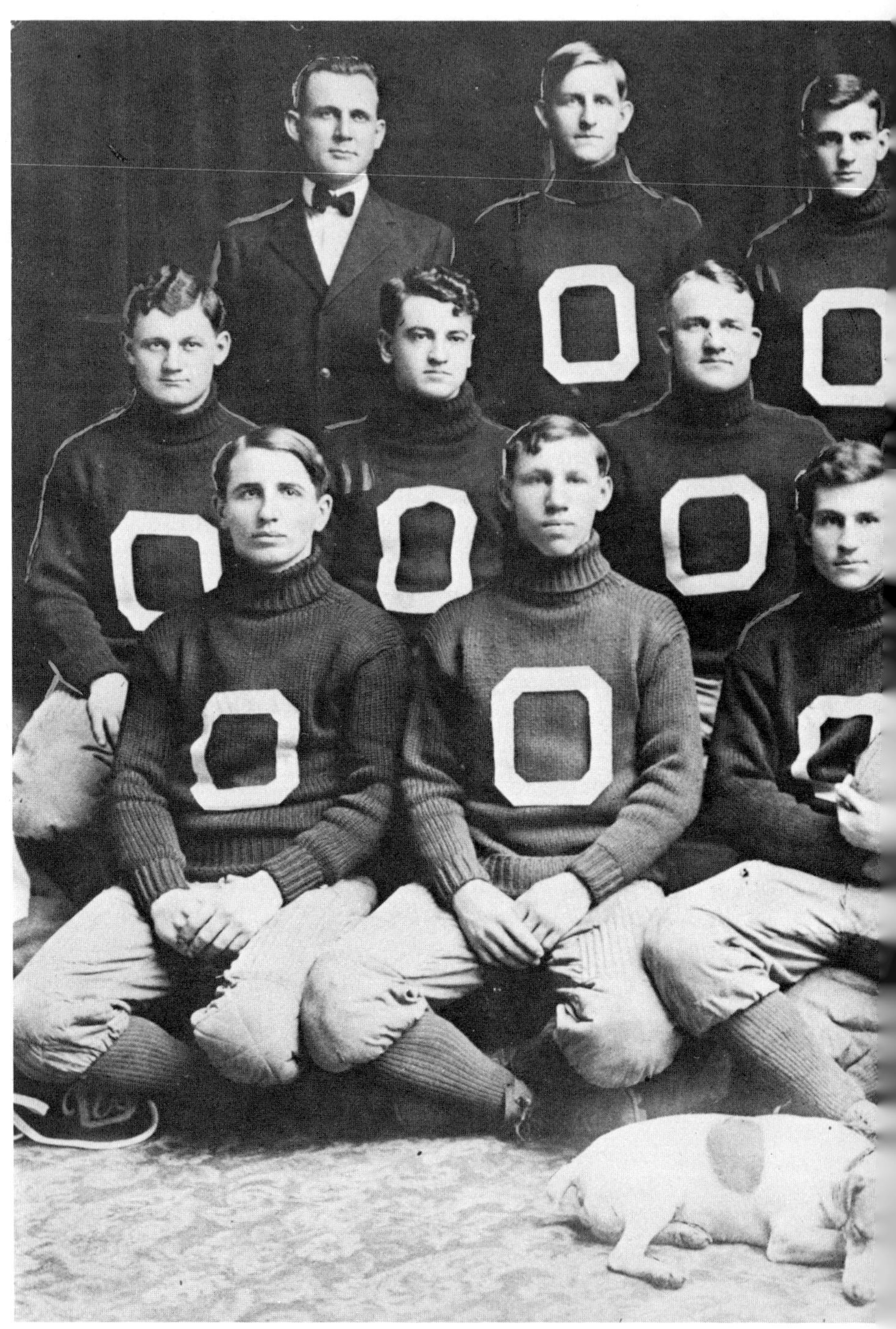

*OU All-Victorious Team
Of 1911*
Front row, left to right: Sabert
Hott, Ray Courtright, Captain
Fred Capshaw, Henry Weedn,
Hubert Ambrister. Second
row: Glenn Clark, Charles
"Chuck" Rogers, William B.
Moss, Roger Berry, James
Nairn. Back row: Manager
Cleve Thompson, Roy Spears,
Claude Reeds, Edgar Meach-
am, and Coach Bennie Owen.

Claude Reeds, OU fullback from 1910 through 1913.

Missouri posted a 7-1 record and shared the championship in the powerful Missouri Valley Conference in 1913.

In 1915 Oklahoma became a member of the Southwest Conference which included Oklahoma A&M College, the University of Texas, Texas A&M, the University of Arkansas, Baylor University, and Southwestern University of Georgetown, Texas.

Oklahoma had been offered a game against Northwestern University at Evanston, Illinois, but the Big Nine Conference school wanted an immediate confirmation and Oklahoma still was trying to arrange its conference schedule. So the game with

Northwestern was not scheduled.

After three lopsided victories over state colleges in 1915, Oklahoma established itself as a power with a 24-0 triumph over Missouri. The Sooners, primarily Geyer, completed 16 of 33 passes for 260 yards that day.

The next week Oklahoma faced Texas in a Southwest Conference game at the Texas State Fair in Dallas, Texas. The contest was attended by 11,000 fans, reportedly the largest crowd to see a football game in Texas to that time.

The Sooners came from behind to win with Geyer passing for 140 yards in the final quarter. Geyer passed to Montford "Hap" Johnson of Norman for a touchdown, tying the score at 13-13. In those days the extra point was attempted from the spot on the goal line at which the touchdown was scored. Geyer kicked the conversion from an extreme right angle for a 14-13 triumph.

When they returned to Norman by train on Sunday afternoon, the Sooners were met at the railroad station by a crowd estimated at 4,000.

Oklahoma defeated Kansas, 24-14, the next week in the first officially recognized Homecoming game at Norman. It appeared then that Oklahoma was home free to another undefeated, untied season, because the Sooners had defeated Missouri, Texas, and Kansas, considered the major powers on the 1915 schedule.

But the next week the Sooners had to come from behind to gain a hard-earned 14-13 win over lightly regarded Henry Kendall College of Tulsa. Elmer "Trim" Capshaw of Norman scored a touchdown from the one-yard line, and Geyer kicked the winning conversion in the fourth quarter.

The Sooners finished the season with a 3-0 record in the Southwest Conference, scoring victories over Texas, Arkansas, and Oklahoma A&M. Oklahoma shared the title with Baylor, which also had a 3-0 conference record. Even so the 1915 team claimed the first official championship in Oklahoma football history.

Oklahoma tried to arrange a postseason game with Nebraska, the Missouri Valley Conference champion, in Kansas City, but conference officials objected to the idea.

The six-foot, two-inch, 162-pound Geyer led the nation in

points after touchdown and was credited with the longest pass of the 1915 season, a 55-yard play to Howard McCasland. An 80-yard return of a blocked placekick by Homer Montgomery of Muskogee against Arkansas was the longest play in its category in the nation in 1915.

No national statistics were compiled on team or individual passing and running. However the Sooners averaged from 30 to 35 passes a game, probably more than any other team at that time. And Geyer became the first Sooner to be selected on an authentic all-America team. He was chosen in the backfield of the 1915 Newspaper Enterprises Association team named by Brown Holmes. Geyer and Montgomery also were on the *Outing* honor roll.

Time Out For World War I

The 10-0 record of the 1915 Oklahoma team helped boost the Sooners to their longest winning streak to that time. The 1914 team had won its final five games starting with the Oklahoma A&M game, the seventh contest of the season. The 1915 team extended the streak to 15 games. And the 1916 team won its first three games before bowing to Henry Kendall College of Tulsa, 16-0. The 18 straight victories remained a Sooner record until 1949.

Following the 1915 season OU teams coached by Bennie Owen had only one other unbeaten, untied campaign and won only two other championships.

The 1917 team suffered the worst defeat in the university's history to that point—a 44-0 loss to the University of Illinois at Champaign, Illinois. The Sooners also suffered their first loss to Oklahoma A&M in 1917. The Aggies won, 9-0, ending OU's winning streak at 11 straight in the series.

But Oklahoma posted a 6-0 record during an unusual 1918 season. It would be the last unbeaten, untied season for the Sooners for 31 years.

Most of the football team's experienced players returning from the 1917 season left school either before or during the 1918 campaign because of World War I. Those leaving included Hugh McDermott of Duncan, the team captain, and Dewey "Snorter" Luster of Chickasha, who returned to be captain of the 1920 Sooners and even later to be OU's football coach.

Fortunately, Oklahoma City High School had one of its

Arlo "Skivey" Davis of Norman who kicked 23 of 26 extra points in OU's 179-0 win over Kingfisher College in 1917.

outstanding teams in 1917, and many of its top players, ineligible for military service, came to OU in 1918. In fact, at times, eight of OU's starters were freshmen.

The closest game of the 1918 season came against an unbeaten Phillips University team of Enid. But Oklahoma won, 13-7, with freshman Russell "Stub" Hardy of Oklahoma City passing to Howard Marsh of Madill and Lawrence "Jap" Haskell of Anadarko for touchdowns. Haskell later became OU's athletic director, and the Sooners' present baseball field, Haskell Park, was named for him.

When a Spanish influenza epidemic reached Oklahoma, games with Texas, Missouri, and Alva Normal were canceled. But in the remaining schedule the Sooners won their only two games in Southwest Conference play in 1918 and tied Texas for the championship. The Longhorns had a 4-0 conference record and 9-0 season mark. Thus the epidemic had forced the cancellation of what might have been the championship game.

In 1920 Oklahoma was accepted as a member of the Missouri Valley Conference. The conference also included the University of Missouri, the University of Kansas, Iowa State University, Drake University, Washington University of St. Louis, Missouri, Grinnell College of Iowa, and Kansas State.

The 1920 Sooners combined several former players who had returned from World War I and the freshmen who had played such a vital role in the unbeaten season of 1918.

Oklahoma established itself as a solid contender for the Missouri Valley Conference championship when it defeated Missouri, 28-14, at Columbia, Missouri. Before the contest Owen came onto the field to shake hands with each of his starters.

Missouri was the defending conference champion and suffered its only loss in eight games to Oklahoma in 1920.

OU played the first Missouri Valley Conference game at Norman the next week, defeating Kansas, 24-9. Kansas, coached by its famed basketball coach Forrest C. "Phog" Allen, led, 9-7, at the half, but Oklahoma unleashed a powerful rushing attack, totaling 425 yards, to claim the win. Kansas was undefeated at the time. The game produced gross receipts of $11,187.22, the highest for a game at Boyd Field.

In the sixth and next to last game of the season Oklahoma received a jolting surprise. Kansas State entered the contest with an unimpressive 3-3-2 record. But the Wildcats took an early 7-0

Dewey "Snorter" Luster was OU captain in 1920.

lead. OU fought back, going 70 yards in eight plays to tie the score at 7-7. And that is the way it remained, although Kansas State missed three drop kicks in attempts to score field goals and upset the Sooners.

The tie with Kansas State meant that OU had to win its final game of the season against Drake or the winner of the Kansas-Missouri clash, scheduled the same day, would claim the conference championship. The Sooners accomplished that easily, handing Drake a 44-7 setback, only its second loss of the season.

So Oklahoma won the Missouri Valley championship in its

Roy "Soupy" Smoot was OU all-American tackle in 1920.

*OU's 1920 Undefeated Missouri Valley Conference
Championship Team
Front row, left to right: Harry "Dutch" Hill, Captain Dewey
"Snorter" Luster, Myron "Little Tub" Tyler, Frank Ogilvie.
Second row: Van Edmondson, Ronald Cullen, Erl Deacon,*

Lawrence "Jap" Haskell, Roy "Soupy" Smoot. Third row: Freshman coach Ed Meacham, Sol Swatek, Paul Johnston, Dwight "Hoss" Ross, Bill McKinley, Coach Bennie Owen. Back row: Arlo "Skivey" Davis, Howard "Tarzan" Marsh, Dow Hamm, Phil White, Clarence "Ram" Morrison.

first season in conference competition. The Sooners finished with a 4-0-1 conference record. Missouri had a 5-1 league mark.

Ohio State of the Big Nine had contacted Oklahoma about the possibility of a postseason game against the Buckeyes at Columbus, Ohio. But in the meantime Ohio State received a more attractive offer to play the University of California in the sixth annual Rose Bowl game, a game incidently that Ohio State lost, 28-0.

Halfback Phil White, one of the 1918 freshmen from Oklahoma City, was named on the Newspaper Enterprises Association all-America first team, becoming the second authentic all-America player at OU. And center Dow Hamm, one of the 1918 freshmen from Muskogee, completed the remarkable feat of never missing a play in one game during the 1919 and 1920 seasons—17 consecutive games. Hamm missed a few minutes in two games in 1918 to allow his substitute enough playing time to gain a letter.

The 1920 Sooners were the last championship football team at Oklahoma for 18 years.

Sooners play Central State in 1921.

Owen Builds A Stadium

Bennie Owen coached for six more years, through the 1926 season, but the Sooners had winning teams only three of those campaigns and were not contenders for the Missouri Valley Conference title. Owen then retired as head football coach following the 1926 season and was OU's director of athletics until 1934 when the Board of Regents forced him to accept the title of director of physical education and intramurals.

Despite the decline of the football program after 1920 Owen made valuable contributions to OU's future athletics as the moving force in the construction of facilities. In 1923 the first football game was played at what is now Owen Field, a game in which the Sooners defeated Washington University of St. Louis, Missouri, 62-7. At the time the field had no stands. But steel bleachers from Boyd Field were erected on the east side, and temporary wooden bleachers were put up on the west side. For the first time cars were not allowed to surround the playing field as had been the custom at Boyd Field. In fact the earlier field was used as a parking lot.

The next year OU attracted its largest home crowd to that time. Some 11,000 fans saw the Sooners bow to Missouri, 10-0. Only 3,750 students were enrolled that year.

Owen also was instrumental in helping raise contributions and sell bonds of $650,000 for a new stadium and $350,000 for a union building. They were promoted in the same package. In 1925 a portion of what is now the west side of the present

Ad Lindsey, OU coach from 1927 through 1931.

stadium was completed. It accommodated 15,000. The stadium was named Memorial Stadium in memory of university associated individuals who died in World War I. Thus OU retains the unique situation of having the playing field known by one name—Owen Field—and the stadium by another name—Memorial Stadium.

The first game played with the new stadium constructed was OU's 7-0 victory over Drake in 1925. However the Kansas

State contest, the fifth game of the season, was declared Homecoming and the dedication game for the stadium. Unfortunately this Homecoming and dedication game was played on a

Athletic Director Bennie Owen helps supervise construction of Memorial Stadium.

cold, wet day, and the teams played to a 0-0 tie on a muddy field before a disappointing crowd.

But in 1926 OU upset previously unbeaten Missouri, 10-7, before 16,235 fans, a Sooner home record. Two seasons later the first portion of the present east stands were added, in 1928, bringing the capacity of the stadium to 32,000. Nebraska defeated OU that season before a record crowd of 18,346.

Although he gave way to less successful coaches, Owen had made his mark on football at the University of Oklahoma. In his 22 years as OU's head football coach, Owen's teams won 122 games, lost 54, and tied 16. Under his guidance the Sooners enjoyed their first undefeated and untied seasons since the early years when only a few games were played. Owen's teams also won the first official championship for the university.

In the latter portion of his career Owen played a major role in starting OU's present athletic facilities. He was inducted into the Helms Foundation Football Coaches Hall of Fame in 1969, a year before his death.

Lewis Hardage, left, OU coach from 1932 through 1934 and Paul Young, right, OU captain in 1932.

Biff Jones Comes To OU

After Owen was discharged as athletic director in 1934, the OU Board of Regents decided that the entire athletic program needed revitalizing. Lloyd Noble, a wealthy oilman from Ardmore and a member of the board, was instrumental in OU's hiring Lawrence McC. "Biff" Jones as head football coach and athletic director for 1935.

In 1935 OU was trying to overcome the effects of the depression and the effects of only two winning seasons in the eight years after Owen had stepped aside as football coach. Jones, a 1917 graduate of the U. S. Military Academy at West Point, New York, and a captain in the Army, had the reputation of a successful coach and a thorough organizer.

The 39-year-old Jones was hired to modernize OU's athletic facilities and teach military courses. He had been the head coach at Army in 1926 through 1929, and his teams had 30 victories, 8 losses, and 2 ties. After being out of coaching for two years, Jones was the head coach at Louisiana State University in 1932 through 1934. There his teams had 20 victories, 4 losses, and 5 ties.

But even his very successful teams did not save Jones after a fatal mistake during the 1934 season. At the half time of one of the LSU games, all-powerful Governor Huey Long wanted to talk to the Tiger team. Jones banned him from the dressing room, and Jones was out of a job at the end of the season.

Gene Corrotto, a Sooner player from Fort Smith, Arkansas, at the time and later one of the state's most

Lawrence "Biff" Jones, OU coach in 1935 and 1936.

successful high school coaches at Norman High, Seminole High, and Tulsa Central High, recalled those days.

"When Biff Jones came in the spring, he made a lot of changes," Corrotto said. "I think he was one man who really did a lot of organization that started OU on an upgrade of big time football. When Biff Jones came, we had another spring practice. We had just finished one. But there were no rules in those days.

"He had lockers built and our training room fixed up. Before that we used to check out a basket to put our clothes in while we practiced. Jones also brought his own equipment manager, Pete "Sarge" Dempsey. Ted Owen had had the overwhelming jobs of trainer and equipment manager.

"Biff Jones was a very staunch coach," Corrotto recalled. "I think he was very smart and very intelligent, and I learned a lot of football from him.

"Most of the boys were scared of the guy," he said of the 6-foot-3, 215-pounder. "He had a voice that would scare you: make you jump plum out of your socks. He's the type that when he hollered at you, you didn't jump once, you jumped three times."

Ironically his two years at Oklahoma were the most

Webber Merrill returns a Nebraska kickoff for a touchdown in 1936.

Double-wing formation used by Oklahoma teams in the 1930s.

ordinary of Jones' coaching career. The Sooners had a 6-3 record in 1935, finishing a distant second in the Big Six Conference race, and had a 3-3-3 record in 1936.

OU had entered the Big Six Conference in 1928 when the Sooners, the University of Nebraska, the University of Missouri, Iowa State University, the University of Kansas, and Kansas State University dropped out of the Missouri Valley Conference to form another league.

Following the 1936 season Jones was transferred to Fort Leavenworth in Kansas. But before the 1937 season he became the head football coach at the University of Nebraska, and his first Cornhusker team won the Big Six Conference championship. A 0-0 tie with OU and a Sooner loss to Kansas made the difference in the race.

Jones' Nebraska teams won 28 games, lost 14, and tied 4. In 1964 he was inducted into the Helms Foundation Football Coaches Hall of Fame.

Sooners Go To "Orange Brawl"

Tom Stidham, a 32-year-old native of Checotah, had been OU's line coach and succeeded Biff Jones as the Sooner head coach in 1937. Stidham had been captain of the undefeated Haskell Indian Institute team of Lawrence, Kansas, in 1926. He also had been an assistant coach at Northwestern University in Evanston, Illinois.

"Tom Stidham just took over where Jones left off," recalled Gene Corrotto of Fort Smith, Arkansas. Corrotto and Earl Crowder of Cherokee were captains of the 1938 Sooners, perhaps OU's best football team to that time.

"We didn't have too much deception," Corrotto said. "We just used the ol' bang, bang football, you know. We'd line up and just try to run over you. However, I'll say this: We did throw the ball a lot. In fact, I think we threw the ball then as much as colleges do now."

Corrotto also recalled that circumstances regarding athletes were different from today.

"You could be on a training table from when practice started until school started," said Corrotto. "That was the Big Six rule then. We lived in boarding houses here and there. There wasn't any athletic dormitory. A scholarship consisted of room, board, books and tuition. But you had to work for your room and board. They got you a job, and when you got your check, you paid your room and board with it.

"Biff Jones organized some jobs. We had some night watchman jobs. We used to watch the campus and the stadium.

Tom Stidham, OU coach from 1937 through 1940.

We had a key. You turned it to punch a clock in. Of course a lot of guys worked different places for their meals. Some of them worked at Rickner's Book Store. Al and I worked in a fraternity house, washing dishes three meals a day," he said, referring to his brother who was the captain of the 1937 Sooner team.

"The biggest deal I ever had when I was in school was

when I started making $40 a month. I thought I was rich. You paid your own room and board, and you could eat where you wanted to. Of course I felt sorry for some of those boarding houses when Gilford Duggan, Red McCarty, Al, and I and some of those other folks would go off to eat some place. You know, that's a lot of food. I didn't eat so much, I don't think. But Duggan could eat quite a bit."

He referred to 220-pound "Cactus Face" Duggan of Benton, Arkansas, an all-America tackle in 1939. But Corrotto recalled that Duggan's eating habits did not hamper his play.

"Duggan was real quick for a big fellow," he said. "In fact he would pull out of the line to lead a play on the double wing. I remember one play where I carried the ball on a double reserve, and he led the play. I'd get behind his big, ol' back. I was just a little fellow, and I'd try to hide."

Pete Smith, OU all-American end in 1937.

Jack Baer, all-Big Six back in 1937.

Corrotto and Duggan were members of the 1938 Sooner team that claimed the Big Six Conference championship, the first for OU in the new conference and the first title for the school in 18 years. The 1938 Sooners completed the regular season undefeated and untied and achieved two firsts in football at OU: They were the first OU team to be nationally ranked and first to go to a bowl game.

The first test of the 1938 season gave an indication of what was to come. OU met Rice Institute at Houston, Texas.

"The previous year Rice had won the Southwest Conference championship," Corrotto recalled. "They had all those boys back, and they were supposed to win it again. I worked with those guys during the summer of 1938 in Houston. They didn't look at me. I was so little. They said that if it was hot weather, they'd beat Oklahoma 30 points."

Corrotto remembered that it was hot, but of course the Owls did not beat the Sooners by 30 points.

"It was so hot that afternoon we didn't even go inside at the half. We had knit wool pants on. They were a little hotter and heavier than they are now. We just stayed out there and poured water and ice on our heads."

Rice took an early 6-0 lead, but then the Sooners stymied the Owls and their heralded passer, 230-pound quarterback Ernie McLain. The Rice star completed only five of eighteen passes for 73 yards and yielded two interceptions. Howard "Red Dog" McCarty of Pauls Valley scored OU's only touchdown on an 18-yard run, and Raphael Boudreau of Purcell kicked the conversion for a 7-6 victory.

OU and Iowa State played for the conference championship. The Cyclones had a 7-1-1 record that season, still the fourth best in the school's history. But OU won, 10-0, at Ames, Iowa, with Bob Seymour of Commerce scoring a touchdown on a two-yard run, Boudreau kicking the extra point, and Hugh McCullough of Oklahoma City kicking a 31-yard field goal.

The Sooner defense was particularly impressive. OU allowed only 12 points in its 10 regular-season games. Rice and Tulsa each scored six. And the Sooners were first in the nation in defense against rushing, allowing an average of only 43.3 yards a game.

Thus OU was ranked fourth in the nation in 1938 and

Hugh McCullough scored against Nebraska in 1938.

received a bid to play in the Orange Bowl game in Miami, Florida. The ranking was by the Associated Press which had started its national rankings two years earlier.

Tennessee, OU's opponent in the Orange Bowl, also was undefeated and untied, had allowed only 16 points all season, and was ranked second in the nation. The Volunteers were coached by the great General R. R. "Bob" Neyland, and their famed single wing attack was led by all-America tailback George "Bad News" Cafego.

Corrotto recalls that the Sooners were not at full strength for their first postseason bowl clash. Bill Jennings of Norman, Corrotto's substitute at wingback, had suffered a broken leg against Washington State in OU's final game of the regular season. And centers Novel Wood of Norman and Cliff Speegle of Oklahoma City had suffered knee injuries against Oklahoma A&M in the next to last game of the regular season. Although they played, neither had fully recovered for the bowl game.

And Corrotto recalls that, "Crowder (OU's starting blocking back) was knocked cuckoo in the first quarter. He didn't know if he was walking or riding."

Nevertheless what probably was one of the greatest Tennessee teams of all-time dominated the game, winning, 17-0, in what became known as the "Orange Brawl." Tennessee was penalized 130 yards and OU 90. Two Tennessee players and OU guard Ralph Stevenson of Ponca City were ejected from the game.

"The officials had to stop the game repeatedly and cool

Wingback Gene Corrotto runs the reverse against Texas in 1938.

OU went to its first bowl game, the Orange Bowl, following the 1938 season but lost to Tennessee.

things off," Corrotto said. "There was a lot of fussin' and hittin' going on. And what they called the angle block, we called clipping up in this part of country. It was the funniest angle I ever saw."

Ironically the Sooners would meet another favored Tennessee team in the Orange Bowl 29 years later in a game that would mean even more to OU football.

Stidham continued to have winning teams at OU and was hired as the head coach at Marquette University in Milwaukee, Wisconsin, following the 1940 season.

Snorter Comes Home

Dewey "Snorter" Luster was never a pacifist, although you hardly could have blamed him if he were. Luster's playing career at Oklahoma was interrupted by World War I. Then his big opportunity as OU's head coach was hampered by World War II.

Luster was the captain of the 1920 Sooners, had been a Sooner assistant coach during the first three years of Tom Stidham's tenure at OU, and had been a highly successful high school coach at Norman and Bixby. He had forsaken a career as an attorney, although he had a degree in the law, after losing the sight in one eye. In 1941 Luster was studying counseling at Columbia University in New York. It was that year that the University of Oklahoma decided to call on one of its own to become the Sooner head football coach. Thus Luster became only the second, and, to this time, the last former Sooner player to become OU's head coach.

"It's a rather funny thing," Luster said, evaluating that decision. "I have never quite been able to understand why everyone who coaches has an insatiable desire to coach his alma mater. Frankly I think it's the worst place in the world he could coach."

Luster recalled that the 1941 Oklahoma team was divided into two groups with the juniors and seniors known as the "Big Red." He believes that that was the first time that nickname was used for an OU team.

The 1941 team is considered the best all-around squad that

Luster had at OU. It posted a 6-3 record, including a 16-6 upset of Santa Clara, coached by the legendary Buck Shaw. The game was played in a drizzling rain, and Luster said the turning point came on a 75-yard punt by Indian Jack Jacobs of Muskogee.

Jacobs, who had averaged a fabulous 47.8 yards a punt in 1940, averaged 50.6 yards on six punts in a 28-0 losing cause in 1941 against Missouri, Big Six Conference champion and ranked seventh nationally.

The 1941 Sooners also scored a 61-14 victory over the Marquette team coached by Stidham that year. It appeared that OU was set for the coming campaign with 30 lettermen returning.

"Pearl Harbor must have come on Saturday night, because I was taking a bath," Luster recalled about the start of World War II, following the 1941 season.

In less than three weeks, 22 OU lettermen had volunteered for military duty. By the start of the 1942 season all of Luster's assistant coaches also had left.

Luster built his teams around students in the Naval Reserved Officers Corps at OU after that.

Indian Jack Jacobs breaks away against Oklahoma A&M in 1941.

Dewey "Snorter" Luster, OU coach from 1941 through 1945.

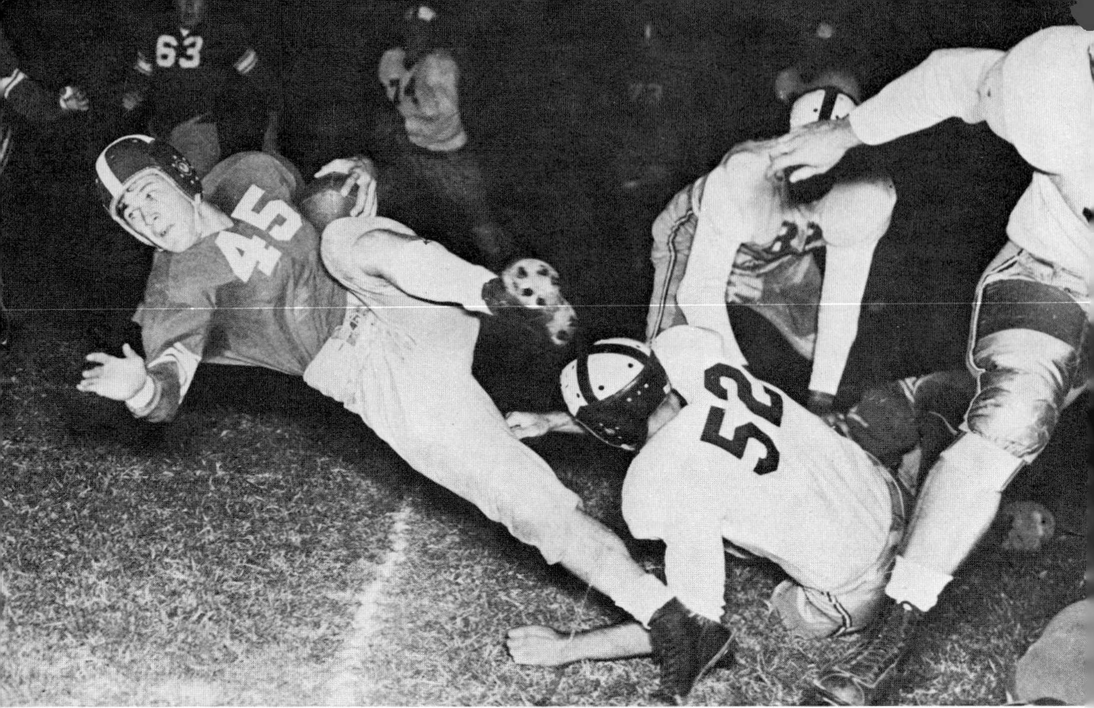

Wingback Charley Heard gains 12 yards against Texas A&M in 1944.

"They were long on brains but a little bit short on brawn," Luster recalled. "If we had a boy who weighed 190 pounds, he automatically played left tackle and we called him 'Big John.' Today the quarterbacks weigh more than that."

Even so, Oklahoma posted winning records and claimed Big Six championships in 1943 and 1944. But by the next year, things had changed. The Sooners had a 5-5 record and lost the final game of the season to nationally fifth ranked Oklahoma A&M, 47-0.

Luster was having health problems, having missed two games in 1945. Some Oklahoma supporters had set their goals on national recognition and were discontent because Oklahoma had not beaten Texas since 1939.

Luster recalled that OU had accumulated more than $125,000 during the war years.

"Jim Tatum (who succeeded Luster as OU head coach in 1946) spent every dime of that before they ever kicked off the next year, and he had to borrow money," Luster said. "But he brought the boys back. Only they weren't boys any more. They were men."

Tatum Recruits Talent

James Moore Tatum hit the OU campus in 1946 somewhat like one of those unexpected spring tornadoes: He was there and gone before too many people knew what happened.

A tornado leaves destruction and death. Tatum left some construction and new life. Many believe that the wealth of talent that Tatum brought to OU in the one year that he was head coach was the cornerstone of the Sooner football dynasty.

When it was determined that Luster no longer would be OU's coach because of health reasons, some supported D. H. "Red" Drew, who later became well-known at Alabama, and Henry Frnka, highly successful coach at Tulsa and Tulane. But Lawrence "Jap" Haskell, who returned from military service to resume duties as athletic director, had his own choice. His choice was Tatum, who had coached the Jacksonville (Florida) Naval Air Station Fliers during World War II. Because of Haskell's strong support, the 32-year-old Tatum became the only candidate seriously considered by the Board of Regents.

Tatum made the most of a unique opportunity. For some four years most of the best athletes in the nation had gone on military duty instead of attending colleges. Several of Oklahoma's best players—Joe Golding of Eufaula, Paul "Buddy" Burris of Muskogee, Plato Andros of Oklahoma City, Jim Tyree of Oklahoma City, Homer Paine of Enid, and Eddy Davis of Muskogee—returned to OU the summer of 1946.

Earlier in the year a group of players from the Jacksonville team had decided to attend the University of Florida. But when

Jim Tatum, OU coach in 1946.

he got the job at OU, Tatum persuaded Wade Walker, John Rapacz, Nute Trotter, John Husak, Johnny Allsup, and Warren Giese, none with Oklahoma ties, to become Sooners.

The 1946 team members were selected during a series of then-legal tryouts during the summer. Some 275 athletes participated. By the end of the summer only 140 remained, and Tatum and his staff selected only 40 of those to make up the varsity the next fall.

"Jim Tatum was a super, super forecaster of what a youngster would do some two or three years later in his growth

and in his ability to perform," said Wade Walker, who became
OU's athletic director in 1971. "I think he was one of the best
organizers that I have ever been around. He was flamboyant.
Maybe a little bit overboisterous."

Golding recalled: "He figured if you can do him any good,
that's fine. If you can't, there's the door."

And end Jim Tyree, the captain of the 1946 team,
expressed the reaction of some: "He didn't think he was doing a
good job unless he had everybody mad at him. And he was
gifted at that."

The Sooners' top 33 players included 31 military veterans.
But they went through the growing pains of becoming a team,
losing two of their first three games before tying Kansas for the
Big Six Conference championship and defeating North Carolina
State, 34-13, in the Gator Bowl.

Joe Golding scores against Missouri in 1946.

The first game of the 1946 season gave a hint of what was to come. OU met Army, the scourge of the war years and mythical national champion in 1944 and 1945, in the opening game of the season. President Harry S Truman was among the 24,500 fans at Army's Michie Stadium at West Point, New York, and became the first U. S. president to attend a game there.

Those were the days of Army's Mr. Inside, fullback Felix "Doc" Blanchard, and Mr. Outside, halfback Glenn "Junior" Davis. The Cadets entered the game with a 19-game winning streak and as solid favorites against the unknown Sooners. Blanchard, who was Tatum's cousin, did not play because of an injury.

The Sooners, still trying to master the techniques of the Split-T formation, fumbled 12 times and lost 4 of them. And

Jim Tyree returned to OU with a family after World War II.

OU center John Rapacz runs down Missouri's Bob Hopkins in 1946.

many believe that one of those errors may have saved Army from what would have been one of its most devastating upsets.

The Sooners had marched to the Army 18-yard line with the Cadets leading, 14-7, in the fourth quarter. But Army quarterback Gerald Tucker intercepted a Sooner lateral and raced 86 yards for a touchdown and a 21-7 triumph. It was reported that Tatum, racing down the sideline, followed Tucker the length of the field, shouting that the play was illegal.

A few years later, Plato Andros jokingly remarked: "We had too many coaches and not enough players in the lineup."

The Sooner roster included seven players who later became major college head coaches. They were Darrell Royal at Mississippi State, Washington, and Texas; Jim Owens at

Darrell Royal gains 21 yards against Texas.

Washington; Jack Mitchell at Wichita State, Arkansas, and Kansas; Dee Andros at Oregon State; Wade Walker at Mississippi State; Warren Giese at South Carolina; and Pete Tillman at Wichita State.

Two weeks after the defeat at Army the Sooners bowed 20-13 to the last Texas team coached by the famed Dana X. Bible. But, nonetheless, in 1946 OU and a veteran re-enforced Kansas team coached by George Sauer tied for the Big Six title. And an 8-3 record, what was considered a strong showing against Texas, an overwhelming 73-12 victory over Oklahoma A&M, and the first bowl win in OU history led Tatum to believe that he was in a position of almost unchallengeable power.

However, he did not count on two factors. Tatum had underestimated the native independent spirit of many of the Oklahomans with whom he worked. And he had brought with him the ready-made popular successor, who had worked as an assistant coach at OU in 1946.

Flight To Keep Bud

Even if he had never achieved such success during the 1946 season, Jim Tatum would have made his mark on the history of OU football by bringing in Bud Wilkinson.

After being discharged from the Navy in the fall of 1945, Charles B. "Bud" Wilkinson had entered the mortgage business with his father in Minneapolis. Wilkinson had played on the great Minnesota teams coached by the famed Bernie Bierman in the late 1930s. And he and Tatum had been assistant coaches of Don Farout at Iowa Pre-Flight during World War II.

Tatum invited Wilkinson to help him during the tryout sessions at OU in the summer of 1946, and the 30-year-old Wilkinson accepted with the idea of being a part-time coach. But football was too much a part of his life, and Wilkinson soon accepted a job as an assistant coach on a full-time basis.

Two days before the Sooners were to meet North Carolina State in the Gator Bowl game following the 1946 season, Lloyd Noble, a wealthy oil man from Ardmore and president of the OU Board of Regents, called Dr. George L. Cross, OU's president. Noble had heard a rumor that following the bowl game Tatum and his entire staff were to be interviewed for jobs at the University of Maryland.

Cross, president for only two years at the time and deeply involved in the myriad of problems faced by colleges following World War II, had not planned to attend the bowl game. But Noble explained that he and the regents had been very favorably impressed by Wilkinson throughout the season, and that Noble wanted Wilkinson to know that he could become OU's head coach, if Tatum decided to become the head coach at Maryland.

So Noble sent his single-engine, private airplane to fly Cross to Jacksonville for a conference with Wilkinson on the eve of the Gator Bowl game. It was during this meeting that Cross made the first of many vital decisions that would help shape OU athletics. He was authorized to offer a three-year contract, if Tatum left. Wilkinson asked for a four-year contract, and Cross agreed on his own authority, without approval of the regents.

Despite the plans going on around him Tatum, following the bowl game, decided to stay at OU. But he misjudged his influence by demanding a 10-year contract and a reorganization of the athletic department that would have given him almost unquestionable power.

Tatum nearly got what he wanted except that the regents voted 4-3 to support a proposal by Cross. It offered a six-year contract and no shake-up of the athletic department.

His plan not accepted, Tatum decided to take the job at Maryland. Thus Bud Wilkinson became OU's head football coach, and the Sooners were on the verge of making collegiate football history.

Bud Wilkinson, OU's new coach in 1947.

OU Goes National

When a blond, dashing, 30-year-old Bud Wilkinson became OU's head football coach early in 1947, Oklahoma was considered by many to be just another team in the hinterlands of the United States. The Sooners had appeared in the wire service polls once in the 11 years of rankings. When the gray-haired, respected Wilkinson resigned 17 football seasons later, Oklahoma had won about every honor that existed and was established as one of the nation's great football powers.

The high point of the Wilkinson dynasty came during the 1950s, a decade in which OU won three mythical national championships and posted an incredible 93 victories, 10 losses, and 2 ties. That record is even more impressive when it is realized that five of those losses came during two seasons.

The Sooners amassed unequaled records. OU set the NCAA record for consecutive victories—47 straight triumphs.

The Sooners lost to Notre Dame, 28-21, in the first game of the 1953 season and then tied Pittsburgh, 7-7, in the next game of that campaign. Then the Sooners won 47 straight contests before bowing to Notre Dame, 7-0, in the eighth game of the 1957 season.

Another NCAA record also fell in that game. Oklahoma had scored in 123 straight games, 112 with Wilkinson as coach, before that fateful day. The Sooners had not been shut out since the final game of the 1945 campaign when they lost to Oklahoma A&M, 47-0.

Previously Oklahoma had amassed a 31-game winning

Coach Bud Wilkinson with quarterback Jack Mitchell in 1947.

streak with Wilkinson as coach. OU lost to Santa Clara, 20-12, in the first game of the 1948 season and did not bow again until it lost to Kentucky, 13-7, in the Sugar Bowl game following the 1950 season.

No team ever dominated a major college conference as the Sooners did the Big Six and Big Seven in Wilkinson's first 13 years as head coach. The Sooners shared the Big Six title with

Kansas in 1947. Then Oklahoma won the championship each of the next 12 years when the conference was the Big Seven.

Wilkinson's teams did not lose a conference game the first 12 years that he was head coach. They were tied by Kansas, 13-13, in 1947, and by Colorado, 21-21, in 1952. They won 44 straight conference games from the tie with Colorado in 1952 to the 25-21 loss to Nebraska in 1959. And they went a remarkable 74 conference games without a loss, having lost to Kansas, 16-13, in 1946 and then not again until the 1959 setback at Nebraska.

The Sooners also received continual national recognition during the period that Wilkinson was head coach. The Associated Press ranked OU fifth in 1948, second in 1949, first in 1950, tenth in 1951, fourth in 1952 and 1953, third in 1954, first in 1955 and 1956, fourth in 1957, fifth in 1958, eighth in 1962, and tenth in 1963.

The United Press International ranked the Sooners first in 1950, the first year of its national poll, and then eleventh in

Safety Wilbur "Buddy" Jones eludes Iowa State pursuers.

1951, fourth in 1952, fifth in 1953, third in 1954, first in 1955 and 1956, fourth in 1957, fifth in 1958, seventeenth in 1959, seventh in 1962, and eighth in 1963.

During the same period Oklahoma won six of eight postseason bowl games. The Sooners defeated North Carolina, 14-6, in the 1949 Sugar Bowl; Louisiana State, 35-0, in the 1950 Sugar Bowl; lost to Kentucky, 13-7, in the 1951 Sugar Bowl; defeated Maryland, 7-0, in the 1954 Orange Bowl; Maryland, 20-6, in the 1956 Orange Bowl; Duke, 48-21, in the 1958 Orange Bowl; Syracuse, 21-6, in the 1959 Orange Bowl; and lost to Alabama, 17-0, in the 1963 Orange Bowl.

But there are many stories behind all those championships, national rankings, records, winning streaks, and bowl games.

For Lack Of A Chinstrap

Of course when Bud Wilkinson faced that first season as Oklahoma's head football coach in 1947, no one could have foreseen the significant role the Sooners were to play in college football.

Although their personalities were quite different, the adjustment from Tatum to Wilkinson apparently was made with no major problems. Wade Walker, a Sooner captain in 1947 while he was a sophomore, recalled some of the differences.

"Tatum was a lot more outgoing," Walker said. "He would bring himself down to the players' level a lot easier than Coach Wilkinson would.

"Coach Wilkinson was a person that you didn't feel like you could sit down and talk to. I could, but I was captain for two years. He put a lot of pressure on the captains to help. Coach Wilkinson was quite reserved."

Walker, a veteran of World War II, compared the coaching styles by saying: "Tatum would be a lot more vocal if you broke a play, if you missed an assignment. He wouldn't curse you. I don't mean that. But he would be a lot more vocal to single you out and gig you.

"Wilkinson wouldn't say anything. He just simply put someone in your place."

As a 31-year-old head coach, Wilkinson was concerned about people thinking that he might be too young for the job. Wilkinson looked even younger than he was. Walker recalls the first time they met during the summer of 1946 when Tatum and Wilkinson were sharing a room in the basement of the home of Lawrence "Jap" Haskell, then OU's athletic director.

"Bud, what position do you play?" Walker recalls asking the new assistant coach.

Wilkinson's great career started on something of a shaky note. Oklahoma never trailed in that first game of the season against an unheralded Detroit University team but fought off a late Titan rally to win, 24-20.

The Sooners took a 17-7 lead after quarterback Jack Mitchell of Arkansas City, Kansas, returned a punt 60 yards for a touchdown just before the end of the first half. Some of the

Darrell Royal gains against Nebraska in 1947.

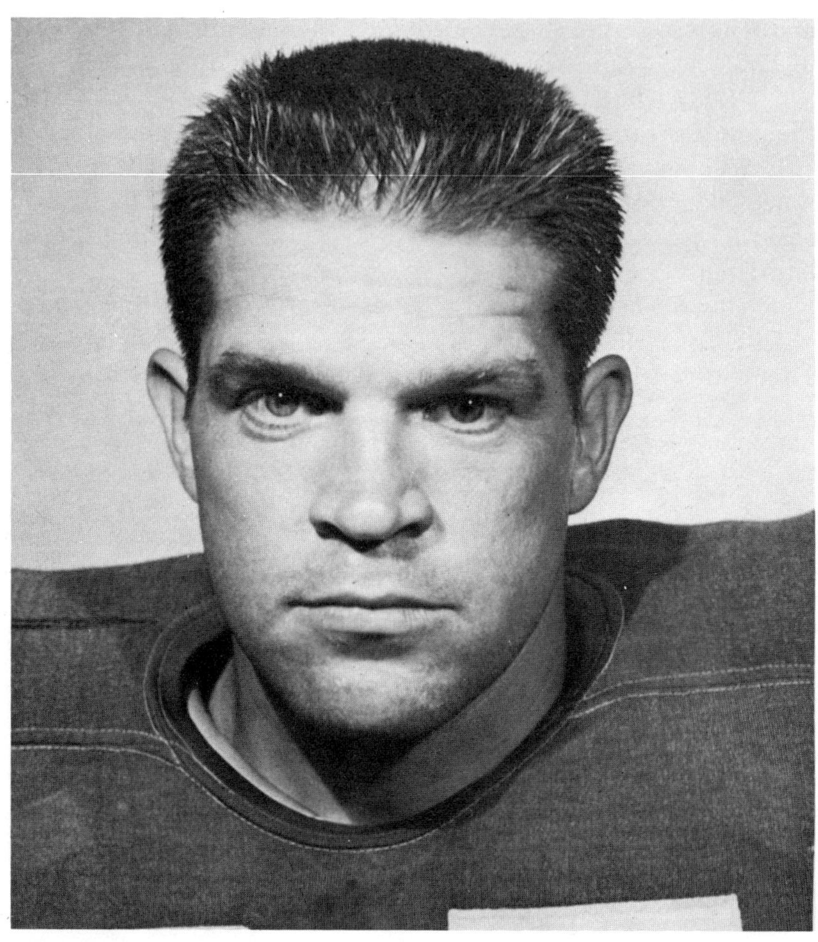

Paul "Buddy" Burris, all-American guard in 1946, 1947, and 1948.

Detroit players reportedly did not try to stop Mitchell because, they later said, they thought they had heard a horn, indicating an infraction on the play. The game was not decided until halfback George Thomas of Fairland intercepted a pass by Detroit quarterback Harry Peterson on the OU 12-yard line on the last play of the game.

The Friday night contest was televised in the Detroit area. It was estimated that there were approximately 5,000 television sets in Detroit at the time.

OU Captain Jim Tyree gains against Texas A&M after receiving a pass in 1947.

Wilkinson recalled that one Detroit touchdown came on a play on which Sooner linebacker Myrle Greathouse of Amarillo, Texas, was on the sideline replacing a chin strap and did not get back on the field in time for the play.

"Well, if we lose the game for having 10 guys on the field—my first game as head coach..." Wilkinson said, not finishing the sentence.

It was at this early point in his career that Wilkinson started to devise his plan of playing more substitutes throughout the game so that the starters would not be tired if the outcome still were in doubt in the final quarter. The strategy of alternating linemen paid off the next week as the Sooners overcame a 14-6 deficit to defeat Texas A&M, 26-14, in the home opener for Wilkinson as head coach before 30,000 fans at Owen Field.

But the Sooners went the next three weeks without another victory. OU bowed to Texas, 34-14, in a game involving the famous Sisco incident; tied Kansas, 13-13, before a record crowd of 34,547 at Owen Field; and then lost to Texas Christian, 20-7. The tie with Kansas eventually meant that the two would share the Big Six Conference championship.

The so-called Sisco incident in the Texas game in 1947 occurred at the end of the first half with the teams tied, 7-7. Texas had marched 57 yards to the OU three-yard line with only seconds remaining. Longhorn Randall Clay was stopped for no gain on the next play, and the field clock showed no time remaining. However Jack Sisco, one of the game officials, declared that Texas had called timeout with three seconds remaining and that the Longhorns should have another play.

On the extra play Texas halfback Jim Canady was stopped at the line of scrimmage, but he fumbled the ball and it bounced backward. In the confusion Texas quarterback Bobby Layne recovered the ball and tossed it to Clay who ran for the touchdown, giving Texas a 14-7 lead at half time. Wilkinson protested the play, claiming that Layne's knees had touched the ground when he recovered the fumble and that the play should have been ended there.

Some claim the disputed play turned the tempo of the game in favor of the Longhorns. In the third quarter, when an OU gain was nullified because of a holding penalty, Sooner fans

OU Coach Bud Wilkinson and Sooners hold Cowboy Hat after 1948 victory over Texas.

threw bottles and seat cushions on the field. After the game the officials were escorted to safety by the police. The following Monday Sisco was burned in effigy on the OU campus.

Wilkinson said that the coaches and officials had agreed before the game that the field clock would indicate the official time. On that basis he believes that Sisco had no right to give Texas the extra play.

"If I had been a more experienced coach, I would have taken our team off the field and let Sisco decide what he was going to do," Wilkinson said.

Wade Walker was all-American tackle in 1949.

After the tie with Kansas the next week, Wilkinson said: "We still haven't got it. We're looking better every week, of course, but take that game today for instance: We shook halfbacks loose, but none of them could go all the way like Joe Golding used to do."

Golding, who set an OU record by rushing for 902 yards in 1946, had decided to forego the 1947 season at OU and play professionally.

The next week OU's downfall against Texas Christian

involved the passing game, something seldom associated in abundance with teams coached by Wilkinson. The Sooners passed 13 times, completing 4 but yielding 5 interceptions to Texas Christian.

But OU's 21-12 victory over Missouri at Columbia in the eighth game of the season stands out in Wilkinson's mind as the key game of his first year as head coach. The game pitted the Tigers of Coach Don Faurot, credited with being the innovator of the Split-T offense, and the Sooners of Wilkinson, whose teams would be the most successful Split-T units in the history of the game. The Sooner defense was stacked on the line and held Missouri to only 81 yards rushing.

Wilkinson recalled the punting of halfback Darrell Royal of Hollis as being the key to the outcome. Royal, who later would achieve great success as head coach at Texas and, in fact, coach teams that would defeat the Sooners late in the career of Wilkinson, punted out of bounds on the Missouri one-yard line and again on the Tiger four-yard line. Missouri lost a fumble after the latter, setting up an easy touchdown for Oklahoma.

"Royal probably is the best punter I've ever seen," Wilkinson now claims. "That was really a pivotal game—not only for that season, but it was the springboard to our becoming a fine good football team," Wilkinson analyzed. "It gave the team and coaching staff confidence and gave the public confidence in our program. And the environment of the players is one of the essential elements in the successful program."

Wilkinson believed that he was on trial as a coach that first year as far as the public was concerned. He passed the test with the Sooners posting a 7-2-1 record and tying for the Big Six championship.

1949 — "A House Afire"

As long as there are OU football fans, there will be discussions of which Sooner team was the greatest. And this certainly is not intended to end that argument or put a damper on continued discussions. But Wilkinson considered the 1949 Sooners his best team with one qualification.

"I would say that 1949 probably was the strongest team with this reservation: All the athletes from 1941 through 1945 went into the service and were back together," said Wilkinson, analyzing the situation.

"So you had the unusual situation of four or five classes of seniors coming together at one time. It's unlikely that it will ever happen again. So it is really unfair to compare this team with what I call a normal college team.

"Many of the 1949 players had combat experience (in World War II) and had been athletes in the service. It was the last big group of veterans, and they were mature, highly competent, and unflappable. We did not have any weakness."

But there were serious questions going into the 1949 season. After all, the 1948 season had been a great one.

Following losing to Santa Clara, 20-17, because of what has been described as a breakdown on pass defense, the 1948 Sooners scored 10 straight impressive victories.

OU defeated Texas, 20-14, providing the first victory for the Sooners over the Longhorns in nine seasons and first by a team coached by Wilkinson.

And, in a game that decided the Big Seven championship,

OU defeated Missouri, 41-7, as a record crowd of 39,297 watched at Owen Field.

Then the Sooners defeated North Carolina and the great Charley "Choo Choo" Justice, 14-6, in the Sugar Bowl.

The Sooners had been ranked fifth in the nation and the Tarheels third going into the contest. But no polls were conducted following bowl games in those days.

The 1948 Sooners set a conference record by averaging 43.4 points a game in Big Seven contests and averaged 33.6 points a game for the season, OU's highest scoring average since it started playing a national schedule.

The losses from that team were not many, but they could have been crucial. For one thing OU would be without Jack Mitchell, who was considered the best T-formation running quarterback of his time. Mitchell had started for three seasons.

End Frankie Anderson tackles Kansas' Dick Gilman while Norman McNabb (65) races to help.

End Jimmy Owens gains on a pass against Texas A&M.

And the Sooners would have to replace three-time all-America guard Buddy Burris; Homer Paine, called by many the greatest defensive tackle OU had had to that time; and the strong linebacking of Myrle Greathouse and Pete Tillman.

The vital job of succeeding Mitchell fell to 170-pound

Darrell Royal, a 25-year-old military veteran who had played quarterback and halfback previously. However Royal was best known for his skillful punting and performances as a defensive back. In fact, going into the 1974 season, Royal's 17 interceptions remain the Sooner career record, and he still shares the school record of seven interceptions in one season.

Only one player in what was the starting line most of the 1949 season was not a military veteran. The starters were Jim Owens of Oklahoma City at left end, Leon Manley of Hollis at left tackle, Dee Andros of Oklahoma City at left guard, Charley Dowell of Tulsa at center, Stan West of Enid at right guard, Wade Walker of Gastonia, North Carolina, at right tackle, and Bobby Goad of Muskogee at right end.

Walker and Goad also were 25 years old and Andros was 24. Key reserves Ken Tipps of Oklahoma City at left end was 26, Norman McNabb of Norman at left guard was 25, and Harry

Wade Walker (70) tackles Oklahoma A&M's Toy Ledbetter. Other Sooners are Myrle Greathouse (44), Buddy Burris (67), Stan West (64), and Homer Paine (71).

Moore of Blackwell at center was 26. Dowell was the only non-veteran in the No. 1 line.

Left halfback Lindell Pearson of Oklahoma City, right halfback George "Junior" Thomas of Fairland, and fullback Leon "Mule Train" Heath of Hollis, the only offensive starter who was not a senior, were not military veterans.

Twenty-two of the varsity players were married.

The Sooners posted an 11-0 record including important

Fullback Leon Heath catches a 38-yard pass against Oklahoma A&M.

George "Junior" Thomas gains 10 yards against Santa Clara.

triumphs over Texas, Missouri, Santa Clara, and over Louisiana State in the Sugar Bowl.

OU defeated Texas, 20-14, the same score as the previous year. Texas took a 7-0 lead but did not score its final touchdown until only 29 seconds remained. A record crowd of 75,347 fans watched the OU victory as the Oklahoma-Texas game took its incredibly significant role in the history of OU football.

The clash with Missouri settled the Big Seven championship for the second year in a row. A record crowd of 37,152 at Columbia, Missouri, saw the pass-happy Tigers tie the score at 7-7 in the second quarter before Oklahoma won, 27-7.

The stage was set for OU's revenge-seeking contest against Santa Clara at Owen Field the next week. Earlier in the year Owen Field had been enlarged from 30,000 to 55,000 seats.

The cinder track was taken out, the playing surface was lowered by six feet, and some 7,000 ringside seats surrounding the playing area were constructed. Also the north end zone was closed and a new three-deck press box was added.

Dr. George L. Cross, OU's president at the time, recalled there was major opposition to the expansion and the including of an elevator for the press box. The elevator was added, not for television which did not play a key role in college football at the time, but to encourage the *Daily Oklahoman* to use its huge, long lens play-by-play camera at OU games.

Cross recalled that some people called the whole project "Cross' Folly" and said that Cross would never live to see the stadium filled. But Santa Clara, the last team to defeat the Sooners, made an attractive drawing card against the undefeated Sooners in the ninth game of the season. And a record crowd of 60,145 fans crowded into Owen Field, and news reports said hundreds of others were turned away.

The Sooners, led by touchdown runs of 81 yards by Heath and 24 yards by Thomas (Pearson had one of 65 yards called back), won, 28-21, holding off repeated threats by Santa Clara for the final 11 minutes.

The victory was the 19th in a row and bettered the previous Sooner best established during the 1914, 1915, and 1916 seasons.

But OU was ranked second to Notre Dame in the final national rating by the Associated Press. When an attempt to match the Sooners and the Fighting Irish in the Sugar Bowl game following the regular season failed, OU and Louisiana State, ranked ninth in the nation, were selected for the clash in New Orleans.

The New Orleans press corps was upset because Wilkinson had it and everyone else barred from the Sooner practices. Some stories hinted that Oklahoma players were not taking Louisiana State seriously.

The Tigers had defeated three 1949 conference champions, Tulane of the Southeastern Conference, Rice of the Southwest Conference, and North Carolina of what was then the Southern Conference, and some thought an upset might be in the making.

But three days before the game Piggy Barnes, a former Louisiana State player, was accused of spying on OU practices.

Barnes later claimed that he was scouting Oklahoma players for
the professional Philadelphia Eagles.

Wilkinson accused LSU officials of attempting to discover
OU's plans. And the OU coach in turn was accused of inventing
an incident to fire up the Sooners.

Nevertheless the game was not even close. The Sooners
won, 35-0, providing the biggest romp in Sugar Bowl history
and before a sellout crowd of 85,000 fans.

OU rushed for 286 yards and gained a total of 360,
compared to only 38 yards rushing and a total of 159 by
Louisiana State. Heath rushed for 170 yards on 15 carries, and
his 86-yard touchdown run set a Sugar Bowl record.

After the game the Sooners visited Havana, Cuba, in what
was described as the longest, largest, and most expensive trip in

*Dr. C. B. McDonald, Oklahoma City dentist and ardent OU fan,
helps police arrest Piggy Barnes, former Louisiana State player,
who was accused of spying on OU's preparations for the Sugar
Bowl game.*

Halfback Lindell Pearson gets ready to pass against Louisiana State in the 1949 Sugar Bowl game.

bowl history.

Having observed his former teammates during the 1949 season, Mitchell recalled:

"When OU walked out on the field, they looked like a bunch of noncommittal, couldn't care less, slouch around guys. They looked like they were going to a funeral. But it was the damnedest revelation you've ever seen. When they blew that whistle, it was like a house afire."

Weatherall:
First Outland Winner

Jim Weatherall arrived at OU in 1948 as one of the biggest players the Sooners had to that time and left in 1951 with the first major individual honor beyond all-American recognition ever won by an Oklahoma player.

Weatherall's career was a great one. He was the only sophomore on the first two teams of the great 1949 team, still considered by him as OU's greatest. He was an all-American selection on the 1950 team that won OU's first mythical national championship. And in 1951 he was awarded the Outland Award, presented annually to the college guard or tackle considered the best in the nation. He was only the sixth recipient of the honor.

At 6-foot, 4-inches, 220 pounds, the 19-year-old Weatherall was the tallest player and the second heaviest player on the 1949 team. Only 22-year-old, 236-pound guard Stan West was heavier.

Weatherall played during the period when OU was converting from teams dominated by military veterans to teams composed of players just out of high school.

"One of the things that I think helped me most was that we had a lot of older type fellows from the standpoint that they had been in the service," Weatherall said of the 1949 season. "I felt that it helped me in that I was in with an older type crowd. I mean their thinking was more mature, and this seemed to be passed on to the younger guys. I think we had more of a mature attitude, and I think that this prevailed over the years.

Tackle Jim Weatherall, 1950 Outland Award winner, is greeted by OU President Dr. George L. Cross.

"But gradually it faded out, because you lose that and it gets back more into your stage of regular kids coming out of high school. I gained a lot of experience by playing with guys like this: not only a more mature attitude but guys were helpful, they taught you.

"I think I learned a lot more football quicker. With that old bunch, you nearly had to or you'd get killed."

Weatherall believes that he was aided by two other factors. He had played high school athletics in White Deer, Texas, a Panhandle community of only 733. This gave him the opportunity to compete in all sports at the school. And during his first two years at OU, Weatherall competed in what was a new sport for him—collegiate wrestling. OU's freshman football coach at the time was Port Robertson, who also was the Sooner wrestling coach.

"The wrestling taught me a lot as far as balance, agility, and lateral movements are concerned," Weatherall said.

Although he played on both offense and defense during a period of limited substitutions, Weatherall was best known for his overpowering defensive play. He remained a huge player physically by OU standards at that time.

He also played a significant role as an extra point kicker. In fact one kick he missed and another he made played key roles in OU's quest for the national title in 1950.

While playing Texas A&M at Owen Field in the second game of the 1950 season, OU scored with only three minutes, 36 seconds remaining, but Weatherall missed the kick for the conversion, and the Aggies led, 28-27. Weatherall left the field, crying, thinking the game had been lost.

But he recalled: "Bud (Wilkinson) said he thought it was the thing that won the ball game for us. Otherwise we might have settled for a tie."

As it was the Sooners scored again with only one minute, 46 seconds remaining for a thrilling 34-28 triumph.

Wilkinson was quoted as saying: "That was the finest football finish I have ever seen. I still don't see how we did it. You just don't move 69 yards in one minute and nine seconds against a team as good as the Texas Aggies."

The next week against Texas, OU scored with only three minutes, 46 seconds remaining to tie the score at 13-13.

"The goal posts looked like they were nearly together," Weatherall recalled. But he kicked the winning extra point.

Weatherall also remembers Wilkinson as a master of psychology, both with working with the team and individuals. Weatherall recalled an incident at the half time of one game when the Sooners trailed at the intermission.

"Every guy on the ballclub knew that we had just stunk," he said. "We hadn't played good at all.

"We knew we deserved it, and we were waiting for him to come in and really chew us out good. We waited and waited and waited. And to this day he hasn't come into that dressing room.

"By this time everyone realized that if he was so ashamed of us that he won't even come in and talk to us, we'd better get

Linebacker Sam Allen tackles Missouri's Tony Scardino while Fred Smith (67) and Ed Rowland (74) come to help.

on the ball. We went out there and just tore them apart (and won the game)."

Weatherall had been selected as an all-American as a junior in 1950 but faced an unusual challenge at the start of the 1951 season.

"I never will forget it, but I later realized what he (Bud) had done," Weatherall said. "At the first practice in the fall of my senior year, Bud called off the names of the players on each team. When he finished calling off the last full unit, he still hadn't called my name.

"For about the first week there I was one of the guys holding the dummies for the fifth and sixth ballclubs. I don't guess I ever worked and practiced and tried as hard in my life, trying to work up. I was really getting worried: You know, I made all-American last year, and I'm not even going to make the ballclub this year."

But three days before the opening game Weatherall was promoted to the starting team.

"I looked back, and I see he was very effective in what he was trying to accomplish," he said.

That year Weatherall won the Outland Award selected by the members of the Football Writers of America.

"He was everything you're looking for in a football player," Wilkinson recalled. "Highly intelligent. Very strong

OU Coach Bud Wilkinson and quarterback Claude Arnold talk on sideline during 1950 Texas game.

Sooner Jim Weatherall tackles Kentucky runner in Sugar Bowl game.

physically. And he had that desire to excel. He became just a superb lineman."

Jim Weatherall had grown up wanting to play football at Oklahoma A&M.

"All they had to do was invite me, and I wouldn't have considered anyone else," he recalled.

So Weatherall took second choice and became one of the great linemen in college football.

Billy The Kid Rides Again

They called him "Billy the Kid." They called him "Curly." While growing up in Cleveland, Oklahoma, Billy Vessels had virtually no home life with stability. He was raised by the townspeople as a whole, living from time to time with different families. But Vessels was an incredible football player.

"He is one of the classic examples of what athletics will do for you," Wilkinson said, recalling Vessels' great career. "Without athletics there wasn't any way."

Vessels became OU's starting left halfback in the third game of the 1950 season, his sophomore year. In that game against Texas in the Cotton Bowl in Dallas, Vessels raced 11 yards, breaking two attempted tackles in the open field, to score the winning touchdown with only three minutes, 46 seconds left in the Sooners' 14-13 triumph before a record crowd of 75,969 fans.

Vessels continued to be sensational that year as the Sooners scored 10 straight victories and were ranked No. 1 in the final polls by the Associated Press and United Press International.

However, Oklahoma's first mythical national championship was somewhat tainted by a 13-7 loss to Kentucky in the Sugar Bowl. But in those days the wire services did not conduct a poll following bowl games, and OU remained No. 1 for 1950.

Vessels passed to halfback Merrill Green of Chickasha for Oklahoma's only touchdown in the bowl loss to preserve the Sooners' scoring streak. The loss ended OU's winning streak at

Halfback Billy Vessels is on his way on a 51-yard touchdown run against Kansas State.

31 straight games, a school record that would not stand for long.

Vessels' greatest individual performance as a sophomore came against Nebraska in what ranks as one of the great duels between backs in college football and one of the most exciting games in OU history. The Sooners defeated the Cornhuskers, 49-35, before 54,000 fans at Owens Field, and Vessels and Bobby Reynolds, Nebraska's great sophomore halfback, put on a brilliant show before the largest crowd ever to witness a Big Seven Conference football game to that time.

Reynolds ran for 81 yards on 14 carries in the first half to boost the Cornhuskers to a surprising 21-14 lead at half time. But Reynolds, an all-America selection as a sophomore who was hampered by injuries his next two seasons, gained only one yard in the second half. Meanwhile Vessels gained an OU record of 208 rushing, averaging 11.4 yards a carry and scoring three touchdowns.

Vessels had a great sophomore season, rushing for 870 yards, scoring 15 touchdowns, and passing for three other touchdowns. However, although Vessels was an all-Conference selection, other Sooners gained the national honors. Tackle Jim Weatherall of White Deer, Texas, and fullback Leon "Mule Train" Heath of Hollis, were consensus all-America choices, and end Frankie Anderson of Oklahoma City and defensive back Buddy Jones of Holdenville were named on other NCAA-recognized all-America teams.

Vessels' junior season was abruptly ended in the third game of the 1951 season when he suffered a disabling knee injury in OU's 9-7 loss to Texas. On the same play on which Vessels was injured, Oklahoma lost Eddie Crowder of Muskogee, who was emerging as one of the great Sooner quarterbacks. However, Crowder played the rest of the season, while Vessels

OU halfback Billy Vessels is carried from the field after suffering a knee injury in 1951 OU-Texas game.

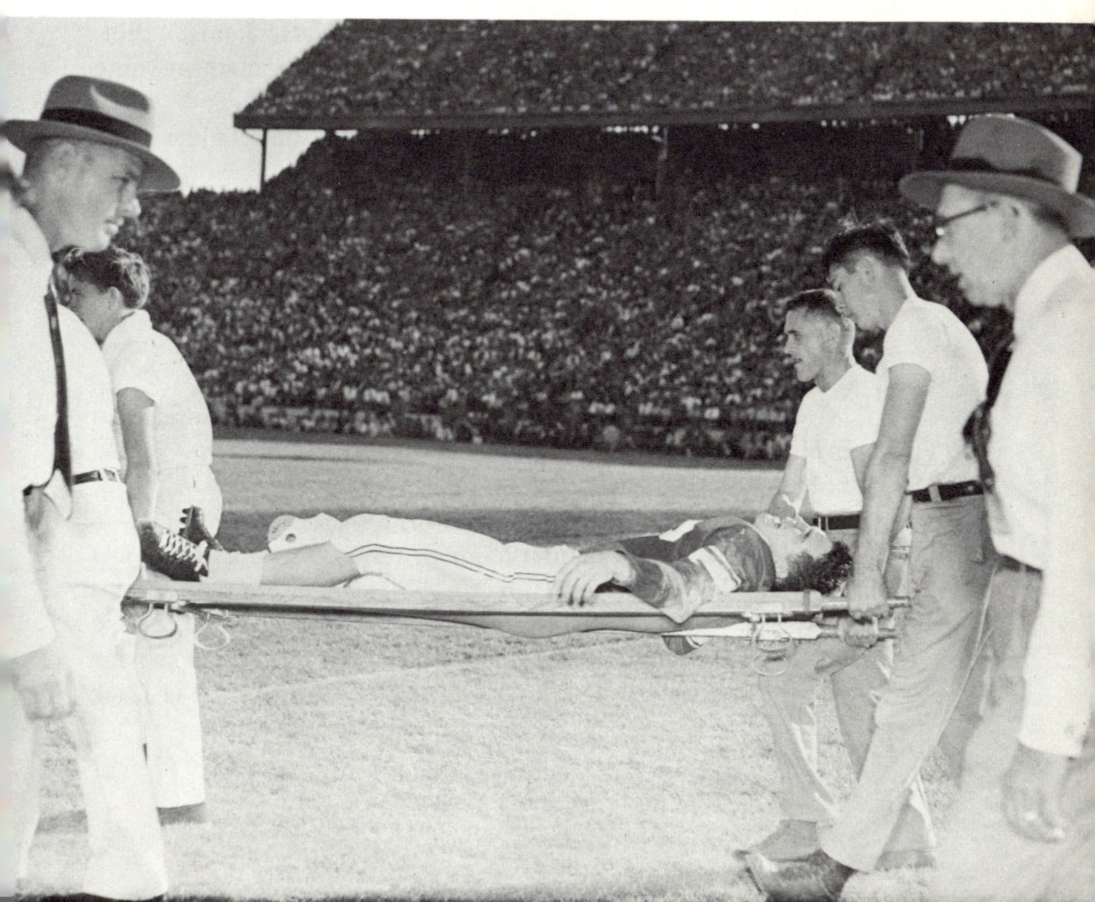

sat it out with his leg in a cast.

The week before, Oklahoma had lost, 14-7, to Texas A&M at College Station, Texas, with Vessels racing 74 yards to a touchdown on the final play of the first half to again add to the Sooners' great scoring streak.

But the Sooners won the rest of their games in 1951, and it is said that it was at this point that Vessels told friends that for the first time he realized the Sooners could win without him.

Vessels returned for his senior season in 1952 with a healthy knee and renewed desire. However, things started on a shaky note as OU lost six of seven fumbles in the opening game of the season against Colorado at Boulder, Colorado.

With the Sooners leading, 14-7, Vessels appeared to make a diving catch in end zone of a 21-yard pass from right halfback Buddy Leake of Memphis, Tennessee. But officials ruled that Vessels had trapped the ball, and OU did not score.

Vessels did score on a one-yard run, and Leake kicked the extra point with one minute, 51 seconds remaining to tie the score at 21-21 in what was a disappointing start for the Sooners.

But the Sooners amassed an incredible attack after that, scoring 40 or more points in seven of their remaining nine games.

Oklahoma had one of its all-time great backfields. Dick Cullum of the *Minneapolis Tribune* wrote:

"When Buddy Leake, the right halfback, was well, the Oklahoma backfield of Eddie Crowder, Billy Vessels, Leake, and Buck McPhail was the best-balanced, most versatile backfield I have ever seen. Every one of them was at the all-American level. Oklahoma had the best offensive platoon of the season and as far as I know, the best ever."

Crowder, now a senior, was often described as a magician when his ball-handling skills were discussed. He also was a fine passer and superb leader.

Leake, who had substituted for Vessels in 1951 as a freshman, was a strong runner at right halfback and an excellent placekicker who would leave OU in 1954 with the school record of 241 points with 28 touchdowns and 74 extra points. Leake scored 78 points as a freshman and shared the individual scoring lead in the Big Seven Conference. And the fullback was Buck

McPhail of Oklahoma City who was overshadowed by Vessels throughout a brilliant career.

A stubborn, rugged runner, McPhail rushed for 1,018 yards in 1952. No other Sooner had ever gained more than 1,000 yards in one season. But 1952 was Billy Vessels' year. He gained 1,072 yards. Vessels and McPhail did become the first two players on one team to gain 1,000 yards or more in the same season.

McPhail survived with one record of his own, however. He rushed for 215 yards against Kansas in 1951, erasing Vessels' school record of 208 set the previous year against Nebraska.

What perhaps was Vessels' greatest performance came in Oklahoma's only loss in 1952. The Sooners bowed to Notre Dame, 28-21, at South Bend, Indiana, in a setback that may have cost OU the national title.

The Sooners were plagued by fumbles and injuries in the

Fullback Buck McPhail is attended by trainer Joe Glander.

Quarterback Eddie Crowder gains 13 yards against Oklahoma A&M.

hard-hitting nationally televised contest that some termed the greatest game in college football history to that time. Vessels ran for 195 yards, the most ever by an individual against Notre Dame and a record that stood until 1973. He scored touchdowns on runs of 62 and 44 yards and on a pass from Crowder on a play that covered 28 yards.

But OU lost five fumbles and was the victim of what was called the "sucker shift," a maneuver outlawed by the NCAA the next year because it was believed its basic purpose was to draw the opposition offside.

Leake, tackle Ed Rowland, and Merrill Green, Leake's

understudy, were injured during the game, and guard J. D. Roberts was ejected. Notre Dame tied the score 21-21 and recovered an OU fumble by Larry Grigg on the Sooner 24-yard line, setting up a one-yard run for the winning touchdown by reserve quarterback Tom Carey.

Wilkinson recalled that OU had one last, desperate drive, but it was foiled when what might have been a perfect play failed because of a freak mishap. OU called a screen pass, but left end Max Boydston of Muskogee, who was to be the receiver, did not hear the screen portion of the call because of the crowd noise.

The screen was formed, but Boydston was blocking instead of being behind the screen, and Crowder had to throw the pass away. Afterward, Vessels with tears in his eyes, faced Wilkinson

OU's Carl Allison (83) and Tom Catlin (54) knock Notre Dame's Neil Worden out of bounds in the Sooners' loss in 1952 at South Bend, Indiana.

Tom Catlin, all-American center in 1951 and 1952.

in the dressing room and said:

"Remember, coach, when I was a freshman, and you told me it was the team that counted and not the individual? I know what you mean now."

Vessels Wins The Heisman

Billy Vessels became an all-American in 1952 and became the first Oklahoma player ever to win the coveted Heisman Trophy, awarded each year to the college player considered the best in the nation.

"It's what every football player dreams of," Vessels said of the award. "Much of the credit goes to Eddie Crowder. I don't see how they could ignore him and Buck (McPhail). Those guys, and all the rest of the team, are really great. The greatest I ever saw.

"Of course I owe more to Coach Wilkinson than anybody else. He took me as a green kid and made me what I am—both on and off the field. Then there's Mrs. (C. R. "Kitty") Roundtree. She's a second coach. She knows more about football than most men. She makes me train even during the summer."

Mrs. Roundtree of Oklahoma City adopted Vessels in every way except legally, helping him to avoid the pitfalls common of a youngster of his background and encouraging him in his academic work.

Vessels' record as an athlete is a great one. At 6-foot-1, 185 pounds, Vessels was big and powerful for a halfback in the early 1950s. Yet he also had great speed and was a rugged competitor.

Many considered him the best passer and perhaps the best defensive player OU had at the time. Vessels sometimes played on defense in key situations in crucial games.

Billy Vessels prepares to throw a touchdown pass to Merrill Green as fullback Leon Heath leads the way in the Sugar Bowl game against Kentucky.

Billy Vessels is on his way to one of three touchdowns against Notre Dame in 1952 loss at South Bend, Indiana.

He rushed for 2,085 yards in 24 games and scored 35 touchdowns to tie the school record held then by George Thomas of the 1946, 1947, 1948, and 1949 teams. But Vessels' 210 total points stood alone. He also passed for 327 yards, gained 391 yards in receptions, returned kickoffs for 528 yards, returned punts for 221, and returned intercepted passes for 39 yards.

In rare unqualified praise Wilkinson said:

"Billy was a remarkable athlete. He was the first player that I had ever been around who was the fastest man on the field and also the toughest. Those two things don't normally go together.

"But Vessels was just unbelieveably strong and tough and also the fastest man we had. And totally dedicated. A truly great player. He really was. His senior year he was just unreal. He could do everything."

And perhaps the most remarkable one thing Vessels did was to rise above his background.

J. D. Roberts: Late Bloomer

For the third straight year a Sooner gained one of the two coveted national individual honors in 1953. The career of that player, guard J. D. Roberts of Dallas, Texas, was very similar to the type of season Oklahoma experienced in 1953. Roberts had been an excellent player in his sophomore and junior seasons, but he became a great player in his senior year and won the Outland Award in 1953. Likewise the 1953 Sooners started slowly but finished with one of the great victories in the history of OU football.

"In our games I noticed that I was always about two steps slow on downfield blocking," Roberts recalled of his first two seasons. "I remember Gomer (assistant coach Gomer Jones) said, 'J. D., you need just a little more speed.'"

Roberts played at 230 pounds as an offensive guard in 1951. Changes in the collegiate rules in 1953, limiting substitutions, meant that players had to perform on both offense and defense.

"I could react pretty well, but I still needed to be faster so I could help our guys cover to the outside when the opponents ran our ends," Roberts said following the 1952 season. "So I decided to come down to 200 pounds."

During Marine Corps reserve camp that summer, Roberts reduced to 200 pounds.

"J. D. was a boy who really was not physically as impressive as Weatherall, for example," Wilkinson said of the 5-foot, 10-inch Roberts. "He was not tall. Yet he had extremely

Guard J. D. Roberts was Outland Award winner in 1953.

fast reflexes. Again that burning desire to excel. A super competitor.

"He played his first couple of years at about 230 and 220. He was an excellent player, but he was just a little bit slow in relative terms. He was still an excellent player. But his senior year he got down to 200 pounds, and that gave him that extra couple of steps in speed that he had not had up to that time. With that little bit of added speed he became just remarkable.

"He was the first dominant type nose guard that I recall. We didn't play him the way Nebraska played Rich Glover (in 1970 and 1971), but he was that important to us and he was that effective."

The 1953 season started with a jolt as OU lost to Notre Dame, 28-21, at Owen Field, in an ironic repeat of the score of the Sooners' stunning loss at South Bend, Indiana, the preceding season. The Fighting Irish, who ended the campaign ranked second in the nation to Maryland, also ended OU's 25-game winning streak at Owen Field.

The next week Buddy Leake of Memphis, Tennessee, converted from halfback to quarterback, completed a pass to right halfback Larry Grigg of Sherman, Texas, on an 80-yard touchdown play in a 7-7 tie with Pittsburgh.

But the following week OU defeated Texas, 19-14, in their classic, annual clash at Dallas, Texas, and the Sooners were off to a successful season, although not without some struggles, the

Larry Grigg scores a touchdown against Notre Dame in 1953.

Merrill Green starts on a 51-yard run for a touchdown in the final 36 seconds of OU's 27-20 victory over Colorado in 1953.

remainder of the 1953 campaign.

Merrill Green raced 51 yards for a touchdown with only 36 seconds left in OU's 27-20 triumph over stubborn Colorado.

And Grigg scored from the one-yard line with only four minutes, 28 seconds remaining in the Sooners' 14-7 victory over Missouri.

But the real triumph came after the regular season.

The Sooners were ranked fourth in the nation and were selected to face Maryland's mythical national champions of former Oklahoma head coach Jim Tatum in the Orange Bowl.

Maryland had a more impressive record, 10 straight victories without a loss. The Terrapins' closest contest was a 20-6 triumph over Missouri in the opening game of the season. And Maryland handed Alabama's Southeastern Conference champions a 21-0 loss.

The Terrapins were known for their great defensive play, having allowed only five touchdowns the entire season. Maryland allowed only one more touchdown, but that was enough for Oklahoma to gain a 7-0 upset victory.

Grigg, the senior co-captain, fittingly ended his collegiate career by scoring the touchdown on a 25-yard end run. The Sooners halted two scoring threats by Maryland, stopping the Terrapins at the one-yard line on one series and then seeing Maryland miss an 11-yard field goal attempt to end another drive.

Three days before the Orange Bowl game second-team quarterback Pat O'Neal of Ada suffered an injury and could not play. Early in the second half of the game, starting quarterback Gene Calame of Sulphur was injured and could not play. This meant that third-team quarterback Jack Van Pool of Oklahoma City would have to play the remainder of the contest.

Van Pool had been Oklahoma's first three-sport high school all-Stater, but he now was a senior and had played very little in college. When he came into the huddle the first time, Van Pool said, "I know I'm not very good but I promise you guys if you'll stick with me through this, I won't fumble."

He extended his hands at the time and they were trembling. The humor of the situation relieved the tension, and Van Pool made good on his promise.

Polls were not taken following bowl games then, but Oklahoma's time was coming.

Start Of The Streak

For all its own achievements the 1953 Oklahoma football team probably will be remembered best as the team that started the Sooners on their unequaled dynasty of that decade—47 straight victories. The 1953 team won its final nine games, and although no one could have known it at the time, those victories would be significant in setting a record never achieved before or since in the history of collegiate football.

The 1954 Sooners had a different situation. They did not start the fabulous winning streak. They did not end it. And unlike their immediate successors, they did not win a mythical national championship.

Forecasts called for uncertainty for Oklahoma football in 1954. Six starters returned from the 1953 team, but vital depth would have to be provided by unproven sophomores. Some sophomores. They included Tommy McDonald, Jerry Tubbs, and Jimmy Harris, players who were to become legends to Sooner fans.

And it was during 1954 that a certain feeling began among Sooner fans: It was not a question of whether Oklahoma would win. The question concerned by what margin the Sooners would win.

Dr. George L. Cross, Oklahoma's president at the time, recalled how that sometimes was a mixed blessing. The Sooners were on their way to another Big Seven Conference championship, but Oklahoma was ineligible to return to the Orange Bowl because the contract between the conference and the bowl

Kurt Burris, all-American center in 1954, and Bob Burris, all-Big Seven halfback in 1955.

forbade one school playing two years in a row.

When Nebraska came to Norman for the final game of its regular season, the Cornhuskers already had clinched second place in the conference and had accepted the bid to play in the Orange Bowl. Cross recalled that his guests at the game were Dr. Clifford M. Hardin, the newly named chancellor at Nebraska,

Halfback Bob Burris races for a touchdown against Nebraska.

and his five small children. Cross bought the youngsters Nebraska pennants before the contest.

Cross recalled Hardin's saying: "I know we're not going to win this ballgame, but I hope that we're just not humiliated."

Cross replied, with what he remembered was great sincerity, "I hope so, too."

When Nebraska scored late in the first quarter to tie the score at 7-7, Hardin said he already felt better about the game.

"Sure enough, here it came," Cross said, describing the Oklahoma rally.

And as the score mounted, Cross said: "I just sat there literally praying that we wouldn't score again. Bud played everyone he had, but it didn't matter. All of the conversation had died down. There was nothing I could think of to say that wouldn't have sounded silly. And, of course, there was nothing Hardin could think of to say.

"Those little kids looked like they were going to cry, and their pennants were down in the box. It was the damnedest thing. I was just sick. It was the worst game I ever sat through."

Oklahoma won, 55-7.

But not all the 1954 games were runaways. In the second game of the season starting quarterback Gene Calame of Sulphur suffered a broken collar bone, and the Sooners trailed Texas Christian, 16-7, going into the final quarter. Calame was replaced by one of those unproven sophomores, Jimmy Harris of Terrell, Texas.

The Sooners scored two touchdowns in the final quarter with halfback Bob Herndon of Medford scoring the winning touchdown on a 10-yard run with six minutes remaining. But Oklahoma did not clinch the victory until linebacker Kurt Burris of Muskogee tackled Texas Christian's Ron Clinkscale inside the Sooner five-yard line on the last play of the game.

Harris' great performance sparked the Sooner comeback. He scored Oklahoma's first two touchdowns, one on an exciting 69-yard punt return.

The Sooners also came from behind to defeat Texas, 14-7, but many believe the key play of the game came on Oklahoma's first touchdown drive. Faced with a fourth down one yard short of a first down on its own 36, Oklahoma gambled and made the first down.

Harris still was the quarterback, and another of those unproven sophomores, Jerry Tubbs of Breckenridge, Texas, made his starting debut against the Longhorns that day. Tubbs was a center but he started at fullback the remainder of the season, primarily because of his skills as a linebacker. Players had to perform on both offense and defense. Tubbs did that, averaging 6.1 yards a carry.

Colorado, troublesome more than once during this fabulous streak, gained a 6-0 lead and was halted at the Oklahoma 13 in an attempt to widen the margin. Finally halfback Buddy Leake of Memphis, Tennessee, and reserve quarterback Pat O'Neal of Ada scored touchdowns in the fourth quarter for a 13-6 triumph by the Sooners.

And, although it was virtually overlooked at the time, the

End Max Boydston was Sooner all-American in 1954.

Sooners set a national record by scoring in their 90th consecutive game when they defeated Kansas State, 21-0. Catawba, a small college in Salisbury, North Carolina, had set the record with a streak of 89 spanning the 1944 to 1953 seasons.

Another game may have had a significant role in Oklahoma's being ranked third in the nation although it posted a 10-0 record. The Sooners defeated California, 27-14, in the opening game of the season for Oklahoma. Ohio State was ranked No. 1 and UCLA No. 2 in the Associated Press poll. And the order was reversed with UCLA No. 1 and Ohio State No. 2 in the United Press poll. Oklahoma was third in both. All three played California.

Ohio State defeated California, 28-0, in its first game of the campaign, and UCLA beat the Golden Bears, 27-6, late in the season.

As it happened UCLA and Ohio State did not meet in the Rose Bowl, because UCLA had played in the postseason game the previous season and was not eligible to return.

Oklahoma came close to another first in 1954. Center Kurt Burris finished second to Wisconsin fullback Alan Ameche in the voting for the Heisman Trophy. That was higher than any interior lineman had ever placed in the voting for the award.

Quarterback Gene Calame gains 20 yards against Kansas.

And only one other interior lineman has finished that high since then. Iowa tackle Alex Karras was second to Texas A&M's John David Crow in 1957.

"If anybody had told us before the season began that we would go through all-victorious, I'd have thought they were crazy," said Wilkinson. "But our 1954 team had a world of fight and was always able to show a little more of it than the other team when the going became tough and the chips were down. That's the mark of a champion."

Halfback Buddy Leake runs for a touchdown against Kansas.

Wave Flag,
Sing "Boomer Sooner"

Clendon Thomas sat in the small office of the receptionist in the southeast corner of the OU Field House. Only a thin wall separated him from the office of Bud Wilkinson, Oklahoma's head football coach. He was a sophomore and had been asked to report to Wilkinson this afternoon during the preseason practices in 1955.

Thomas did not consider himself to be what is commonly referred to as "a highly sought" prospect in high school. He attended a new school named Southeast in Oklahoma City. And in his senior year, the football team had an unimpressive 2-8 record.

He had had some problems his freshman year. He entered spring training in 1955 as an "a.o.," meaning he was one of the players not listed on a team on the depth chart. Such players were called "all others" or "a.o." He was not considered the ideal halfback at the time. At 6-foot, 2-inches, 185 pounds, Thomas took long strides and did not appear to be moving fast or going full speed. Actually he was, but it just did not look like it.

"They didn't know it then, but I was going to play," Thomas recalled.

And things changed after a particularly bruising tackle by Thomas in a scrimmage got the attention of the coaches. In the early fall practices he was challenging junior Tommy McDonald, a more flashy runner from Albuquerque, New Mexico, for the starting left halfback position.

Looking back Thomas recalled what meetings with Wilkinson were like. "He would do a snow job on you," he said. "He would call you in to talk to you. And you knew why he was going to talk to you, and you knew everything he probably was going to tell you. But you appreciated it.

"He would make a point to tell you that you were going to be a good ball player and that you were going to do good things for them. And that they expected certain things out of you. He just had a way of making you wave the flag and come out singing, "Boomer Sooner.""

On this particular day Wilkinson asked Thomas to make a sacrifice. Thomas was told that he probably could be a starter, but that he could contribute more to the team by playing on the second team. The second team, which Wilkinson referred to as the alternate team, would play almost as much as the first team anyway.

However, the choice was up to Thomas. Clendon Thomas played on the second team in 1955. Actually, there was not a great deal of difference between the first and second teams as a whole. In fact Wilkinson found that out one day.

"He had a scrimmage one day between the first team and alternate team, and he made the mistake of saying whoever won that scrimmage was going to start," Thomas recalled.

"It was good psychology, except that our second unit was whipping the first unit. We had them down a touchdown, and they couldn't come up. And Wilkinson didn't want to start the second unit. He didn't intend to get caught like that.

"Well, it was going to be the next morning before we got off that field, if we (the second team) didn't let them score. And finally the guys let Tommy (McDonald) run for one so we could go in. It was already dark. That tied the score and gave him an out. It dawned on us that we had better let them score and call this thing a tie or we never are going to get off that field."

That scrimmage probably was the biggest challenge either team faced all year. The 1955 Sooners extended Oklahoma's all-victorious streak to 30 straight games with eleven wins and no losses. The Sooners were overpowering, averaging 35 points a game and allowing their opponents an average of 5.5 points a contest. Oklahoma shut out five of its eleven opponents.

Sooners Clendon Thomas, Tom Emerson, and Jerry Tubbs close in on Kansas State's Jerry Hayes.

The closest game came in the season opener against North Carolina. The Tarheels scored with only five minutes, 21 seconds gone when quarterback Jimmy Harris of Terrell, Texas, fumbled on the center snap and North Carolina's John Bilich recovered the ball in the end zone. But the Sooners scored twice in the second half to win, 13-6.

Thomas recalls that most of the games were much more challenging than the scores indicate.

"Any time anyone plays the University of Oklahoma, it didn't matter who they were, they were going to be five times better than they were going to be any other time of the year. They'd do things that day that they weren't capable of doing. If they were 10 flat sprinters, they were running 9.8s. If they won that one ballgame, their whole season was a success. We never played a team that wasn't ready to play us. And they could play us head to head for a half a lot of times.''

Two major-college teams finished the regular season all-victorious in 1955. Oklahoma was ranked No. 1 and unbeaten Maryland No. 2 in the final wire service polls. That, of course, set the stage for another classic confrontation between the Sooners and the Terrapins in the Orange Bowl.

Halfback Tommy McDonald worries on the sideline.

Quarterback Jimmy Harris stiff-arms Texas' Don Marony on an eight-yard touchdown run.

The game was a natural, since Oklahoma had upset Maryland's 1953 mythical national champions in the Orange Bowl. And it gave Jim Tatum, the former head coach at Oklahoma, an opportunity to gain revenge.

Maryland had an even more impressive defensive record than the Sooners. The Terrapins had shut out four opponents and had allowed only 57 points in 10 games.

The bowl contest was billed as a battle between Oklahoma's high-scoring offense and Maryland's stingy defense. The game also provided an opportunity for the Sooners to show off their hurry-up offense on a national scale. The idea for the hurry-up attack apparently grew out of McDonald's fantastic hustle. The 169-pound speedster always ran back to the huddle. And before long the entire team ran to line up for the play and then ran back to the huddle after the play.

Interestingly, McDonald, who was an consensus all-America selection for his great play in 1955, was not a highly sought high school player either.

"Tommy only weighed 155 pounds in high school," Wilkinson said. "We recruited a teammate of his named Rhodes (end Ted Rhodes). We thought he was the real prospect. But Tommy was convinced that he was going to win, and that rubbed off on the people around him."

The hurry-up offense, used only at certain times in a game, had a devastating effect on the opponent's defense. It caused confusion and fatigue and gave the impression that the Sooners might be something other than human.

"It was all you could do to last through it," Thomas recalled. "After four of five quick plays, if they hadn't called timeout, we'd had to. We were just as tired as they were. They

Sooners celebrate after defeating Maryland, 20-6, in the Orange Bowl game following the 1955 season.

Guard Bo Bolinger was OU all-American in 1955.

just didn't know it."

Then Thomas laughed. "I remember in the Maryland game that we ran one play so quick that Harrison (Oklahoma second team center Bob Harrison of Stamford, Texas) hit Pellegrini (Maryland's all-America center Bob Pellegrini) right in the back while he was calling defensive signals."

The fired-up Maryland team threatened early when halfback Ed Vereb raced 66 yards but was knocked out of bounds at the Oklahoma 10-yard line on a desperate, diving tackle by reserve quarterback Jay O'Neal of Ada. Then Oklahoma end Don Stiller of Shawnee recovered a fumble to end the threat.

Later, Jerry Tubbs of Breckenridge, Texas, blocked an attempted field goal. But Maryland was persistent and gained a 6-0 lead at half time. In the second half the Sooners came back, scoring once in the third quarter and twice in the final quarter for a 20-6 victory. Reserve halfback Carl Dodd of Norman put the outcome out of question when he returned an intercepted pass 82 yards for Oklahoma's final touchdown.

Nationally syndicated columnist Bob Considine wrote: "If his forebears had run that fast in the Oklahoma run, he'd own half the state," referring to Dodd's Indian heritage.

Of the victory, Wilkinson said: "That's the most satisfying victory we've ever had."

Tatum was gracious in defeat, remarking: "Oklahoma is definitely the best team in the country. I've never seen a team with all the equipment this one has."

Smiling, Wilkinson said: "I don't know if we're the best. But we haven't been beaten yet."

Tubbs Makes
Keynote Address

It seemed incredible that the feats of the 1955 Sooners could be matched, much less exceeded, the very next season, but they were. Most observers classify the 1956 Sooners on a par with the great 1949 team. And some even believe the 1956 team was Oklahoma's all-time best.

Analyzing the teams today former OU Head Coach Bud Wilkinson avoided a direct comparison by saying that the 1956 team was the best "normal college team" he coached. The 1949 team had mature, military veterans and the best of several years of high school players. The 1956 team was formed from only three years of recruiting and had no older players.

Six starters returned from the 1955 team. They were Ed Gray of Odessa, Texas, who moved from right tackle to the left side which had been wiped out by graduation; center Jerry Tubbs of Breckenridge, Texas; right end John Bell of Enid; quarterback Jimmy Harris of Terrell, Texas; left halfback Tommy McDonald of Albuquerque, New Mexico; and fullback Billy Pricer of Perry.

Clendon Thomas of Oklahoma City was moved to the starting right halfback position, providing an added striking force. The other starters were left end Don Stiller of Shawnee; left guard Joe Oujesky of Fort Worth, Texas; right guard Bill Krisher of Midwest City; and right tackle Tom Emerson of Wilson. The Sooners had great depth with 16 other lettermen, some of whom had played as much as the regulars on other teams.

Center Jerry Tubbs was all-American in 1956.

"The odds of a coach acquiring that much talent at one time on one roster," said Clendon Thomas, not finishing the sentence or even offering a guess at the odds. "There were many on the bench that could have played anywhere else."

This great depth allowed Wilkinson to continue to use two units almost equally with little sign of a drop-off in skill. The opening game of the campaign was to provide former OU head coach Jim Tatum his last of three unsuccessful and frustrating opportunities to defeat the Sooners. After the 1955 season Tatum left Maryland to become the head coach at North Carolina, his alma mater. But, unlike the great clashes with Maryland, this game was no contest with the Sooners winning, 36-0.

The Sooners scored their third straight shutout, outclassing Texas, 45-0, the second widest winning margin for Oklahoma in the series.

"I remember some guys coming off the field crying when someone would score on us that year," Thomas said.

Oklahoma scored one of its great victories against a below-par Notre Dame team at South Bend, Indiana.

OU's First Team At The Start Of The 1956 Season
Front row, from left: John Bell, Tom Emerson, Bill Krisher, Jerry Tubbs, Ken Northcutt, Ed Gray, and Don Stiller. Back row: Clendon Thomas, Jimmy Harris, Bill Pricer, and Tommy McDonald.

"They had just kinda embarrassed us a few years ago," Thomas said of Notre Dame's victory over Oklahoma in 1952 on national television. "They just needed what we were fixing to give them.

"He didn't have to say much," Thomas said of Wilkinson. "He had us ready. He knew when to say things and when not to. There was no rah rah stuff.

"They were in for it. We had an outstanding ball team. We had unbelievable depth.

"I guess Jerry Tubbs was as good a collegiate player as I've ever seen. First play out of the hat he stuck Hornung (Notre Dame's 1956 Heisman Trophy winner and quarterback Paul Hornung) in the face and chest. That was the keynote address that ball game."

The Sooners rolled to an easy 40-0 victory, the worst ever suffered by a Notre Dame team to that time. Even so Oklahoma gained only 235 yards rushing and passing, about half its average to that time in 1956.

Reserve end Steve Jennings of Ardmore blocked a punt to set up one touchdown. And the Sooners intercepted four Irish passes. McDonald returned one 55 yards for a touchdown, and Thomas returned another 35 yards for a touchdown. Notre Dame suffered through a 2-8 record that season.

The next week against Colorado the Sooners faced their stiffest test of the campaign. Orange Bowl bound Colorado had lost only once previously in 1956 and was determined to score its first victory over the Sooners since 1912.

Folsom Field in Boulder, Colorado, had been enlarged to

Halfback Clendon Thomas races past Notre Dame's Paul Hornung on an 11-yard touchdown run in OU's 40-0 victory in 1956.

Sooners show where they think they rank after their 40-0 triumph over Notre Dame in 1956.

hold a sellout crowd of 47,000, and the Sooners added to their delight by yielding a blocked quick kick and fumble, allowing the Golden Buffaloes to gain a 19-6 margin at half time.

"That's one of the few times in my career with Mr. Wilkinson that he ever really got mad," Thomas said, referring to Wilkinson's talk at half time. "That day he made a comment to the effect that we didn't deserve to wear the red jerseys that we had on our backs. He was mad. He was speaking, and everybody knew it, about the tradition, the winning streak, and as ball players."

From there the game changed. On the first series of the second half the Sooners went for a first down on a fourth down play with two yards to go at their own 28-yard line. Thomas made three yards on the crucial play and Oklahoma was off to a 27-19 triumph.

Next the Sooners triumphed 53-0 over Oklahoma A&M (now Oklahoma State). It was Oklahoma's 40th straight victory, establishing an NCAA record. The University of Washington

Halfback   Tommy   McDonald   leaps   to   avoid   a   Colorado defender.

held the record until then, winning 39 straight games during the 1908, 1909, 1910, 1911, 1912, 1913, and 1914 seasons. But Washington's record was amassed against high school, military, and athletic club teams as well as collegiate teams. All of Oklahoma's victims were major-college teams.

McDonald and Thomas entered the Oklahoma A&M game tied for the national lead in scoring, each with 16 touchdowns and 96 points. Fullback Billy Pricer raced 37 yards for Oklahoma's first touchdown of the contest, and Thomas recalls that McDonald trailed him the entire way, yelling for a lateral.

"Pricer had never scored on a run that long, and he wasn't about to give up the ball," Thomas said.

Thomas and McDonald each scored one touchdown on running plays. Ironically, McDonald passed eight yards to Thomas for the touchdown that gave the junior halfback the national scoring title.

Thomas finished the season with 18 touchdowns and 108 points, and McDonald placed fourth with 17 touchdowns and 102 points. For two years there had been a friendly rivalry between the two excellent players.

Earlier in the season, when a photographer had asked him to pose for a picture, McDonald suggested that the photographer lie on his back and McDonald would leap over him. "You could say these are the cleats that are going to run over Texas," McDonald said.

The photographer had other ideas, but McDonald insisted. Then the photographer suggested: "Well, I guess I could get Clendon Thomas for this picture."

McDonald reacted immediately: "What kind of picture do you want?" he said.

Late in the Oklahoma A&M game co-captain Ed Gray, an all-America tackle, came back to the huddle and said:

"I want to carry the ball. I've never scored."

Thomas traded places with him, and Gray scored a touchdown on a two-yard run.

"Wilkinson went crazy," Thomas recalled. "He loved it. We loved it, too."

The Sooners were overwhelming that year. Oklahoma set NCAA and Big Seven records in rushing with an average of 391 yards a game. The Sooners also led the nation and set a Big

Coach Bud Wilkinson and quarterback Jimmy Harris talk during flight.

Seven record with an average of 481.7 yards a game in rushing and passing. And they led the nation in scoring with an average of 46.6 points a game. Although it is often overlooked, the Sooners also were second in the nation in total defense, allowing an average of only 193.8 yards a game rushing and passing. Oklahoma allowed its 10 opponents only 51 points. National statistics were not kept at the time in defense against scoring.

Twelve seniors completed their careers as three-year lettermen who had been all-victorious in their collegiate days. They were left ends Bob Timberlake of Tulsa and Delbert Long of Ponca City; left tackles Ed Gray of Odessa, Texas, and Wayne Greenlee of Breckenridge, Texas; center Jerry Tubbs of Breckenridge, Texas; right tackle Tom Emerson of Wilson; right end John Bell of Enid; quarterbacks Jimmy Harris of Terrell, Texas, and Jay O'Neal of Ada; left halfback Tommy McDonald of Albuquerque, New Mexico; right halfback Robert Derrick of Woodward; and fullback Billy Pricer of Perry.

Two other players missed that distinction simply by

Tackle Ed Gray shouts encouragement from the sideline.

chance. Ken Northcutt of Wichita Falls, Texas, started the first game of the season at left guard but was injured and allowed to play in 1957 under the Big Seven Conference hardship rule. And right end Hugh Ballard of Memphis, Tennessee, completed his senior year and gained his third letter in 1956, but he had lettered as a sophomore in 1951 when Oklahoma was not undefeated.

During 1954, 1955, and 1956 Oklahoma's record was an unequaled 31 victories, no losses, and no ties. And the Sooners had averaged 37 points a game to an average of less than 6 points for the opponents.

Harris had been the starting quarterback in 23 of those games, and he did not even make the all-Big Seven Conference team as a senior, an honor he had obtained as a junior.

Remembering those days, Wilkinson commented: "Jimmy Harris was probably the most underrated athlete who ever played."

"You Don't Like Ties"

One football fan leaned over to the man next to him and said: "Father, why don't we just call it a tie? Why don't we go home and have a cool drink?"

The other fan replied: "No, I'd rather lose than have a tie."

The questioner concluded: "Okay, we'll just play it."

And they did, and the game made college football history.

They were no ordinary football fans—Dr. George L. Cross, OU's president, and his guest that day, the Reverend Edmund P. Joyce, C.S.C., executive vice president of Notre Dame. The scene was Owen Field in Norman, Oklahoma. The day was November 16, 1957. It was a gray, chilling day. But it did not start unlike many days for Oklahoma's football at that time.

The Sooners had posted seven straight victories that season and were ranked second in the nation. They had been No. 1 the previous two seasons, and the goal was clear.

After all, Oklahoma entered the contest with 47 straight victories and was an 18-point favorite.

The Sooners could not be beaten. So believed the 62,800 fans at Owen Field.

Sports Illustrated also was a believer. That very week the national magazine had published a cover story entitled: "Why Oklahoma is Unbeatable."

Oklahoma's opponent was another traditional great among the nation's collegiate teams—Notre Dame. But this year's Fighting Irish team was not considered among the school's greatest. Many of its players had endured the humiliating 40-0 defeat by the Sooners the previous season. That was the worst defeat ever inflicted on the proud Irish to that time.

This year's Notre Dame team had won its first four games but had bowed to Navy and Michigan State in the two weeks preceding the clash at Owen Field.

Oklahoma's most serious scoring threat came on its first possession when the second team marched to the Notre Dame 13-yard line only to be halted there on downs. The Sooners repeatedly put the Irish in peril, hoping for a game-breaking mistake. Notre Dame was pinned back on its 15- and 4-yard lines on punts by halfback Clendon Thomas of Oklahoma City and back on its 3- and 7-yard lines on punts by quarterback David Baker of Bartlesville. But Notre Dame survived each test without yielding a score.

The Sooners repeatedly turned down threats by the Irish, stopping Notre Dame on downs at the OU one-foot line once and intercepting a pass in the Sooner end zone on another drive. Thomas punted into the Notre Dame end zone early in the fourth quarter, and the Irish began a grueling, decisive drive from their own 20-yard line with 12 minutes, 51 seconds left in the game.

In 19 time-consuming plays, only one a pass, Notre Dame moved to the Oklahoma three-yard line with a fourth down. When Notre Dame reached the eight, Oklahoma's first team was sent into the contest to perform another miracle.

But on the fourth-down play Notre Dame halfback Dick Lynch, running to his right, took a pitch-out and, to the surprise of nearly everyone, found no one threatening his path to the end zone. Lynch scored the touchdown, and Monte Stickles kicked the extra point for a 7-0 lead for the Irish with only three minutes, 50 seconds left in the game.

Oklahoma made one last, desperate attempt to preserve its streak of 47 straight victories and 123 games in which it had scored. Oklahoma reached the Notre Dame 24-yard line in the closing minutes, but a pass by quarterback Dale Sherrod of Odessa, Texas, was intercepted by Bob Williams in the Notre Dame end zone.

A stunned, partisan crowd sat not believing as college football's longest winning and scoring streaks came to an end on

Notre Dame's Dick Lynch runs for a touchdown in the Fighting Irish's 7-0 victory in 1957. The loss ended OU's 47-game

winning streak and the shutout ended OU's record of scoring in 123 consecutive games.

one bleak afternoon. Following the game Cross and Father Joyce visited the dressing rooms of each team. Cross recalled Wilkinson's comments to Father Joyce.

"Father, I want to congratulate you," the OU coach said. "You have a great ball team. We played as well as we could every minute of the game."

The two university officials left and started the short walk across the OU campus to the residence of Cross.

"In all my years, and there are many, I've never heard a losing coach say his team played as well as it could," Father Joyce said.

"They always explain how the team didn't play so well. What a fine spirit it was for a coach to have. How gentlemanly and sportsmanly his boys were."

Then Joyce put his arm around Cross' shoulders and said: "It's tough to lose. Isn't it too bad when you have two such fine schools, two such fine coaches, and two such fine teams, that both can't win the same day?"

Cross replied: "That's right, Father, but that's the name of the game: You can tie but you can't both win. And you don't like ties."

End Of An Era

Oklahoma's 1957 football team won the Big Seven Conference championship, was ranked fourth in the nation in both wire service polls, and defeated Duke in the Orange Bowl following the regular season. However, unfortunately, the 1957 Sooners probably always will be remembered for their one loss—the 7-0 upset by Notre Dame.

Clendon Thomas, the brilliant halfback from Oklahoma City, recalls the situation.

"At that time we had a tradition to uphold," he said. "There were three seasons of teams that had set that thing in motion. You were letting those guys down, if you didn't continue. You felt obligated, and you're under a lot of strain. The whole team for some reason was just dead that day.

"The guys never really felt all that guilty about losing to Notre Dame. They felt bad because that streak was over. But we also felt a sigh of relief, too. That was a big strain and it was over.

"Had we been able to walk into that game without the pressure being on so much, I believe we would have played a different ball game that day. I think the strain finally caught up with a bunch of guys."

Only three weeks earlier the Sooners made one of those miracle comebacks to avoid having the winning streak ended at 44 straight. Before 61,700 fans, a Big Seven Conference record, at Owen Field, Thomas scored on an eight-yard run, and Carl Dodd of Norman kicked the extra point with only four

OU stops Notre Dame's Nick Pietrosante in 1957.

minutes, 34 seconds left in Oklahoma's 14-13 triumph over Colorado. Once again the ever-challenging Golden Buffaloes had been denied their place in history.

Another noteworthy event also occurred in 1957. The Sooners defeated Texas, 21-7, giving Oklahoma its sixth straight triumph and ninth victory in ten years against the Longhorns. However, it was to be the last victory scored against Texas by an OU team coached by Bud Wilkinson.

Thomas recalled that the Sooners voted not to accept the bid the Orange Bowl at the end of the 1957 season. "For some reason, they felt obligated to let you vote," he said. "I don't know who thought that one up, because it's worth so much to your university to go. But the guys who had gone before (in 1955) remembered the bowl trip was worse than two-a-days.

"When we got down there, he (Wilkinson) decided we would get the kinks out from flying by having a little workout on the traffic island across from the Bal Harbour," Thomas said of the 1955 bowl trip. "Ask anyone on that football team about the traffic island. Ask them if they got a nice workout on that traffic island. I thought I was going to die. We were going to get loosened up, and he killed us.

"The most difficult thing is the end of the season. Your legs are tired, and you don't get your quickness back at the end of the week. The mere fact that you're young is the only thing that saves you.

"A lot of it is mental. You've played your whole season. You've got a strain on you every week to win. You've got to win. That's just the name of it. So we voted not to go to the Orange Bowl in 1957.

"He just grinned," Thomas said, recalling Wilkinson's reaction.

Duke would have been better off if the Sooners had stayed at home. Oklahoma led only 21-14 going into the final quarter but unleashed a furious attack to defeat the Blue Devils, 48-21.

Oklahoma football remained devastating in 1958.

Halfback Clendon Thomas races past Texas' Maurice Doke in OU's 21-7 victory in 1957.

Bill Krisher, all-American guard in 1956 and 1957.

Oregon nearly ruined the season in the second game of the campaign. But guard Dick Corbitt of Altus recovered a fumble on the Oregon 17-yard line, and quarterback Bobby Boyd of Garland, Texas, passed one yard to halfback Jimmy Carpenter of Abilene, Texas, for a touchdown in the first half of the 6-0 decision.

Texas pulled one of Oklahoma's miracle finishes the next week. Longhorn quarterback Bobby Lackey passed 16 yards to end Bob Bryant for a touchdown, and then Lackey kicked the extra point with only three minutes, 10 seconds remaining for a 15-14 triumph by the Longhorns, their first victory over Oklahoma in the last seven seasons. It also marked the first victory over the Sooners for a familiar name—Darrell Royal, the Sooner star of the 1940s who was in his second season as the

Longhorn head coach.

In the final game of the regular season Boyd ran 31 yards for a touchdown with only five minutes remaining as the Sooners defeated Oklahoma State, 7-0.

Then, the Sooners, ranked fifth in the nation, defeated Syracuse, ranked ninth, in a convincing 21-6 struggle in the Orange Bowl.

However, Oklahoma's fortunes were to change, and the Sooners would not be ranked among the nation's top ten teams for the next three years.

"No Simple Issue"

In the summer of 1956 Bud Wilkinson faced a difficult decision. He knew he was going to produce one of the greatest teams in Oklahoma history the next fall. But this decision involved more than football. His decision was to prove to be a monumental one. It was a decision that would affect the lives of every athlete at Oklahoma not only for the next few years but far into the future of Oklahoma athletics.

"Prentice Gautt was probably the best player in Oklahoma that year," Wilkinson recalled. "We're now faced with the problem of do we or don't we give him a scholarship. This was no simple issue."

The problem was Prentice Gautt was black. No black athlete had ever played football at Oklahoma. Not only that, many influential supporters of Oklahoma's program openly opposed the idea of a black ever playing for the Sooners.

Wilkinson was secure. He did not need Prentice Gautt to continue Oklahoma's football success. Not only that, the University of Oklahoma already was involved in controversial integration issues in other areas.

Gautt's potential was obvious for any who were willing to look. He had helped Oklahoma City Douglass, a black high school playing in the state's segregated league, to 76 straight victories. He was not eligible to be named to the all-State team because he was black, but was asked to play in the all-State game in August when the North team did not have any fullbacks because of injuries. Gautt was named the outstanding player in the game.

Gautt had received scholarship offers from Oklahoma A&M, Michigan State, and Maryland State. He was thinking seriously about going out of state to play football. But Gautt recalled what influenced his decision to attend Oklahoma. His mother became ill, and he did not want to be far away from his home in Oklahoma City. Merrill Green, an assistant coach at Wichita State and former Sooner star halfback in the early 1950s, contacted Gautt in an attempt to get him to attend Wichita State.

Gautt recalled Green's saying: "They've got some great players down at OU, and I doubt if you'll be able to play down there."

Gautt reacted: "That was just like a challenge. I said to myself, 'I know I can go down there and play. I know I can.'"

Then for what appeared to be no apparent reason, members of the Black Medi-Pharm Association, a group of black professional men in Oklahoma City, offered to pay Gautt's expenses for four years at Oklahoma.

Wilkinson had avoided the issue of offering an athletic scholarship but had gotten Gautt to Oklahoma. Without public fanfare and without Gautt's knowing, Wilkinson had struck a bargain with the opposition among the Oklahoma supporters: Gautt would be allowed to try out for the team, and if he made it he would be given an athletic scholarship.

Wilkinson recalled: "I knew he would make it."

A Lasting Contribution

Of course Prentice Gautt did make it in more ways than one. He remembers feeling "very much alone" during his freshman year when the other blacks on the Oklahoma campus were commuters. But by October he had received his athletic scholarship, and he moved into the athletic dormitory the next year. Gautt played as a reserve fullback and linebacker as a sophomore.

"I can remember a conversation I had with him when I was a sophomore," Gautt said, referring to Wilkinson. "He told me, 'The way that you're performing now, you're not going to make our squad.'

"Boy, that really shook me up. It was sorta like a self-fulfilling prophesy: I was just falling in line with what others had said about my ability. A lot of people had said, 'He won't make it neither academically nor athletically.'

"From that point on it seemed like I started to pick up.

"Of course there was lots of positive re-enforcement coming from guys like Bob Burris (then a freshman coach) and Eddie Crowder (former head coach and now athletic director at Colorado who was a varsity assistant coach at the time). And, of course, Bud.

"I was caught up in accepting myself: How much I could really let go in terms of hitting on defense, in terms of running, in terms of the friends that were saying they were friends.

"It was almost like a state of paranoia to some extent. And yet there was something there that kept me going, kept me

Fullback Prentice Gautt races 42 yards to a touchdown against Syracuse in the Orange Bowl.

relatively integrated and pretty well stable.

"I still say that Bud had a lot to do with my emotional stability. It was almost like he was protecting me. I think he tried to see to it that I never had any real pressures placed on me. At least, none that I couldn't handle."

Gautt started at fullback and linebacker in 1958 in his junior year. He rushed for 627 yards, averaging six yards a carry as the Sooners posted a 10-1 record, won the Big Seven title, and defeated Syracuse in the Orange Bowl game.

The 21-6 triumph over Syracuse in the Orange Bowl was one of the games Gautt remembered as one of his best. He raced 42 yards for a touchdown, gained 94 yards rushing, and made key blocks and tackles on other crucial plays.

Gautt also recalled that one of the most significant games to him was OU's 23-7 triumph over Colorado at Boulder in

OU Coach Bud Wilkinson sometimes surprised opponents with unusual formations. Here is a spread formation used against Oregon in 1958.

1958. The Sooner fullback rushed for 117 yards, including a 48-yard touchdown run that tied the contest at 7-7. Gautt recalls that Colorado had an outstanding black guard, John Wooten, who was named all-Big Seven in 1957 and all-America in 1958.

Gautt also played a key role in OU's 6-0 win over Oregon earlier in the season. He pulled down Oregon's Willie West from behind on a 53-yard run and prevented what might have been the winning points for the Ducks.

Gautt was an all-Big Seven selection in both 1958 and 1959 and rushed for 674 yards and averaged 5.2 yards a carry in 1959. He led OU in rushing in both his junior and senior seasons.

But all was not winning and honors for Prentice Gautt at Oklahoma in those days. During the 1959 season Gautt recalled that Wilkinson ended practice early one day because of what Wilkinson considered the players' poor performances. Wilkinson held a squad meeting immediately afterward.

"He gave a speech," Gautt said. "He said, 'I'm ashamed. I don't want to be associated with some of you, because a lot of you have been talking about this guy.' And he pointed at me. I was really surprised, because I didn't know what this was all about.

"He said, 'Now, a lot of you have been talking about this guy behind his back.' He said, 'If you're a man, you'll stand up and tell him what you said in front of his face and apologize.'

"It really took me back, because I think in a situation where a person is a first, you have to be oblivious to some things. You can't become paranoid and think people are doing certain things to you, unless you can't exist at all.

"So evidently I had really done a job on myself. I had just said, 'Everybody loves me and no problems at all.'"

Wilkinson left the room and closed the door. Gautt recalled that hardly anyone moved, and the room remained silent for maybe five minutes. "Then, all of a sudden, guys started hopping up and apologizing," he said. "Guys that I was really surprised to see some of them stand up and say some of the things that they had said."

But make no mistake there also were strong supporters during those perilous days. Gautt never had a roommate in the

Bob Harrison, (left) all-American center in 1958 and Joe Rector, (right) captain in 1958.

athletic dormitory, but Jakie Sandefer, a starting halfback from Breckenridge, Texas, was his roommate on road trips during 1957 and 1958, and Ronnie Hartline, Gautt's fullback understudy from Lawton, was his roommate on road trips in 1959.

There still were moments of uncertainty. Texas laws prohibited Gautt from staying at the same motel with the team in Fort Worth, Texas, where the Sooners spent Friday night before the annual OU-Texas clash.

Gautt believes that Sandefer took a chance of risking his own great popularity among his teammates when he became Gautt's first white roommate.

"I think Jakie was asked if he wanted to be my roommate," Gautt said. "I believe that he accepted that as sort of a modeling thing for my acceptance."

Gautt also recalled the enthusiasm of halfback Brewster Hobby of Midwest City. Of reviewing films of playing days at OU, Gautt remarked: "It's amazing how many times Brewster, such an elated and enthusiastic kind of person, comes and just jumps all over me (after Gautt made a successful play). I think about him quite a bit. I thought that we were pretty good friends."

But Wilkinson remains the central figure in Gautt's recollections of his experiences at Oklahoma.

"He got some awfully nasty letters," Gautt said of his former college coach. "Of course, I got some too, but I didn't realize the pressures that he was enduring. I really didn't realize the pressures that he went through in terms of getting me to play there.

"I guess I got the feeling that he really wanted me to make it. Otherwise I don't think he would have talked to me the way he did.

"Maybe it's because I wanted to see him that way. But I

Jim Davis scores a touchdown after recovering a fumble by Texas in 1958.

don't think that he did that kind of thing with other players. So he was something special to me. And I guess I kinda looked at him as a father-image to some extent."

But Gautt says that he never really considered the significance of his success at Oklahoma until he was out of school.

Wilkinson said: "I've never felt that this was like the stories I've read of Jackie Robinson and Branch Rickey at all. The professional situation is different than the amateur.

"You're talking about a relatively young person who wanted to do it, but I don't think he really knew at the start what he was getting into either. But he grew with it. We all did."

Trouble In Evanston

The 1959 season opened as none other in Oklahoma history. The Sooners, again considered challengers for the mythical national championship, were scheduled to play Northwestern of the Big Ten Conference in Evanston, Illinois. Many thought Northwestern was to have one of its best teams in years, and Oklahoma was installed only a six-point favorite.

The week of the game started normally. But from Thursday evening until the Sooners arrived in Norman Saturday night after the game nothing was to be normal. It was a week many Sooner fans would rather forget and one that still is draped in mystery and suspicion.

The Sooners, victors of their last eight games after suffering their only loss of the 1958 season to Texas, worked out early Wednesday afternoon in Norman before flying to Chicago. The team left earlier than usual because classes had not started.

After Thursday's workout the Sooners were scheduled to dine at the Chez Paree, then one of the famous night clubs in Chicago. Only two of the 40-player traveling squad did not attend the dinner. Fullback Prentice Gautt was excused, and right end Edward "Wahoo" McDaniel missed the team bus, not an uncommon occurrence.

It was one of Wilkinson's policies that members of the coaching staff not attend meals with the team. He believed the team would be more relaxed if the coaches were not present.

However, Ken Farris, then OU's athletic business manager,

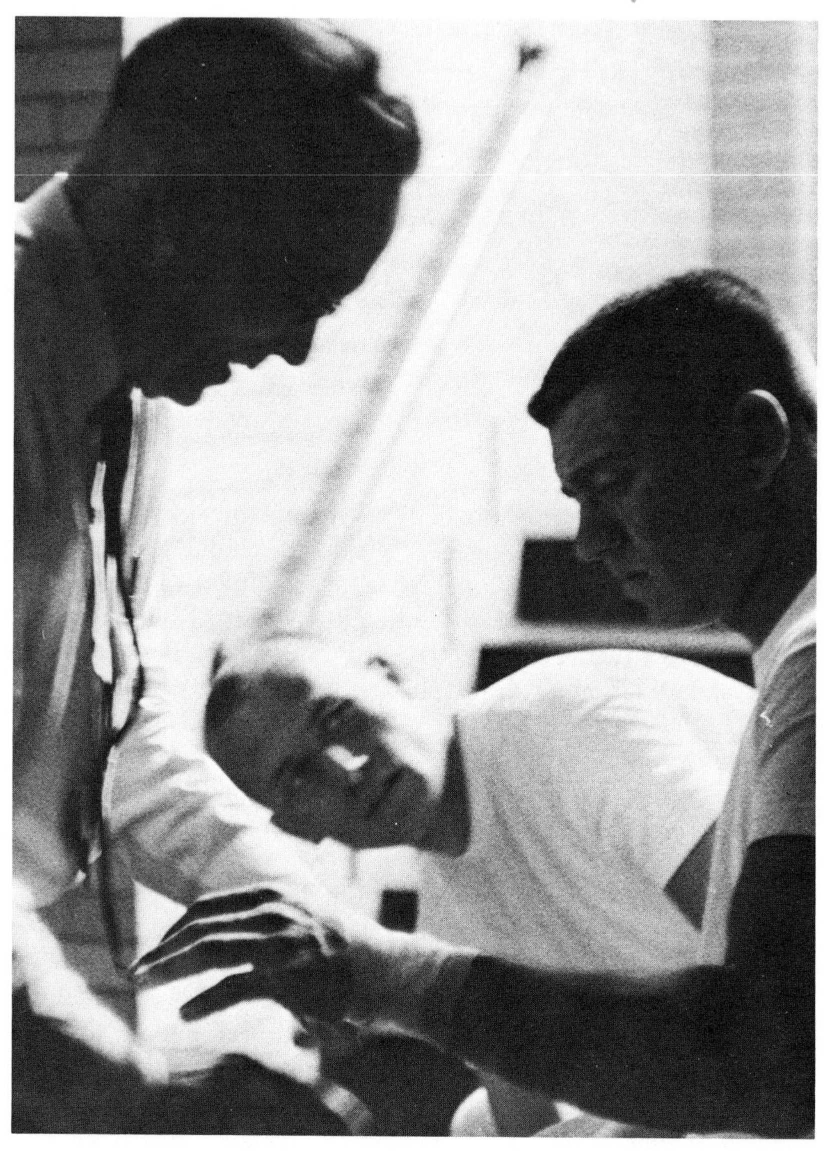

Wahoo McDaniel is assisted by trainer Ken Rawlinson.

did attend the meal. In fact Farris was in charge of selecting the site and the menu. As late as four that afternoon, Farris changed the menu, substituting steak for roast beef.

The menu also included a fruit cup, tossed salad, mashed

potatoes, roll and butter, and ice cream. The Sooners also were scheduled to attend the performance of vocalist Patrice Wymore, who was entertaining at the Chez Paree. But none of them was to be around for that treat.

Shortly before the Sooners were to be served dinner, a man and a young woman approached the area. The man introduced himself as a Sooner fan from Oklahoma and the woman as his daughter. He said his daughter wanted to meet the players, and each Sooner was asked to stand and introduce himself. Such hero worship and gracious response were not uncommon. But considering what was to happen, the incident became very suspicious.

Jerry Thompson, all-American tackle in 1959.

Shortly afterward the Sooners were served the fruit cup and tossed salad. One by one players excused themselves. Before long eight players and student coach Jimmy Harris, who had begged special permission to attend, had become violently ill.

They were taken to a Chicago hospital, and their stomachs were pumped. The players were first-team center Jim Davis, second-team center Bob Scholl, first-team quarterback Bobby Boyd, second-team quarterback Bob Page, first-team left tackle Gilmer Lewis, second-team fullback Ronnie Hartline, second-team right end Paul Benien, and third-team right tackle Bill Watts. Boyd and Lewis were co-captains.

Trainer Ken Rawlinson says he will never forget seeing Boyd so ill that the stocky, powerful quarterback had to be strapped into a hospital bed.

Rawlinson returned to the hotel to find four other players ill. They were first-team left halfback Brewster Hobby, first-team right halfback Jimmy Carpenter, second-team left guard Jerry Payne, and third-team left tackle Max Morris. Rawlinson believes that the illnesses may have been caused by seeing their teammates ill.

News reports state that among the ill players only Hartline worked out with the team Friday.

The game was as much a disaster for the Sooners as the evening out. Northwestern gained a 13-0 lead in the first quarter. The Sooners struggled to trim the score to 13-7 as a spring-like storm blew in before the end of the first half. Northwestern gained a 45-7 margin before OU reserves scored a meaningless touchdown late in the game.

The Sooners had lost, 45-13. It proved to be the worst loss in terms of points by an opponent and in losing margin in Wilkinson's fabulous career as head coach at Oklahoma.

Oklahoma had contributed significantly to its own setback. The Sooners fumbled 12 times and lost 5. Northwestern recovered OU fumbles within 8, 9, 20, and 37 yards of the Oklahoma goal.

How significantly the poisoning contributed still is an open question to some. After the game Wilkinson and some of the Sooner players discounted the illnesses.

Reports show that all the stricken players except Watts,

Benien, and Morris played in the game. However, Rawlinson said many made what he called "only token appearances."

To this day many Oklahoma officials and fans do not discount the illnesses. They claim there still are too many unanswered questions. The game was taken out of betting circulation within an hour after the incident. Specimens of food and player waste mysteriously disappeared before they could be examined.

Northwestern officials of course were never suspected of being involved.

Ironically the return flight to Norman was to be little better. The plane had to change its original flight plans to avoid severe storms.

Perhaps the incidents were storm warnings of things to come.

In one of Oklahoma's better games, halfback Brewster Hobby races past Missouri's Ed Hehrer.

Bud's Last Years

From that disastrous 1959 beginning against Northwestern the Sooners bounced back to post a 7-3 record and claim the last championship before the Big Seven Conference added Oklahoma State and became the Big Eight. OU had reason to regret the passing of the Big Seven Conference. In the 12 years that the conference was known as the Big Seven, Oklahoma had won all 12 championships.

Yet the 7-3 record in 1959 was the worst in the 13-year career of Bud Wilkinson as head coach at Oklahoma, and perhaps was an omen of things to come. The year 1959 was the year that the idea that the Sooners could be beaten by a conference team became reality.

In a game played before a disbelieving homecoming crowd of 34,000 at Lincoln, Nebraska, the Cornhuskers took advantage of a blocked punt, two field goals, and a 61-yard punt return for a touchdown by Pat Fischer to upset the Sooners.

Oklahoma fought back to trim the score to 25-21 with its only touchdown in the second half. But Nebraska's Ron Meade intercepted a pass by the Sooners in the Cornhusker end zone with only 25 seconds remaining to prevent another miracle victory by Oklahoma.

The setback was the first loss in conference play by the Sooners since 1946 and in 74 games. It was the first time a Sooner team coached by Wilkinson had ever lost in conference play.

Wilkinson's teams had a record of 70 victories, 2 ties, and

no losses in conference play going into that game. The loss also ended what still stands as the conference record of 44 straight victories in league play.

Had it not been for a 21-21 tie with Colorado in 1952 Oklahoma would have had 70 straight victories in conference play. The victory was Nebraska's first over the Sooners since 1942.

In 1960 Wilkinson suffered his only losing season as a head coach and the first at Oklahoma since 1942. The Sooners had a 3-6-1 record and finished fifth in the Big Eight Conference race.

Billy White, captain in 1961.

Oklahoma suffered its first loss to Colorado since 1912, its first loss to Iowa State since 1928, and its first loss to Missouri since 1945.

The Sooners made a remarkable comeback to post a 5-5 record in 1961 but suffered their first loss to Kansas since 1946.

After Oklahoma lost the first five games of that season, Wilkinson, who was very cautious, even pessimistic, in his public statements, announced on statewide television that the Sooners would win their remaining five games.

"The pressures of losing were getting heavy," Wilkinson said, remembering the incident. "I said we were going to win the next five games in an effort to give everybody the feeling we

Halfback Jimmy Carpenter gains seven yards against Kansas State in 1961.

Halfback Mike McClellan races for touchdown against Army in 1961.

could."

The next week Oklahoma defeated Kansas State, 17-6.

"That was one game we didn't have to play well to win," Wilkinson recalled.

But the next game was the crucial one as the Sooners met Missouri at Columbia. The Tigers, the defending Big Eight champions, entered the game with a 5-1-1 record and were attempting to rebound from a 7-6 loss to Colorado and stay in the title race.

Left halfback Jimmy Carpenter of Abilene, Texas, passed

Wayne Lee (left) and Leon Cross, OU's 1962 captains, chat with Morris Tenenbaum who has guarded the entrance to OU's dressing room for years.

14 yards to right halfback Mike McClellan of Stamford, Texas, for the only score of the game in Oklahoma's 7-0 triumph, perhaps one of the biggest upsets in Sooner history.

The next week the Sooners caught Army's defense completely offguard when they ran a play without a huddle, and McClellan raced 75 yards for a touchdown in the 14-8 victory. Victories over Nebraska and Oklahoma State by a margin of one touchdown each completed the remarkable comeback.

"Our teams in the early 1960s just did not have enough quality athletes." Wilkinson said, analyzing the situation years later. He attributed the situation to what he called "poor recruiting."

"In retrospect I believe the ease of traveling by air had extended recruiting boundaries tremendously, and we just hadn't realized it at the time," he said.

But it appeared that during the last two years of

Wilkinson's coaching career at Oklahoma the Sooners were on their way back to the glory days of the past.

Combining the experience of a few seniors and the skills of an excellent sophomore crop including future all-Americans Jim Grisham and Ralph Neely, the 1962 Sooners rebounded from two losses in their first three games to win Oklahoma's first conference championship in four years, return to the nation's top 10 for the first time in four years, and gain a bid to the Orange Bowl.

The Sooners, ranked eighth in the nation, faced the rising forces of Alabama, ranked fifth, in the postseason meeting in Miami, Florida. Led by linebacker Lee Roy Jordan and quarterback Joe Namath, the Crimson Tide scored a surprisingly easy 17-0 triumph over the Sooners.

Paul "Bear" Bryant, on his way to making his alma mater a perennial national power, won the second of two meetings with teams coached by Wilkinson. Ironically Bryant coached the Kentucky team that ended Oklahoma's 31-game winning streak in the 1950 Sugar Bowl game when Wilkinson was a young

President John F. Kennedy visits OU's dressing room before the Orange Bowl game against Alabama following the 1962 season.

Joe Don Looney, all-American halfback in 1962.

coach.

Now a team coached by Bryant had robbed Wilkinson, near the end of his career at Oklahoma, of his last opportunity for a victory in a bowl game 12 years later. But the 8-3 record was a big improvement over the previous two campaigns.

Hopes were high for the 1963 season. In the second game sophomore quarterback Mike Ringer led the Sooners to a 17-12 triumph over defending national champion Southern California before 52,245 fans in the Coliseum in Los Angeles and a nationwide television audience.

The temperature got up to 110 degrees during the game, and Wilkinson believes that was a deciding factor.

"Southern California just couldn't maintain the pressure," he said, remembering the contest. "And that's one thing we knew how to do. If the game had been played in 75-degree weather, I don't think we had the athletic ability to beat them."

Even so, the victory boosted the Sooners into first place in the national wire service polls the next week. But that same week Ringer accidently stuck his right elbow into an electric fan in his room and was out for the remainder of the season.

"He would have been a super player," Wilkinson said, bemoaning the incident.

The next week the Sooners were completely dominated in

Halfback Larry Shields is led by cheerleader Vicki McNeeley on a 65-yard touchdown run on a punt return against Missouri in 1963.

a 28-7 loss to Texas, the eventual 1963 national champion.

The following week in an unprecedented move for Wilkinson, a starter, 1962 all-America halfback Joe Don Looney, was dismissed from the squad. Reports said that Looney was dismissed because of his unconventional attitudes about not attending practices or not fully participating in practices and because of complaints from his teammates.

But the Sooners still had an opportunity to repeat as champions of the Big Eight. This despite the fact that a one-time early day power of the Midlands, Nebraska, was being revived by Bob Devaney, who was in his second season as the head coach of the Cornhuskers.

Nebraska won the game that decided the title, 29-20. Actually the game was not that close, since Oklahoma scored all of its points in the final quarter.

In January of 1964 Wilkinson resigned to enter what proved to be an unsuccessful race for the United States Senate.

New Challenges For Bud

During the 17 years he was the head football coach at the University of Oklahoma, Bud Wilkinson was the best known and perhaps the most popular man in the state of Oklahoma. He had all the characteristics necessary for success.

He played on the great Minnesota teams of 1934, 1935, and 1936 coached by the redoubtable Bernie Bierman. The Gophers had a record of 23 victories and only 1 loss during those years. Minnesota was ranked No. 1 in the first national rankings poll conducted by the Associated Press in 1936.

Wilkinson also was the quarterback on the first College all-Star team to defeat the national professional championship team in the annual game played in Chicago in 1937.

At 6-foot-2, 190 pounds, Wilkinson always stayed in excellent physical condition. He had a disarming smile. He was a spell-binding public speaker. He was a thorough organizer. He was a master at convincing people to at least try to do what he wanted done.

He believed in the sanctity of practice, more often than not closing such sessions to the public. Some observers contend that the only thing that could drive the Sooners from the practice field in those days was a storm containing lightning.

Wade Walker, now Oklahoma's athletic director, recalls Wilkinson in the early days of his coaching career as being "mild, standoffish, serene."

"The worst thing I ever heard Coach Wilkinson say in my four years with him was what he said to one youngster," Walker said. "Instead of saying, 'you're a gutless coward.' Man, he'd never say that. It was simply: 'It just looks like you don't want to hit them.'"

Clendon Thomas, who played on the great teams of the mid-1950s, had other memories of Wilkinson. "You weren't going to be buddy buddy," Thomas said. "It was going to be Mr. Wilkinson, which is the way any smart head coach stays with his people.

"Gomer was a super guy," he said of line coach Gomer Jones. "If you had a problem, go see Gomer, go see Port (Port Robertson, then the freshman football coach and wrestling coach)."

But Thomas also recalled Wilkinson's manner at practices. "One day I wasn't hustling and wasn't practicing hard," Thomas said. "He would never get on you in front of people. He would take you aside. He'd ask you about everything, but he'd never tell you you were loafing.

"His approach was: Are you having trouble in school? Have you got financial problems? Did you have a fight with your girl friend? Anything I can help you with?

"He'd never, though, get down to the fact that the real problem was that you were just out there doggin' it. He gave you 300 excuses just to make you feel bad. He was giving you a way out. But you knew what he meant."

However, Walker and Thomas each remember another side of Wilkinson, the coach.

"His philosophy was to beat the other team down so hard that it won't pay the price to win in the fourth quarter," Walker said. "A champion finishes the job."

"'The fourth quarter's ours,' was one of his pet sayings," Thomas said.

"He developed in these guys a phenomenal thing. That was a killer instinct. You get a team down, you don't just beat 'em by three points, you beat 'em by 50. That was something he taught. He put 'em away.

"I felt sorry for some of those teams when the third team came in during those good years. They were so hungry. If I was an opposing coach, I'd rather have the first or second team in because we were tired. But he'd stick the third team in, and they'd score, invariably they'd score."

Although his teams sometimes used trick plays and formations, Wilkinson basically was a conservative coach.

He believed in consistency and the running attack. He selected his players primarily for their skills on defense. During

Bud Wilkinson (right) and Gomer Jones test field before game.

Coach Bud Wilkinson is consoled by one of his sons, Jay, an all-American back at Duke in 1963.

most of his coaching career college rules limited substitutions. He believed that if a team had a strong defense and sound kicking game, it would not have to have a good offense to win.

However Wilkinson's teams probably were best known for their offense, perhaps because he was so closely associated with the Split-T attack. During his tenure the Sooners averaged 28.7 points a game, an unusually high scoring average during a period of limited specialization.

But it also should be noted that Oklahoma's opponents averaged only 10.1 points a game. And during five seasons the opponents averaged less than a touchdown a game.

During 15 of the 17 years Wilkinson coached, Oklahoma ranked in the top ten in the nation in rushing. During his first 12 years the Sooners posted a remarkable 114 victories, only 10 losses and 3 ties. The Sooners' overall record during his 17 seasons as head coach was 145 victories, 29 losses, and 4 ties.

In 1949 Wilkinson was named Coach of the Year by the National Football Coaches Association. He was the Associated Press Coach of the Year in 1950. He was the president of the National Football Coaches Association in 1958 and also served as a member of the national rules committee.

Even so, Dr. George L. Cross, then president of the University of Oklahoma, recalls: "Wilkinson worried that what he was doing would not be a source of satisfaction to him later in life. We often talked about this. I think he really lost his zest for coaching near the end of his career. Recruiting fell off. The probation was a handicap. He even considered accepting the job at Stanford, because it would be a different type of challenge."

Thomas recalled that two years before Wilkinson resigned they sat in an otherwise empty dressing room following Oklahoma's annual spring game with its alumni team. Thomas repeated Wilkinson's words: "I'm probably smarter as a coach that I've ever been. But there are other challenges in life, other areas of activity where one can be of service."

So at the age of 47 Bud Wilkinson resigned as the head coach at the University of Oklahoma.

Wilkinson's achievements are many. Certainly his introduction of the black athlete into Oklahoma football must be considered a master stroke when one looks at the Sooner teams of today. His OU football teams' established records that may never be equalled in collegiate history. Yes, the Wilkinson era stands as the emergence of Oklahoma football onto the national scene.

Number Two
Becomes Number One

One of the first decisions made by Bud Wilkinson after he became OU's head football coach early in 1947 proved to be one of the most important in his coaching career. He had been impressed by the work of a young line coach at the University of Nebraska and hired him as OU's line coach.

Thus began the meshing of the coaching careers of Wilkinson and Gomer Jones and the building of one of college football's great dynasties. Jones was OU's line coach and Wilkinson's right-hand man during the 17 years Wilkinson was OU's head coach.

"They were both tremendous fellows," said Jim Weatherall, OU's all-America tackle of 1950 and 1951. "They formed a tremendous team. Gomer was closer to the boys, while Bud stayed a little more aloof. Gomer was kind of a go-between. If a guy had problems, he'd go to Gomer and he'd say, 'I'll talk to Bud.'

"Personally, I can't think of one and not think of the other. Either one of them would have been hurting without the other."

Dr. George L. Cross, former OU president, stated: "I doubt if any football team will ever be as dominant as Oklahoma was during the period when Wilkinson and Jones coached here. It would be unlikely that any school would have that combination that complement each other for so long. It also gave the school a great advantage in attracting athletes."

Thus Jones became perhaps the best known and most

respected assistant coach in college football in the nation at that time. He turned down several opportunities for head coaching jobs, stating:

"Why should I become a head coach? I already have an ulcer."

However, Jones apparently did not feel that coaching at Oklahoma would give him an ulcer. When Wilkinson resigned as OU's head football coach, January 11, 1964, Jones made himself available, with Wilkinson's blessing.

Controversies surrounding the replacement of head coaches at major institutions are legendary. But the decision by Jones, backed by Wilkinson, to seek to replace Wilkinson perhaps added new dimension. Jones and Wilkinson promptly found themselves on one side and the OU Board of Regents on the other. Because of Oklahoma's great success and reputation in college football, OU fans believed that the Sooners could hire just about any coach in the nation. An added factor may have been Wilkinson's suggestion that he might run for the U. S. Senate as a Republican, unless he stayed on as OU athletic director. All the regents had been appointed by a Democratic administration.

So one week to the day after he had resigned as head football coach, Wilkinson resigned as athletic director, criticizing some members of the board for their involvement in the political issues and strongly urging that Jones be hired immediately.

Cross, a persuasive leader with powerful influences, also supported the hiring of Jones. "I believed that he deserved the opportunity if he wanted it," Cross said. "But I didn't know if he could be successful."

Strong public support also had been mustered for Jones by this time. So one day after Wilkinson was completely out of the situation, Gomer Jones was hired as head football coach at the University of Oklahoma. At 49 years old Jones succeeded one of the nation's most successful coaches at a school whose fans thought in terms of undefeated seasons.

Gomer Jones was OU coach in 1964 and 1965.

Gomer Steps Aside

Oklahoma entered the 1964 season with high expectations. The Sooners were returning seven starters from a 1963 team that was ranked 10th in the nation after losing only to national champion Texas and Big Eight Conference champion Nebraska, which had lost only once in 11 games.

But the Sooners lost three of their first four games. First came a devastating 40-14 loss to Southern California at Norman in the second game of the season. Then OU lost to Texas, 28-7, in a series then being dominated by the Longhorns of Coach Darrell Royal. Next week at Lawrence the Sooners lost to Kansas.

In that third Sooner loss the Jayhawks beat them, 15-14, by scoring on the first and last plays of the Big Eight Conference opener for the Sooners. Gale Sayers returned the opening kickoff 93 yards for a touchdown. Then on the final play of the game Bob Skahan scored on a 26-yard screen pass. And, with no time remaining, Mike Johnson scored the winning two points on the conversion on a double reverse. It was Kansas' first victory over the Sooners at Lawrence since 1946.

Despite their poor season opening the Sooners could have shared the conference title in 1964 had it not been for a 14-14 tie with Missouri at Norman in the eighth game of the season. The Tigers' Gus Otto scored on a one-yard run with three minutes, 45 seconds left in the game to pull Missouri within one point, 14-13. Instead of attempting to score a two-point conversion for the victory, Missouri settled for a kick and a 14-14 tie.

The Oklahoma-Missouri tie clinched the conference title for Nebraska, but the regular season was not over. Nebraska, which was then unbeaten in Big Eight Conference play, had an encounter with the Sooners remaining. And that encounter was to be Jones' finest moment as a head coach.

When Oklahoma met Nebraska the following week, 55,000 loyal Sooner fans turned out in 20 degree weather on a bleak Thanksgiving Day. And they were rewarded, though not at first as things started badly for the Sooners. OU lost all-American fullback Jim Grisham of Olney, Texas, and starting right halfback Lance Rentzel of Oklahoma City because of injuries in the first quarter.

But the Sooners won convincingly, 17-7. Butch Metcalf of Garland, Texas, kicked a 23-yard field goal. He had missed a field goal attempt from 29 yards with only 13 seconds remaining against Missouri. Quarterback Bob Page of Wolfe

Fullback Jim Grisham scores a touchdown against Kansas State.

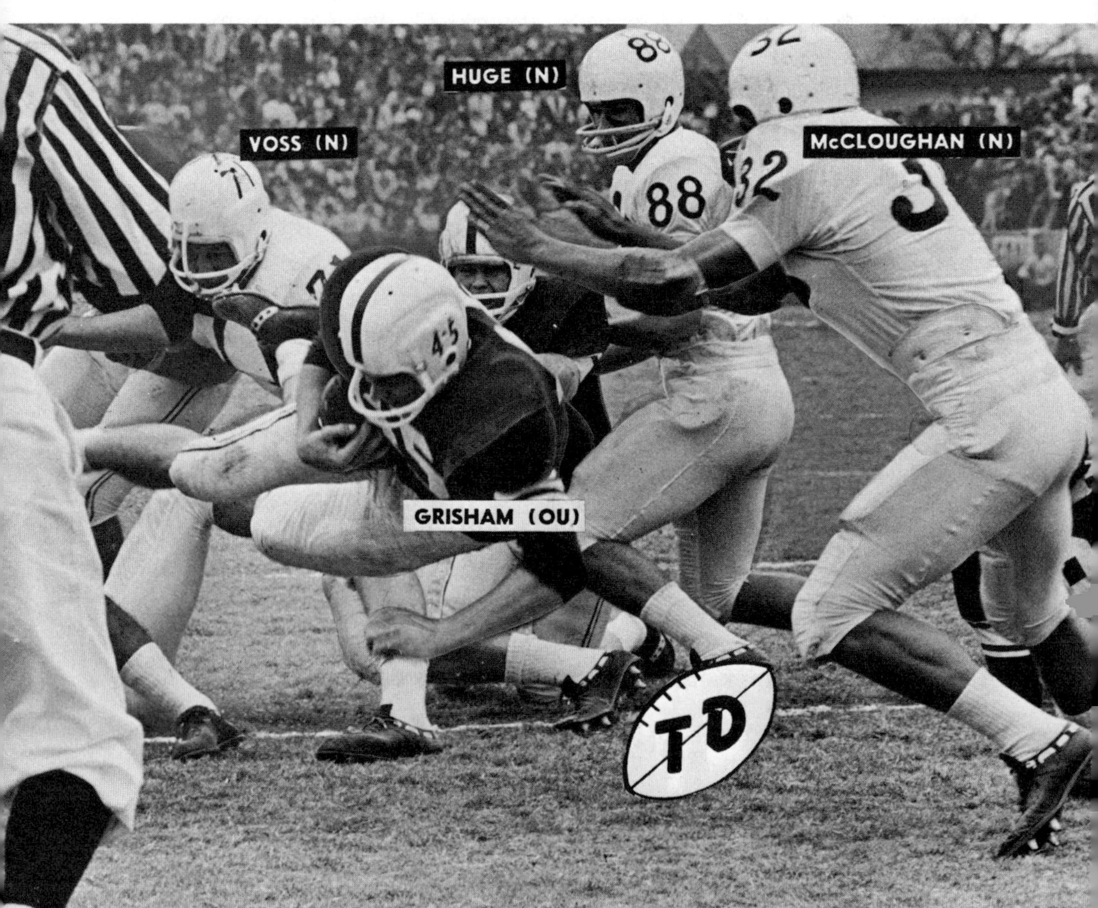

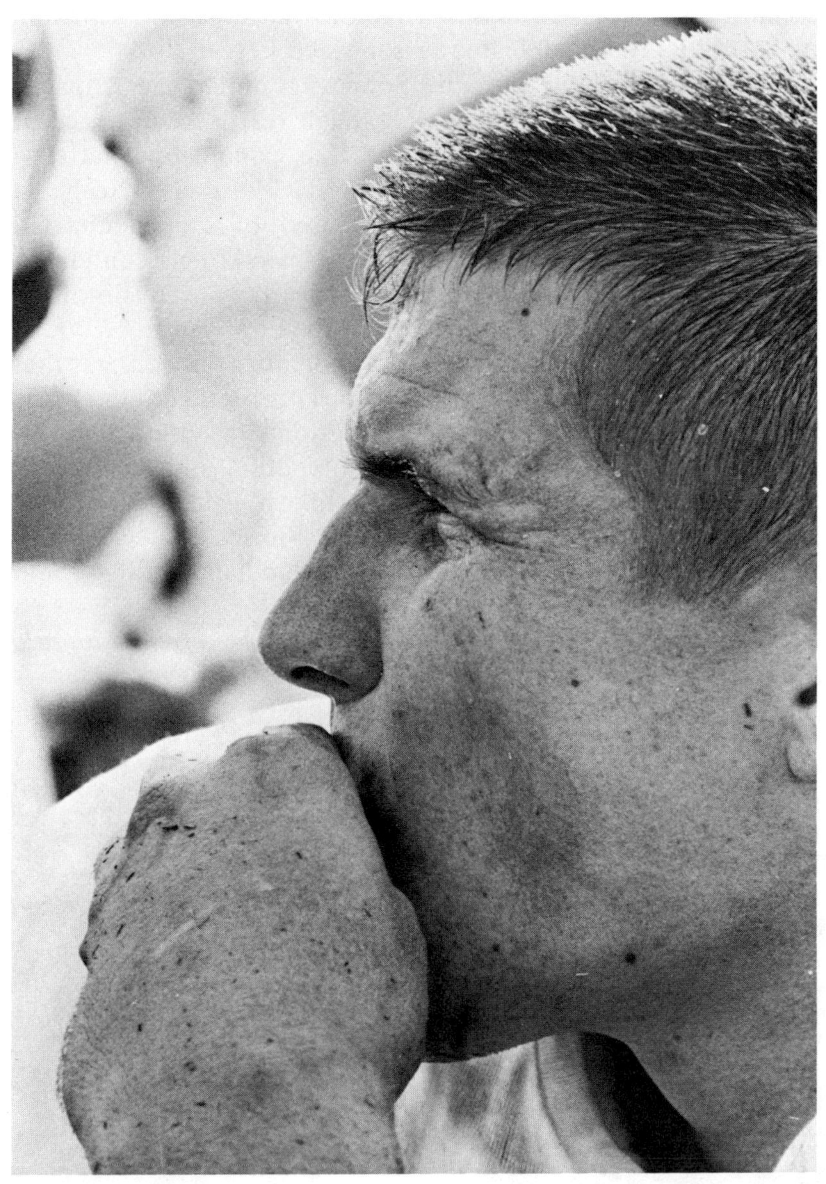

Tackle Ralph Neely was all-American in 1964.

City, Texas, and left halfback Larry Brown of Jenks scored OU's touchdowns.

Thus Nebraska, ranked sixth in the nation, and already

committed to meet Arkansas in the Cotton Bowl, was denied in its bid for its first undefeated season since 1915.

The victory did earn the Sooners a bid to meet upstart Florida State in the Gator Bowl, though the decision to accept proved ill-advised. Two days before the game, three starters—Grisham, Rentzel, and all-American tackle Ralph Neely of Farmington, New Mexico—were accused of signing undated contracts with professional football teams. After a conference with the players, Jones announced that they were dismissed from the squad and would not play in the bowl game.

Jones was praised for his quick, forthright action, but that did not help the Sooners against ambitious Florida State. While 50,408 fans at the Gator Bowl and national television audience watched, Florida State's great combination of quarterback Steve Tensi and flanker Fred Beletnikoff gained 303 yards passing, resulting in five touchdowns. Florida State's starters remained in the entire game although it won handily, 36-19.

Linebacker Carl McAdams intercepts a pass against Florida State in the Gator Bowl game following the 1964 season.

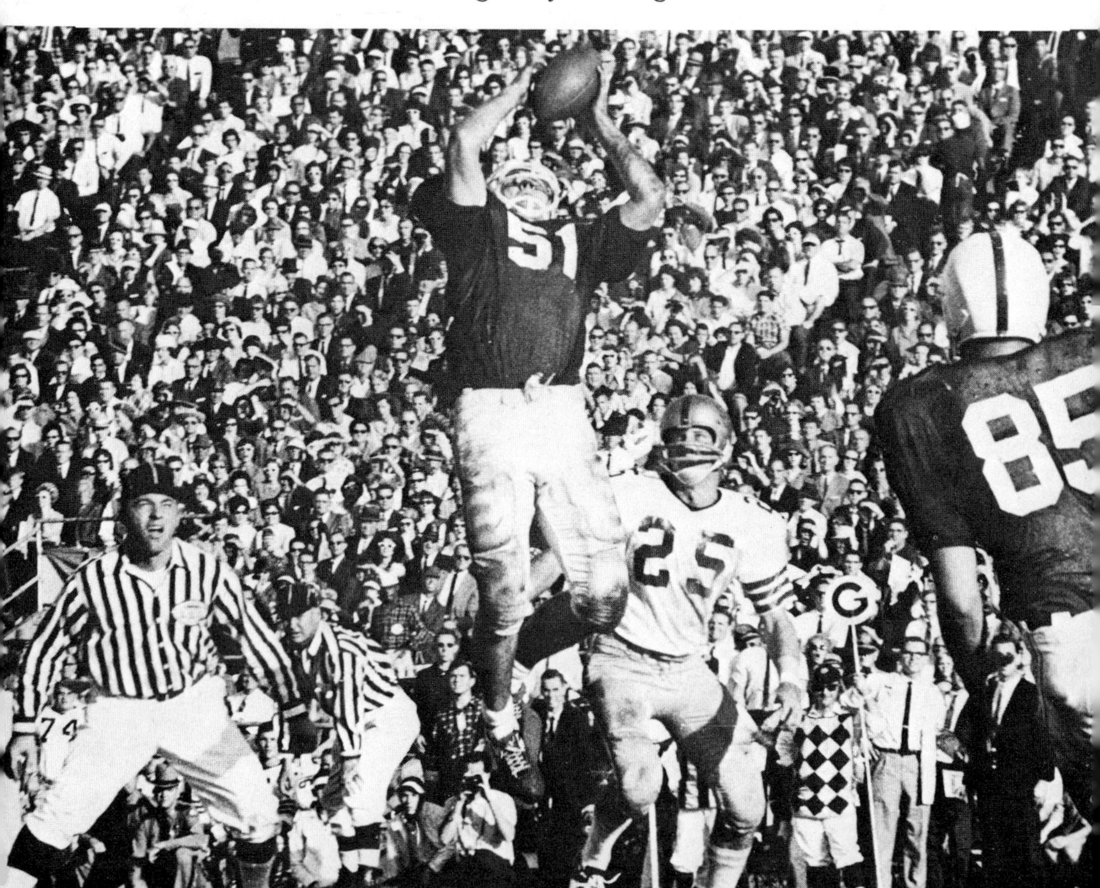

With many of its starters gone, its pride and confidence severely damaged, Oklahoma struggled to a 3-7 record in 1965. The offense sputtered as OU was shut out in four of its ten games, more than the Sooners had been shut out in the previous seven seasons.

Coach Gomer Jones and Carl McAdams, all-American linebacker in 1965.

Mike Ringer, captain in 1965.

But the worst disaster of all came in the final game of the season when the Sooners lost, 17-16, to Oklahoma State at Norman. Some 57,000 fans watched the battle of the bitter, intrastate rivals as the Sooners sought to salvage a victory.

Left halfback Ron Shotts of Weatherford, who rushed for 163 yards despite suffering a separated shoulder during the game, kicked a 27-yard field goal to give the Sooners a 16-14 lead with only three minutes, 56 seconds remaining. But Cowboy Charles Durkee kicked a 35-yard field goal with one minute, 41 seconds left to provide Oklahoma State with its first victory over the Sooners in 20 years.

Two days later, on December 6, 1965, Jones resigned as

head football coach. Some believe that he was forced to resign
because certain booster groups threatened to discontinue their
support to the OU athletic program.

In a portion of his brief statement of resignation, Jones
said: "I just got tired of the criticism and of constantly reading
and listening to all the untrue rumors concerning my position as
head coach here."

Jones remained as OU's athletic director until he suffered a
fatal heart attack in March of 1971.

But before his brief tenure as a head coach, Gomer Jones
had established himself as a great coach. His contributions to
OU's great success in the 1950s are immeasurable. Jones was the
designer of the 5-4 defense, now commonly referred to as the
Oklahoma Defense. In 1949 he devised the defense in which the
linebackers played more toward the center of the line and
defensive backs took on more responsibility outside the ends at
the line of scrimmage. Since then nearly every college in the
nation has used some form of that defense at some time.

Wilkinson claimed that Jones was the greatest teacher of
football that he had ever known. Jones also served as a father
away from home for innumerable OU football players.

Mackenzie
Never Disinterested

After Gomer Jones resigned in early December in 1965, certain factions of Sooner supporters remained convinced that OU still could hire nearly any coach in the nation.

One of the factions maintained that Darrell Royal, whose University of Texas teams had won three Southwest Conference championships and tied for another in the previous seven years, was anxious to return to OU as head coach.

Dr. George L. Cross, OU's president, did not believe that Royal would leave Texas. Cross figured that Royal was earning about $50,000 a year, everything considered, and Royal had tenure.

But Cross also was wise enough to know that if the Royal backers were not satisfied that the new OU coach, whomever he might be, might never gain their full support. So Cross devised an ingenious plan and convinced the members of the Athletic Council and the Board of Regents to allow him to try it.

After a special meeting of the regents, Cross announced publicly that Royal would be offered a six-year contract calling for $32,000 a year, more than any OU coach had ever been paid. Four days later Royal graciously turned down the offer.

Now the Royal supporters were convinced that there was no way to get the former Sooner star to return, and they were ready to support another coach.

Doug Dickey of the University of Tennessee had the inside track for a while because of the early day relationship between Cross and Dickey's father in South Dakota. But Dickey was

Assistant Coach Pat James brought fire and brimstone to OU's 1966 spring practice.

involved in preparing his Volunteers for the Bluebonnet Bowl, and OU could not wait. Then Vince Dooley of the University of Georgia became the primary candidate, but four days after interviewing with OU officials, Dooley withdrew from contention.

Then onto the OU scene in 1965 came a gentleman named

Jim Mackenzie tries to see around assistant coach Chuck Fairbanks.

Jim Mackenzie. Not many Oklahomans had noticed Mackenzie, a tackle from Gary, Indiana, playing at the University of Kentucky when that school ended OU's 31-game winning streak in the Sugar Bowl following the 1950 season.

But this was 1965 and Mackenzie had gotten a thorough second look. Now assistant head coach of Frank Broyles at the University of Arkansas, Mackenzie was asked to interview for the OU job. He overslept on his flight to Oklahoma City and had to return from Denver, Colorado, to meet with the search committee. Mackenzie immediately tipped his personality by explaining the incident.

"I had read about Royal and Dooley and thought I'd act disinterested, too," he said.

But he was not disinterested and won the unanimous support of the OU search committee. So on December 22, sixteen days after Jones had resigned, the 35-year-old Mackenzie was hired as OU's head football coach.

Mackenzie had all the credentials. He had played football at Kentucky when Paul "Bear" Bryant was head coach there. And he had been Broyles' right-hand man the previous eight years while Arkansas was emerging as a national power. During that time the Razorbacks had won three Southwest Conference championships and shared another with Texas and were ranked in the nation's top 10 teams six of the eight seasons.

Mackenzie was a firm believer in a strong coaching staff. He brought his former Kentucky teammate, Pat James, from Alabama where he had forged some of the nation's great defensive units. And three of his other assistant coaches were to become head coaches—Homer Rice at the University of Cincinnati in 1967 and Chuck Fairbanks and Barry Switzer later at OU.

Although Mackenzie liked to call himself "just a country boy," the description was lacking. Many veteran observers considered him ideally prepared and ready for a head coaching job. And his outgoing personality helped gain immediate, widespread support.

But as soon as Mackenzie accepted the position he was surprised and disappointed by what he considered OU's lack of outstanding athletes. Convinced that added quickness might help overcome this shortcoming, Mackenzie installed a rigorous offseason training program. By the start of spring practice in 1966, the Sooner squad had lost nearly 1,000 pounds. The training caused several young prospects to leave the already shorthanded team.

OU Coach Jim Mackenzie gets a ride after 1966 victory over Texas.

Even so, Mackenzie's changes appeared to be paying off. OU won its first four games in 1966, including an upset 18-9 triumph over Texas, the Sooners' first victory over the Longhorns in nine seasons. A stubborn defense and field goals of 43, 41, 31, and 25 yards by OU sophomore Mike Vachon of Amarillo, Texas, were the difference.

By the fifth game of the season the Sooners were ranked 10th in the nation and appeared ready to host No. 1-ranked Notre Dame, the eventual mythical national champion in 1966.

However the Sooners were out-weighed 20 pounds per player, and Notre Dame was on its way to one of its great campaigns. The crowd of 63,439 fans at Owen Field was the largest to witness a football game in the state of Oklahoma. They saw the scrappy Sooners hold Notre Dame on downs at the OU nine-yard line with only a minute left in the first quarter of the scoreless tie. But Notre Dame's overall strength was too much, and the Irish won, 38-0, the worst OU defeat in 21 years.

When he entered a press gathering following the game, Mackenzie stated: "Well, gentlemen, it's not far from the castle to the outhouse."

That shattering defeat and the rugged schedule took its toll on the lightweight Sooners, and OU won only two of five games the remainder of the season. One of the few bright spots occurred when the Sooners, for the second time in three years, foiled a bid by Nebraska for an undefeated season. Again the Cornhuskers had clinched the Big Eight Conference championship and had accepted a bid to the Sugar Bowl. But Vachon kicked a 21-yard field goal with only 48 seconds remaining to give the Sooners a 10-9 victory on Thanksgiving Day over the Cornhuskers, then ranked fourth in the nation.

The next week was not a bright spot. OU suffered a stunning defeat when the Sooners bowed for the second straight season to Oklahoma State, 15-14, this time before 38,000 fans at Lewis Field in Stillwater. In the fourth quarter the Sooners did not score on four straight running plays from the Cowboy one-yard line.

On another series OU finally scored on a one-yard touchdown by tailback Ron Shotts of Weatherford with only one minute, 29 seconds remaining. That narrowed the score to

15-14 in Oklahoma State's favor. Quarterback Bobby Warmack of Ada passed to Shotts in an attempt to score the winning two extra points, but Shotts was stopped at the two-yard line by Cowboys Charles Trimble and Willard Nahrgang.

Such a defeat might have ended Mackenzie's coaching career had it not been for other factors. It was the first season as head coach for the tremendously popular Mackenzie, and nearly everyone had expected a so-called rebuilding season. Also the Sooners had beaten Big Eight Conference champion Nebraska and had ended Texas' galling domination of that series.

The importance of the OU-Texas series may be summed up in a statement by former OU Head Coach Bud Wilkinson, who said: "To put the Oklahoma coaching job in its proper

The annual sellout crowd to see OU and Texas meet each year in the Cotton Bowl in Dallas, Texas.

Quarterback Bob Warmack passes to end Ben Hart.

prospective as a coach, you have to beat Texas to have a good year. If you're good enough to beat Texas, you can win the national championship. It's just that simple, because Texas is that good. You base what you're going on what it takes to beat Texas."

Mackenzie, a tireless worker, had begun to experience increasing discomfort from pains in his chest but had decided to postpone a thorough examination until after the spring practice of 1967. On April 27 he had flown to Amarillo, Texas, in an effort to recruit Monty Johnson, an outstanding high school quarterback who had Oklahoma ties. His ties included the fact that he was the grandson of Montford "Hap" Johnson and grandnephew of Neil and Graham Johnson, OU players from the early 1900s. Johnson played at the University of Texas as a freshman but transferred to OU for his junior and senior seasons.

OU already had started spring football practice, and Mackenzie was working extremely long days at the time. A few minutes after midnight on April 28 Mackenzie's 12-year-old daughter found him unconscious in the bathroom of the family's home. Mackenzie had died of a heart attack, and OU's athletic community was grief-stricken and virtually paralyzed.

It's Chuck
By Executive Order

Being appointed OU's head football coach during the spring training of 1967 may have appeared to be a mixed blessing for 33-year-old Chuck Fairbanks. After Jim Mackenzie's death early one Friday morning, Fairbanks, who had been OU's defensive backfield coach in 1966 and was scheduled to be the offensive coach in 1967, was appointed as his successor the following Tuesday.

So, Fairbanks, schooled as an assistant coach at Arizona State University and the University of Houston, became OU's fourth head football coach in five years.

"I wanted to get someone appointed immediately," recalled Dr. George L. Cross, OU's president at the time. "The regents were reluctant, but I appointed Fairbanks by executive order, subject to the approval of the board."

The regents wanted a coach with an established national reputation but did not want to overrule the appointment by Cross. So the regents gave Fairbanks a contract only until the end of the 1967 football season. The situation was clear: Fairbanks produced to the satisfaction of the regents or they would seek another head coach.

The graduate of Michigan State University was more reserved than was Mackenzie and did not enjoy the great personal popularity of his predecessor. But Fairbanks and the Sooners were up to the challenge.

Fairbanks retained the I-formation on offense and five-man line on defense, both of which had been installed by

All-American Granville Liggins is aided by trainer Ken Raw-linson.

Mackenzie. The Sooners had several veteran players, particularly at key positions. Granville Liggins of Tulsa returned to fill the all-important nose guard spot on defense. And Bob Warmack of Ada had started at quarterback as a sophomore in 1966.

Before the season, Fairbanks told the Big Eight Sky-writers: "I'm very optimistic. Maybe I don't have a right to be, but I think we will have a winning season."

The Sooners won their first two games with ease. However then came Texas, still boiling from the OU upset in 1966. The Sooners took a 7-0 lead on a two-yard run for a touchdown by tailback Ron Shotts of Weatherford with only four minutes, 23 seconds left in the first quarter. But Texas' Rob Layne trimmed the count to 7-3 with a 35-yard field goal with five minutes, 49 seconds left in the third quarter. And Longhorn quarterback Bill Bradley scored a touchdown on a seven-yard run with 14 minutes, 19 seconds left in the game.

Oklahoma had its problems. Mike Vachon of Amarillo, Texas, one of the heroes of the 1966 OU win with four field goals, missed field goal attempts from 27 and 28 yards. And Warmack threw two passes that were intercepted in the Texas end zone and lost a fumble on the Longhorn 31-yard line on what might have been the winning drive. Texas won, 9-7.

Wingback Eddie Hinton gains 12 yards against Colorado.

But the Sooners were not to be denied the rest of the season. The next week OU, then ranked eighth in the nation, won a surprising 23-0 victory of Colorado, then ranked ninth in the country.

The Sooners established themselves as title contenders when they defeated Missouri, 7-0, at Columbia, Missouri. The OU defense was superb, not allowing Missouri in OU territory in the first half and then halting the Tigers on the Sooner 27-, 21- and 10-yard lines in the second half. Shotts scored what proved to be the winning touchdown on a one-yard run with five minutes, 54 seconds left in the second quarter. The score was

set up on a pass play from Warmack to tight end Steve Zabel of Thornton, Colorado. The play covered 51 yards.

But the Sooners' title drive appeared in trouble when a fast-improving Kansas team visited Norman late in the season. The Jayhawks, under the guidance of new Head Coach Pepper Rodgers, had lost their first three games of the season but won four of their last five contests. And things looked even worse for the Sooners when Kansas gained a 10-0 lead. However OU rallied, and Warmack passed 30 yards to Zabel for a touchdown with only one minute, two seconds remaining for a 14-10 victory. OU fans showered the field with oranges, a hint of their

Quarterback Bob Warmack passes to end Steve Zabel for OU's winning touchdown in 14-10 victory over Kansas in 1967.

Tailback Ron Shotts gains against Oklahoma State.

hopes.

Six days later the Sooners met Nebraska at Lincoln, Nebraska. And wingback Eddie Hinton of Lawton, often overshadowed because of the dominant role of the tailback in the I-formation, raced 23 yards for the winning touchdown with 14 minutes, 12 seconds left in the 21-14 triumph.

"I may not live long, but it's fun while it lasts," Fairbanks said afterward. "Two of these in a row is tough on you."

The Sooners finished the Big Eight campaign with a 7-0 record and season with a 9-1 mark. They claimed OU's first Big Eight Conference championship since 1962. OU was ranked third in the final poll by the Associated Press. The Sooners had returned to the nation's top ten for the first time in four years.

The Sooners accepted a bid to play Tennessee in the

Orange Bowl, marking OU's first appearance in the prestigious game in Miami, Florida, in five years. Tennessee was ranked second in the nation after suffering a loss to UCLA in its opening game and then winning its remaining nine contests and the Southeastern Conference championship.

However, the Sooners took a stunning, 19-0 half-time lead over the favored Volunteers. But Tennessee fought its way back, and Volunteer quarterback Dewey Warren scored a touchdown on a one-yard run with only four minutes, five

Quarterback Bob Warmack and tackle and 1967 captain Bob Kalsu celebrate win.

seconds left in the game to trim OU's lead to 26-24.

Tennessee had a chance to win when it stopped the Sooners on downs on OU's 27-yard line with 14 seconds left in the game. But the 43-yard field goal attempt by Volunteer Karl Kremser was wide to the right. And a 26-yard return of a pass interception for a touchdown by Bob Stephenson of Claremont, California, in the fourth quarter assured the victory for OU.

Combined with the outstanding season, the victory immediately established Fairbanks as a highly successful head coach.

Before the bowl game Fairbanks had received a new contract. Now there was no talk at all at Oklahoma about seeking an established coach.

The prestige of the victory, many believed, reopened the door to the vital recruiting of outstanding athletes from Texas, an essential element in OU's resurgence to national power in the early 1970s.

Coach Chuck Fairbanks and quarterback Bob Warmack receive trophy after Orange Bowl victory over Tennessee.

Owens Runs
For The Heisman

Steve Owens came to the University of Oklahoma with a football under one arm and left with the Heisman Trophy under the other. The story of OU football in 1968 and 1969 is the story of Steve Owens of Miami, Oklahoma.

Oklahoma needed a great tailback for its I-formation, and it found him in Owens, perhaps the best tailback in recent college history with the exception of Southern California's great O. J. Simpson.

But it took more than Owens in 1968. OU lost two of its first three games, bowing to Notre Dame, which eventually finished fifth in the nation, and Texas, which eventually was third in the nation.

The Sooners nearly defeated the Longhorns.

Texas, on its way to a mythical national championship a year later, stopped OU, 26-20, when sophomore fullback Steve Worster, running from the newly devised Wishbone-T, scored a touchdown on a two-yard run with only 39 seconds left in the game.

Then the Sooners fell short in a brilliant rally against Colorado at Boulder, Colorado, two weeks later. Trailing, 34-6, after the third quarter, OU bowed, 41-27, to the Buffaloes in a loss that would cost the Sooners their second straight clear-cut conference title.

In the seventh game of the season and the pivotal contest of the conference race, the Sooners met Kansas, undefeated in seven previous games in 1968 and ranked third in the nation, at Lawrence, Kansas. A revenge-seeking crowd was prepared with a barrage of oranges as the Jayhawks expected not only to win but receive a bid to the Orange Bowl.

Kansas got the bid to the Orange Bowl. But OU came from behind twice, and Owens, who rushed for 157 yards, scored a touchdown on a five-yard run with four minutes, 14 seconds left in the game for a 27-23 upset victory by the unranked Sooners.

The Sooner defense, hampered by the loss of 1967 all-American Granville Liggins of Tulsa at the vital nose guard position, had been bolstered by the addition of Steve Zabel of Thornton, Colorado. The 6-foot-4, 212-pound Zabel was an excellent tight end but also was being called on to play defensive end in certain situations.

Kansas, which led the nation at the time with an average of 47 points a game, was held to half that number.

The next week Zabel led another outstanding defensive performance in OU's 28-14 victory before 60,500 fans at Columbia, Missouri. A week later Owens ran wild against Nebraska, scoring five touchdowns and 30 points, both Big Eight Conference records for one game, in OU's 47-0 triumph.

The season was capped by OU's meeting of Southern Methodist University in the first Astro Bluebonnet Bowl game in the Astrodome in Houston, Texas. The Sooners lost, 28-27, before 53,543 fans, largest crowd to see a football game indoors.

Despite the losses of quarterback Bob Warmack of Ada and Zabel because of injuries in the first half, OU almost won. Reserve quarterback Mickey Ripley of Perry passed 30 yards to split end Johnny Barr, of Atlanta, Texas, substituting for another injured Sooner starter, Joe Killingsworth of Oklahoma City, for a touchdown to trim the count to 28-27 with one minute, 16 seconds left in the game. However on the try for the extra points Ripley was forced out of bounds by Southern Methodist's Mike Mitchell.

OU had another chance to win. The Sooners recovered an onside kickoff, but a 34-yard field goal attempt by Bruce Derr of Harvey, Illinois, sailed to the left of the goal posts with only 19 seconds left.

The 1969 season started better but proved even more frustrating. The Sooners won three of their first four games, failing only to overcome the jinx against Texas. OU entered the annual clash in the Cotton Bowl ranked eighth in the nation, and the Longhorns, on their way to their second mythical national championship, were ranked second in the nation at the time. The Sooners gained a 14-0 lead in the first 11 minutes, but for the third straight year Texas came from behind to win, this time, 27-17.

Next came real disaster waiting in what had seemingly always been the safe haven of Manhattan, Kansas. But OU did

End Steve Zabel is aided by Dr. Donald Robinson, OU team physician (left), and trainer Ken Rawlinson.

Tailback Steve Owens, 1969 Heisman Trophy winner, stretches for extra yardage.

not count on two factors. OU's defense had been prepared to play a style that Head Coach Chuck Fairbanks later said the Sooners did not have the personnel to play. And Kansas State had been given "Purple Pride" by Vince Gibson, a product of Florida State who was in his third year of trying to bring life to what had been a seemingly hopeless situation.

Though OU was ranked 11th in the nation, and the surprising Wildcats, winners in four of their first five games, were ranked 18th, this was to be the day of the underdog.

While a capacity crowd of 38,500 partisan, almost hysterical fans chanted, "We've Got Pride," Kansas State defeated once-proud Oklahoma, 59-21, OU's worse loss since falling to Notre Dame in 1966. Kansas State was led by quarterback Lynn Dickey, who completed 28 of 42 passes for three touchdowns and 380 yards, a Big Eight record for one game. Kansas State had defeated OU for the first time since 1934 and caused the Sooners to suffer one of the low points in their proud football history.

But the Sooners escaped disaster in the final game of the 1969 season by defeating Oklahoma State, 28-27. OU had to halt the Cowboys on an attempt for a two-point conversion with only one minute, 15 seconds left in the game to achieve it.

Oklahoma, favored in preseason forecasts to win the Big Eight Conference championship, finished the season with a 6-4 record and in fourth place in the conference race. However in the face of such disappointment, Owens salvaged some pride.

In his brilliant career Owens had established seven NCAA records, five other Big Eight Conference records, and three

Ken Mendenhall, all-American center in 1969.

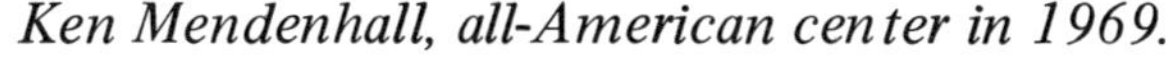

Tailback Steve Owens churns through mud and Oklahoma State.

other school records. The NCAA records consisted of 17 straight regular season games in which he had rushed for 100 yards or more, 56 touchdowns in a three-year career, 336 points in a three-year career, 3,867 yards rushing in his career, 905 carries in his career, 358 carries in one season (1969), and 55 carries in one game (against Oklahoma State in 1969).

In addition to those, Owens established Big Eight records of 30 points and five touchdowns in one game (against Nebraska in 1968), 1,536 yards rushing in 1968, 3,059 yards rushing in 1968 and 1969, and 23 touchdowns in one season. Added to those were school records of 261 yards rushing in one game (against Oklahoma State in 1969), 136 points in one season in 1969, and scoring touchdowns in 15 consecutive regular season games.

On the morning of November 25, 1969, Owens and his wife, Barbara, waited in an office in the university's Memorial Union building. The 1969 winner of the coveted Heisman Trophy, symbolizing the outstanding college football player in the nation, was to be announced that day.

Shortly before noon Owens received a call to come to the office of Dr. J. Herbert Hollomon, then OU's president. He and his wife raced the few yards between the buildings. But the word already was out. Students left their classrooms to run with Owens and congratulate him. In fact his wife reached the office before Owens.

When he raced into the office of the president of the university, Owens, who had his sport coat tucked under his arm as if it were a football, received a standing ovation from the newsmen and friends who had gathered there.

Owens and Fairbanks embraced. Then Owens accepted a

End Jim Files stops Oklahoma State runner.

call from New York City.

"You are the winner," the voice said. No one had to ask of what.

"It's hard for me to realize I'm in this position," Owens replied. "It's the greatest, greatest moment of my life."

When told that Mike Phipps, quarterback at Purdue University, was the runner-up, Owens replied: "I feel for him right now."

That type of statement was typical of the six-foot, two-inch, 215-pound Owens.

Because the OU offense centered on the tailback position and he carried the ball so much, Owens always was in the spotlight. But he was a tireless worker in practice and never lost the respect or his popularity among his teammates and many fans.

When he went to New York to accept the Heisman Trophy, only the second ever won by a Sooner, Owens took fullback Mike Harper of Jenks, who in effect was a blocking back. And in a tearful acceptance speech Owens thanked everyone in the state of Oklahoma.

The Wishbone Explosion

The last years of Chuck Fairbanks' tenure as OU's head football coach were a curious mixture of incredible success and bitter disappointment.

A series of decisions during the 1970 season prepared the groundwork for OU's return to prominence as a national power. In 1970 Fairbanks changed OU's offense from the I-formation to the Houston Veer. He had become well-versed in the formation during his four years as an assistant coach at the University of Houston. The Sooners did not have a tailback replacement for Steve Owens but had Jack Mildren of Abilene, Texas, a quarterback who seemed tailormade for the Veer.

Although OU won two of its first three games in 1970, Fairbanks had become convinced that the Sooners did not have the type of players needed to make the Veer successful against the opposition to be faced. So, with two weeks without a game before the annual clash with Texas, OU secretly changed to the Wishbone-T, developed by Longhorn Coach Darrell Royal.

Texas, on its way to a third straight Southwest Conference championship and 10-1 record, won easily, 41-9. The Longhorns ended the season ranked No. 3 after being the 1969 mythical national champions.

But the Sooners rebounded the next week to upset Colorado, then ranked 13th in the nation, by a 23-15 score at Boulder, Colorado. By then Fairbanks had made more key changes, promoting center Tom Brahaney of Midland, Texas; Dean Unruh of Lakewood, Colorado; and fullback Leon

Fullback Leon Crosswhite leads quarterback Jack Mildren on the option play.

Crosswhite of Hennessey, all sophomores, to No. 1 offensive team.

An inspired Iowa State team gained a 21-0 advantage over OU in the first quarter before a Homecoming crowd of 27,000 fans at Ames, Iowa. However the Sooners fought back and left halfback Joe Wylie of Henderson, Texas, scored on a five-yard touchdown run with only two minutes, 24 seconds left in the game to trim the Cyclones' lead to 28-27.

OU had lost its starting right halfback Everett Marshall of Inglewood, California, during the game because of an injury. But his substitute, Greg Pruitt of Houston, Texas, raced around left end for a two-point conversion and a 29-28 victory. Thus the door was opened for Pruitt to become one of OU's greatest running backs.

"For a team to be 21 points behind and have the ability to come back and win it is something I have never been associated with as a player or coach," Fairbanks said afterward.

The Sooners were improving rapidly and won five of their final seven regular season games. OU suffered an upset loss to Kansas State, bowing, 19-14, when the Wildcats, again led by

Safety John Shelley makes a diving interception against Colorado.

quarterback Lynn Dickey, scored two touchdowns in the final four minutes before 60,800 disappointed fans at Owen Field. The only other loss came against eventual mythical national champion Nebraska, 28-21, at Lincoln.

OU accepted a bid to meet Alabama and return to the Astro Bluebonnet Bowl in Houston, Texas. The game seemed to mean little at the time since the Sooners had a 7-4 record and Alabama a 6-5 record. However, no one could have known that

Quarterback Jack Mildren breaks away from an Alabama defender in the Astro Bluebonnet Bowl game following the 1970 season.

Halfback Greg Pruitt is presented the award as the Outstanding Player in the Astro Bluebonnet Bowl game in his home town of Houston, Texas, after the 1970 season. Weldon Humble, chairman of the Bluebonnet committee, made the presentation.

the same teams with many of the same players were going to become two of the nation's major powers in the succeeding seasons.

The game ended in a 24-24 tie when OU's Bruce Derr of Harvey, Illinois, kicked a 42-yard field goal with only 59 seconds remaining and Alabama's Richard Ciemny missed a 34-yard field goal attempt with only one second left.

Derr, who had missed a field goal in the final minutes in

OU's loss to Southern Methodist in the same bowl two years earlier, redeemed himself in his final collegiate game. The contest also gave a hint of things to come as Pruitt raced for touchdowns on runs of 58 and 25 yards and was named the Outstanding Player in the game.

In 1971 OU's Wishbone attack got in high gear with what may have been the most awesome offense in the history of collegiate football. The Sooners had it all on offense. Mildren reached near perfection in operating the option play. Pruitt's great breakaway speed and mobility made him a constant threat. And Brahaney, who was the all-American center in both 1971 and 1972, led a powerful line.

OU averaged 472.4 yards rushing a game in 1971. Some teams never gain that much rushing in one game, much less average it for a season.

Despite OU's terrific record a combination of injuries on

The fabulous 1971 backfield of left halfback Joe Wylie, quarterback Jack Mildren, fullback Leon Crosswhite, and right halfback Greg Pruitt.

Defensive back Glenn King was OU co-captain in 1971, thus becoming first black to be a Sooner varsity football captain.

defense and a great Nebraska team on its way to its second straight mythical national championship kept the Sooners from being No. 1 in the nation.

Early in the season Pruitt put together three back-to-back performances that never may be equalled in college football, considering the caliber of the opposition. The five-foot, nine-inch, 177-pound Pruitt gained 205 yards on 16 carries and scored touchdowns on runs of 75, 42, and 7 yards in OU's

Quarterback Jack Mildren passes 41 yards to split end Jon

33-20 victory over Southern California, ranked fifth in the nation in preseason polls. The Sooners gained 516 yards rushing before 61,826 fans, the first sellout crowd at Owen Field since 1967.

Harrison for a touchdown against Iowa State in 1971.

In the next game Pruitt gained 216 yards on 20 carries and scored touchdowns on runs of 20, 4, and 1 yard as the Sooners defeated Texas, 48-27, for OU's second win over the Longhorns in the last 15 years. OU had 435 yards rushing against the

Longhorns, ranked third in the nation at the time. That was the most any team had ever gained against a Texas team. And the loss was only the second for Texas in its last 35 games.

"You can't compare outstanding teams, but OU has the best team I've seen since I've been here," Darrell Royal, in his 15th year then as the Texas coach, said afterward.

The next week OU met Colorado, undefeated in its first five games and upset victor over Louisiana State and Ohio State. The Buffaloes were ranked sixth in the nation at the time. Pruitt ran for 190 yards in 14 carries and scored touchdowns on runs of 66 and 14 yards as the Sooners gained a 24-0 half-time advantage before winning, 45-17. OU rushed for 498 yards and had 670 yards in total offense, both the most ever gained against a Colorado team.

Mildren was becoming more prominent by now as he rushed for 74 yards and completed three of four passes for 152 yards. He passed to Wylie for 68 yards and a touchdown and to split end Jon Harrison also of Abilene, Texas, for 54 yards and a touchdown.

The next week the Sooners returned to the site of their 1969 disaster: Manhattan, Kansas. With Pruitt running for 294 yards, a Big Eight Conference record, on 19 carries and scoring on runs of 15, 38, and 15 yards, OU defeated Kansas State, 75-28. The Sooners gained an NCAA record of 711 yards rushing.

Kansas State's 28 points prompted OU defensive coach Larry Lacewell to ask: "Has only an offensive team ever been invited to a bowl game?"

But the big game of the 1971 season came on Thanksgiving Day when No. 1-ranked Nebraska came to Owen Field to face No. 2-ranked OU. They billed it as the Game of the Decade, and the contest lived up to its billing.

The Cornhuskers took an early 14-3 lead, aided by a controversial 72-yard punt return for a touchdown by Johnny Rodgers. The Sooners, boosted by Mildren's passing, fought back for a 17-14 lead at the end of the first half.

Again Nebraska took control early in the second half to gain a 28-17 margin. But OU claimed a 31-28 lead in the final quarter. Then Nebraska, led by tailback Jeff Kinney, quarterback Jerry Tagge, and Rodgers, marched 72 yards on 12 plays,

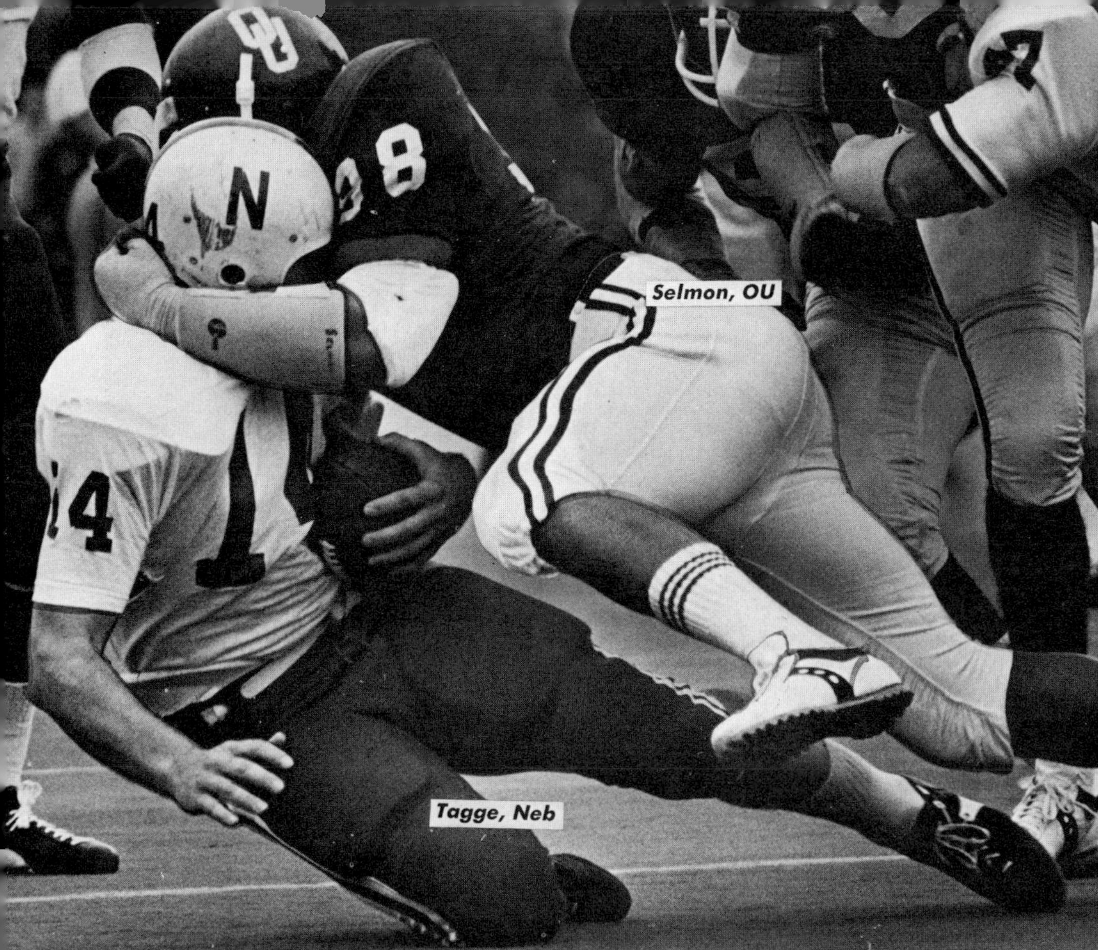

OU's Lucious Selmon tackles Nebraska quarterback Jerry Tagge for a loss in the Game of the Decade in 1971.

and Kinney scored the winning touchdown on a two-yard run with only one minute, 38 seconds left in the game.

Nebraska won, 35-31, to claim its second straight mythical national title. Nebraska's great defense had shut off OU's outside running, but Mildren dealt the Cornhuskers misery, running for 130 yards on 31 carries and passing 24 and 17 yards to Harrison for touchdowns.

In a game that proved anticlimatic the Sooners returned to the Sugar Bowl for the first time in 21 years to meet Auburn, loser in only one of its 11 regular season games, and quarterback Pat Sullivan, the 1971 Heisman Trophy winner. OU raced to a 31-0 lead at half time and a 40-7 margin in the fourth

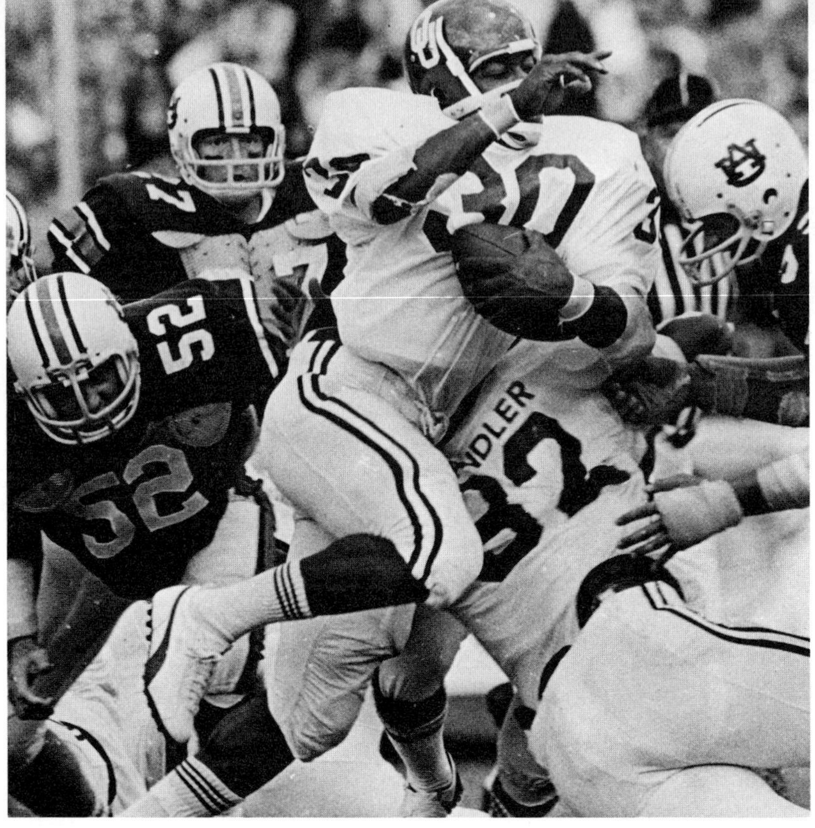

Halfback Greg Pruitt follows a block by end Albert Chandler against Auburn in the Sugar Bowl.

quarter before reserves took over. The final score was 40-22.

The fabulous Pruitt finished the season with 1,665 yards rushing, a Sooner and Big Eight Conference record. He averaged 9.4 yards a rushing attempt.

And Mildren rushed for 1,140 yards to become the first major college quarterback to ever run for more than 1,000 yards in one season. He added 878 yards passing to establish a Sooner record of 2,018 yards in total offense in one season.

Pruitt and Mildren also became only the second players on the same team to rush for more than 1,000 yards in the same season. Sooners Billy Vessels and Buck McPhail had been the first in 1952.

The Big Eight Conference achieved a first in 1971 when Nebraska was ranked first in the nation, OU second, and Colorado third in the final ratings by the Associated Press.

Championship Won, Championship Lost

Although it had missed winning the mythical national championship by only a 35-31 loss to Nebraska the previous year, OU's prospects were brighter for 1972.

The Sooners returned seven offensive starters including center Tom Brahaney of Midland, Texas; left halfback Joe Wylie of Henderson, Texas; right halfback Greg Pruitt of Houston, Texas; and fullback Leon Crosswhite of Hennessey. Brahaney and Pruitt had been consensus all-American selections as juniors.

The major question concerning the offense came at quarterback. Jack Mildren of Abilene, Texas, who had guided OU's explosive Wishbone attack in 1971, had completed his eligibility. However, lanky senior Dave Robertson of Garden Grove, California, proved to be up to the challenge, although he did not possess Mildren's great athletic skills.

Only three defensive starters returned, but the Sooners expected improved defensive play. For one thing OU avoided the nagging injuries that crippled the 1971 defensive team. And there were plenty of experienced players returning. OU also had two sensational sophomore prospects in linebacker Rod Shoate of Spiro and safety Randy Hughes of Tulsa.

The Sooners lived up to their expectations in the first four games as OU defeated its first three opponents by a total of 169 points to only six.

But OU expected, and got, a test in its fourth game of the season—the annual clash with Texas in the Cotton Bowl. The

Center Tom Brahaney was consensus all-American in 1971 and 1972.

Sooners were ranked second and Texas, also undefeated in its first three games, was ranked tenth in the nation.

OU struggled to a 10-0 lead after three quarters. The defense already had played a key role. In the third quarter tackle Derland Moore of Poplar Bluff, Missouri, blocked a punt by Texas, and nose guard Lucious Selmon of Eufaula recovered the ball in the Longhorn end zone for a touchdown.

In the fourth quarter end Gary Baccus of Brownfield, Texas, deflected a Texas pitchout, and Moore recovered the ball in the Longhorn end zone for another touchdown. The Sooners won, 27-0. It marked the first time the Longhorns had been shut out in 100 games and was the only loss for Texas in 1972.

But the next week OU's aspirations for the mythical national title lay in ruins on a wet field at the foot of the Rocky Mountains. The Sooners met Colorado, also considered a strong contender for the Big Eight Conference title and national recognition. The Golden Buffaloes entered the contest with a 5-1 record, having been upset by Oklahoma State, and ranked ninth in the nation. OU still was No. 2.

The already bitter rivalry was spiced by an alleged spying incident, made public by Colorado the night before the game. A former OU player, then a student at Colorado, was accused of spying during the Buffaloes' open practices the week of the

Halfback Joe Wylie eludes Wisconsin defender.

Quarterback Dave Robertson races for gain.

game.

The next day the largest crowd, 52,020, ever to witness a sporting event in the State of Colorado also witnessed the Buffaloes' 20-14 upset victory. The new artificial turf at Folsom Field had been soaked by a heavy rain the morning of the game, and the Sooners great speed was neutralized.

OU led at the half, 7-0, but Colorado's highly emotional team scored two touchdowns in the third quarter and two field goals in the fourth quarter before the Sooners scored again with only one minute, 13 seconds left in the contest.

OU, however, still had an opportunity to claim the Big Eight Conference title. This was because Colorado was knocked out of contention by two more conference losses late in the season. And Nebraska, upset in its opening game of the campaign by UCLA, suffered a surprising 23-23 tie against Iowa State. All this meant that if it could defeat both Nebraska and Oklahoma State in the remaining regular season games, OU could win the conference championship.

But things looked dim when Nebraska took a 14-0 lead in the third quarter before a record crowd of 76,587 fans in Lincoln on Thanksgiving Day.

Though the game was to have been a battle for the Heisman Trophy between him and Nebraska's Johnny Rodgers, Pruitt had suffered an ankle injury before the game and left the contest, not to return. He had carried the ball only twice.

The Sooners' chances seemed to fade even more when split end John Carroll of Norman suffered a knee injury and was

Split end Tinker Owens races for a long gain after receiving a pass against Colorado.

Halfback Joe Washington puts a move on a defender.

replaced by freshman Tinker Owens of Miami, younger brother of OU's 1969 Heisman Trophy winner, Steve Owens. But Owens was up to the task, and he enjoyed a unique advantage. Nebraska's defensive backs had not studied films of Owens and were not prepared to defend against him.

Fortunately the contest also provided Robertson, a reserve quarterback until his senior campaign, with his finest hour. Robertson's passes to Owens set up one-yard touchdown runs by freshman Joe Washington of Port Arthur, Texas, substituting

Head Coach Chuck Fairbanks watches from the sideline with assistant coaches Jim Dickey (kneeling with cap) and Wendell Mosley.

for Wylie, and Grant Burget of Stroud, substituting for the injured Pruitt. Rick Fulcher of Cupertino, California, kicked both extra points, and the Sooners had gained a 14-14 tie.

OU got its next big opportunity when Moore tackled Nebraska quarterback Dave Humm, causing a fumble. Selmon recovered the ball on the Nebraska 27-yard line. And Fulcher kicked a 41-yard field goal with eight minutes, 44 seconds remaining for what proved to be OU's 17-14 winning margin.

When he got on the team bus following the game, freshman Owens, who had caught five passes for 108 yards, got a rare standing ovation from the Sooners players.

The Sooners had little trouble defeating Oklahoma State the next week and claimed their first Big Eight Conference title since 1968. OU finished with a 6-1 conference record and Nebraska with a 5-1-1 mark.

But all of that was erased a few months later when it was discovered that OU had used an ineligible player, reserve quarterback Kerry Jackson of Galveston, Texas, in its games against Colorado, Missouri, Kansas, and Oklahoma State.

So, the Sooners had to forfeit their victories over Kansas, Missouri, and Oklahoma State, changing their conference record to 3-4 and dropping them into a tie for fifth place. The forfeits also changed OU's season record from 11-1 to 8-4 in 1972.

Nebraska then became the official conference champion.

The Sooners still retained hopes of claiming that elusive mythical national championship. In the final rankings of the regular season, OU was rated second behind Southern California. OU hoped to defeat fifth-ranked Penn State in the Sugar Bowl and then hoped to get some help from third-ranked Ohio State, which met Southern California in the Rose Bowl.

The Sooners defeated Penn State, which also entered the bowl contest with a 10-1 record, 14-0, before 82,123 fans in New Orleans, Louisiana. But Southern California remained unbeaten by defeating Ohio State, 42-17.

OU's win was more impressive than the score indicated. The Sooners scored in the second quarter on a 27-yard pass from Robertson to Owens and in the fourth quarter, on a one-yard run by Crosswhite. The second touchdown was set up by a 17-yard pass from Wylie to Owens, who made a disputed, diving catch.

OU's Lucious Selmon (98) and Derland Moore (97) rush Kansas State passer.

The Sooners lost five fumbles, three inside the Penn State five-yard line. The Nittany Lions had averaged 402 yards rushing and passing a game in 1972 but gained only 196 against the Sooners.

Fairbanks called the 1972 Sooners the best "all-around" team he coached in his six seasons as OU's head coach.

Less than a month later Fairbanks resigned to become the head coach and general manager of the New England

Patriots of the National Football League. Fairbanks, a sensitive, almost shy man in many ways, was a demanding leader and superb student of the game of football.

In his six years as head coach OU won 52 games, lost 15, and tied 1. The Sooners won two Big Eight Conference championships and tied for another and were ranked second twice and third once in the final national ratings. Each time OU was only a blink away from the mythical national title.

Although a conservative himself, Fairbanks was wise enough to relax hair and dress codes for the OU players. He also had an excellent relationship with black athletes. The Sooners had had a sprinkling of outstanding black football players since Prentice Gautt first came to OU in 1956. But Fairbanks recruited them en masse, certainly one of the keys to OU's recent success. OU had its first black varsity football captain in Glenn King of Jacksboro, Texas, in 1971.

Yes, in the short span of six seasons Chuck Fairbanks had restored Oklahoma football to national prominence.

Oklahoma
Becomes Switzer-Land

Barry Switzer had not considered coaching as a career until Head Coach Frank Broyles and his No. 1 assistant, Jim Mackenzie, convinced Switzer to give it a try as the coach of the freshman team at the University of Arkansas in 1960. The year before, Switzer had been the center and captain of Arkansas' Southwest Conference co-championship team.

When he came to OU in 1966, Mackenzie brought Switzer with him as an assistant coach. Mackenzie was particularly astute at evaluating coaching capabilities. Even then he foresaw Switzer's future but had advised him to get out of coaching if he had not obtained a head coaching job by the time he was 35 years old.

Although he was a great admirer of Mackenzie, Switzer did not take that bit of advice. When Chuck Fairbanks resigned as OU's head coach on January 26, 1973, Switzer, only five months after his 35th birthday, knew he had found what he had been seeking. Three days later, Switzer, already considered the primary architect of OU's awesome wishbone attack, became OU's head coach. But what seemed like such a great opportunity soon was threatened by several obstacles.

Kerry Jackson of Galveston, Texas, who was scheduled to be OU's starting quarterback in 1973, was declared ineligible because his high school records had been altered to make him eligible for an athletic scholarship.

And the Sooners were barred from postseason bowl competition following the 1973 and 1974 seasons and from

Head Coach Barry Switzer delights Oklahoma Governor David Hall at a Sooner pep rally.

appearing on television during the 1974 and 1975 regular seasons. In the aftermath, Bill Michael, OU's highly capable offensive line coach, resigned.

Before the 1973 fall workouts started it was discovered that LeRoy Selmon of Eufaula, who was scheduled to be the starting right tackle on defense, had pericarditis and could not play, at least, the first part of the season.

Then John Carroll of Norman, the 1972 starting split end, suffered another knee injury in preseason practice and was out for the year. And in the first game against Baylor starting right halfback Grant Burget of Stroud suffered a knee injury and was out for the season.

But Switzer's great enthusiasm and positive approach never waned. When asked about the effect of the probation on the Sooners, Switzer made a prophetic statement before the 1973 season.

"Bowl games and playing on TV, to me, are fine incentives for a football team," he said. "But I'm going to tell you what: There isn't but one reward, one great reward for playing the game of football, and that's winning.

"And winning is a matter of pride. We've been put on

Eddie Foster, all-American tackle in 1973.

probation by the NCAA. The cards have been dealt now. And we have to live by it. But they didn't say that we couldn't beat the teams that are going to play on TV and go to bowl games, and they didn't say we couldn't win the Big Eight championship."

Even so the Sooners were picked to finish only fourth in the conference race. Because of the inexperience of the linemen and sophomore quarterback Steve Davis of Sallisaw, OU's offense was considered suspect. And much of the success on defense would depend on how well LeRoy and Dewey Selmon, sophomore tackles from Eufaula, performed. They were scheduled to flank their older brother, Lucious, who was OU's nose guard. OU had had many brother acts previously. Though never had the Sooners had three brothers side by side in the same line.

Sophomore left halfback Joe Washington of Port Arthur, Texas, added to OU's great reputation of having the nation's best rushing attack year after year. Washington rushed for 1,173

The Selmons, Lucious (from left), LeRoy, and Dewey, get instructions from line coach Rex Norris.

Halfback Joe Washington leaves Iowa State linebacker Brad Storm with nothing but air.

yards, and Clark, a junior college transfer, rushed for 1,014 yards. Thus they became only the third teammates in collegiate history to rush for 1,000 yards or more in the same season. Only OU players have ever achieved that distinction.

A hint of OU's approaching success came early in the 1973 season. The Sooners, ranked eighth in the nation, played No. 1-ranked Southern California to a 7-7 tie before 84,016 fans at the Memorial Coliseum in Los Angeles. The deadlock ended a Trojan victory streak of 14 straight games.

After a shaky start, OU dominated the game. The Sooners lost fumbles on their first two possessions. Another fumble, recovered by Southern California on the OU 25-yard line, set up the Trojans' only score. The Sooners also missed two field-goal attempts in the first half. But Davis finally scored a touchdown on a two-yard run, and Rick Fulcher of Cupertino, California, kicked the tying extra point with seven minutes, 18 seconds left in the third quarter.

"It sounded like trucks running together—big trucks," the colorful Switzer said. "They had semis and we had pickups."

The next week OU narrowly averted disaster against a Miami of Florida team coached by Pete Elliott, a Sooner assistant coach in the 1950s. Miami led the stunned Sooners, 20-7, at the half. But the Sooners shutout Miami in the second half, and Davis passed 52 yards to split end Tinker Owens to tie the score at 20-20 in the third quarter. Fulcher added a 30-yard field goal in the fourth quarter for a 24-20 triumph.

Texas, still smarting from a season-opening upset by Miami of Florida, saw the Sooners as a chance to regain some of its national prominence. OU was ranked sixth and Texas thirteenth in the nation going into the contest at Dallas, Texas.

Led by Washington of Port Arthur, Texas, who rushed for

Quarterback Steve Davis races between Oklahoma State defenders.

The eyes of Texas were on split end Tinker Owens as he raced to a touchdown after taking a pass from halfback Joe Washington.

117 yards, and Davis, who passed for 185 yards, the Sooners routed the Longhorns, 52-13, handing Darrell Royal his worst defeat in 17 years as the Texas coach.

The Sooners clinched the Big Eight Conference championship with a convincing 27-0 defeat of Nebraska in their final appearance on national television for at least two years. It was the Cornhuskers' first shutout since OU had defeated them, 47-0, in 1968.

The unheralded Davis led the offense with 114 yards rushing and 51 yards passing and touchdown runs of 47, 8, and 1 yard. The defense was brilliant allowing Nebraska in Sooner territory only once. And on that play the Cornhuskers lost a fumble.

"I'll take this defense and go fight Russia," shouted Larry Lacewell, OU's defensive coach.

Nebraska, which had averaged 418 yards a game rushing and passing, was limited to only 174 yards.

"The nation had a chance today to see the finest defensive team in the country," Switzer said afterward.

Split end Billy Brooks takes a touchdown pass from quarterback Steve Davis despite a desperate effort by Texas' Tommy Keel.

Head Coach Barry Switzer (left) and assistant coach Gene Hochevar get a victory ride after OU's 52-13 win over Texas in 1973.

The 1973 Sooners won 10 games and tied Southern California, the 1972 mythical national champion, in their other game. It was OU's first unbeaten season in 17 years. Eight of the Sooners' 11 opponents in 1973 were ranked in the nation's top 20 at one time during the season. And Nebraska, Missouri, Texas, and Kansas, each a Sooner victim, and Southern California went to bowl games.

The lack of a bowl bid did cost the Sooners in the national rankings. OU was ranked second behind Alabama in the final rankings at the end of the regular season. But after the bowl games, the rankings by the Associated Press were shuffled with Notre Dame rated first, Ohio State second, and OU third. The Fighting Irish defeated Alabama, 24-23, in the Sugar Bowl, and the Buckeyes beat Southern California, 42-21, in the Rose Bowl.

The Big Eight Conference prides itself on being the strongest in the nation and what it calls the best balanced. The 1973 Sooners made a shambles of the conference race. They won their closest conference game by a margin of 17 points. No team had so dominated the conference in that manner since the 1956 Sooners.

In 1973 OU had a 7-0 conference record. Nebraska and Kansas tied for second place each with a 4-2-1 record. No team has so dominated the conference in that manner since 1943 when OU had a 5-0 record and Missouri and Iowa State tied for second place each with a 3-2 record.

So the free-wheeling, uninhibited, popular Switzer turned what appeared to be a desperate situation into what may be considered in retrospect one of the great seasons in the proud history of Oklahoma football.

Pride And Love

Following the University of Oklahoma's 1973 football season, a season successful in spite of adversity, the people of Eufaula, an Eastern Oklahoma community of 4,000, honored Lucious Selmon. Lucious Selmon is one of their own and was an important member of the 1973 Sooner football team. In some ways he symbolizes many of the reasons for OU's great success.

On that sunny but cold December day in Eufaula, they had a parade and an assembly in the high school gymnasium. They designated that portion of the state highway that goes through Eufaula as "Lucious Selmon Road."

The high and mighty of state politics and the University of Oklahoma joined the people of Eufaula in honoring the son of a former sharecropper. They made speeches. They praised Lucious Selmon for the kind of man he is, not for being an all-American football player. There was a feeling of pride and love.

Lucious Selmon may not be typical of all of OU's football players. And Eufaula may not be typical of all of the towns in Oklahoma. But every one of those towns has youngsters, such as those in that parade in the oversized red and white helmets and uniforms and hoping to be "Future Big Reds."

This has been a story of football at the University of Oklahoma and of some of the young men who through football have brought pride to millions of OU fans around the world.

Appendix

Yr.	W	L	T	Pct.	Pts.	Opp. Pts.	Coach	Captain
1895	0	1	0	.000	0	34	John A. Harts (S.W. Kans).	John A. Harts, Winfield, Kans.
1896	2	0	0	1.000	28	4	None	Ray Hume, Anadarko
1897	2	0	0	1.000	33	8	V. L. Parrington (Harvard)	C. C. Roberts, Medford
1898	2	0	0	1.000	29	0	V. L. Parrington (Harvard)	C. C. Roberts, Medford
1899	2	1	0	.667	61	28	V. L. Parrington (Harvard)	C. C. Roberts, Medford
1900	3	1	1	.750	118	28	V. L. Parrington (Harvard)	C. C. Roberts, Medford
1901	3	2	0	.600	93	29	Fred Roberts (Oklahoma)	Ray Crowe, Deer Creek
1902	6	3	0	.667	175	60	Mark McMahan (Texas)	Clyde Bogle, Norman
1903	5	4	3	.555	126	85	Mark McMahan (Texas)	Clyde Bogle, Norman
1904	4	3	1	.571	204	96	Fred Ewing (Knox)	Byron McCreary, Norman
1905	7	2	0	.777	229	55	Bennie Owen (Kansas)	Byron McCreary, Norman
1906	5	2	2	.714	124	36	Bennie Owen (Kansas)	James Monnett, Yale
1907	4	4	0	.500	181	75	Bennie Owen (Kansas)	Bill Cross, Kingfisher
1908	8	1	1	.888	272	35	Bennie Owen (Kansas)	Key Wolf, Davis
1909	6	4	0	.600	202	110	Bennie Owen (Kansas)	Charlie Armstrong, Kingfisher
1910	4	2	1	.667	163	31	Bennie Owen (Kansas)	Cleve Thompson, Erick
1911	8	0	0	1.000	282	15	Bennie Owen (Kansas)	Fred Capshaw, Norman
1912	5	4	0	.555	197	80	Bennie Owen (Kansas)	Glenn Clark, Comanche
1913	6	2	0	.750	323	44	Bennie Owen (Kansas)	Hubert Ambrister, Norman
1914	9	1	1	.900	440	96	Bennie Owen (Kansas)	Billy Clark, Comanche
1915	10	0	0	1.000	370	54	Bennie Owen (Kansas)	Forest Geyer, Norman
1916	6	5	0	.545	472	115	Bennie Owen (Kansas)	Homer Montgomery, Muskogee
1917	6	4	1	.600	451	103	Bennie Owen (Kansas)	Frank McCain, Ada
1918	6	0	0	1.000	278	7	Bennie Owen (Kansas)	Hugh McDermott, Duncan
1919	5	2	3	.714	275	63	Bennie Owen (Kansas)	Erl Deacon, Tecumseh
1920	6	0	1	1.000	176	51	Bennie Owen (Kansas)	Dewey Luster, Chickasha
1921	5	3	0	.625	127	102	Bennie Owen (Kansas)	Lawrence Haskell, Anadarko
1922	2	3	3	.400	64	114	Bennie Owen (Kansas)	Howard March, Madill
1923	3	5	0	.375	144	111	Bennie Owen (Kansas)	Pete Hammert, Anadarko
1924	2	5	1	.285	28	80	Bennie Owen (Kansas)	Obie Bristow, Ardmore
1925	4	3	1	.571	93	44	Bennie Owen (Kansas)	Eddie Brockman, Tulsa
1926	5	2	1	.714	137	52	Bennie Owen (Kansas)	Pollak Wallace, Oklahoma City
1927	3	3	2	.500	122	101	Ad Lindsey (Kansas)	Granville Norris, Laverne
1928	5	3	0	.625	120	88	Ad Lindsey (Kansas)	Bill Hamilton, Ardmore
1929	3	3	2	.500	81	81	Ad Lindsey (Kansas)	Frank Crider, Durant
1930	4	3	1	.571	100	57	Ad Lindsey (Kansas)	Bob Fields, Ponca City
1931	4	7	1	.363	88	108	Ad Lindsey (Kansas)	Guy Warren, Norman
1932	4	4	1	.500	90	81	Lewie Hardage (Vanderbilt)	Paul Young, Norman
1933	4	4	1	.500	83	70	Lewie Hardage (Vanderbilt)	Bill Pansze, Fort Smith, Ark.
1934	3	4	2	.428	64	43	Lewie Hardage (Vanderbilt)	Art Pansze, Fort Smith, Ark.
1935	6	3	0	.667	99	44	Capt. Lawrence Jones (Army)	Morris McDannald, Electra, Tex.
1936	3	3	3	.500	84	67	Capt. Lawrence Jones (Army)	Connie Ahrens, Oklahoma City
1937	5	2	2	.714	98	39	Tom Stidham (Haskell)	Al Corrotto, Ft. Smith, Ark.
1938	10	1	0	.909	185	29	Tom Stidham (Haskell)	Gene Corrotto, Ft. Smith, Ark. and Earl Crowder, Cherokee
1939	6	2	1	.750	186	62	Tom Stidham (Haskell)	Norval Locke, Ardmore
1940	6	3	0	.667	121	105	Tom Stidham (Haskell)	Gus Kitchens, Purcell
1941	6	3	0	.667	218	95	Dewey Luster (Oklahoma)	Orville Mathews, Chickasha and Rogers Eason, Okla. City
1942	3	5	2	.375	135	78	Dewey Luster (Oklahoma)	Bill Campbell, Pawhuska and W. G. "Dub" Lamb, Ardmore
1943	7	2	0	.778	187	92	Dewey Luster (Oklahoma)	W. C. "Dub" Wooten, Amarillo and Bob Brumley, Edinburg,

Yr.	W	L	T	Pct.	Pts.	Opp. Pts.	Coach	Captain
								Tex.
1944	6	3	1	.667	227	149	Dewey Luster (Oklahoma)	W. C. "Dub" Wooten, Amarillo and Bob Mayfield, Norman
1945	5	5	0	.500	169	138	Dewey Luster (Oklahoma)	Omer Burgert, Enid
1946	8	3	0	.727	309	120	Jim Tatum (North Carolina)	Jim Tyree, Oklahoma City
1947	7	2	1	.778	194	161	Bud Wilkinson (Minnesota)	Jim Tyree, Oklahoma City and Wade Walker, Gastonia, N.C.
1948	10	1	0	.909	350	121	Bud Wilkinson (Minnesota)	Wade Walker, Gastonia N. C. and Homer Paine, Enid
1949	11	0	0	1.000	399	88	Bud Wilkinson (Minnesota)	Stanley West, Enid and Jim Owens, Oklahoma City
1950	10	1	0	.909	352	148	Bud Wilkinson (Minnesota)	Harry Moore, Blackwell and Norman McNabb, Norman
1951	8	2	0	.800	321	97	Bud Wilkinson (Minnesota)	Bert Clark, Wichita Falls, Tex. and Jim Weatherall, White Deer, Tex.
1952	8	1	1	.888	407	141	Bud Wilkinson (Minnesota)	Eddie Crowder, Muskogee and Tom Catlin, Ponca City
1953	9	1	1	.900	293	90	Bud Wilkinson (Minnesota)	Larry Grigg, Sherman, Tex., Roger Nelson, Wynnewood
1954	10	0	0	1.000	304	62	Bud Wilkinson (Minnesota)	Gene Mears, Seminole; Gene Calame, Sulphur; Carl Allison, McAlester
1955	11	0	0	1.000	385	60	Bud Wilkinson (Minnesota)	Bo Bolinger, Muskogee; Cecil Morris, Lawton; Bob Loughridge, Poteau
1956	10	0	0	1.000	466	51	Bud Wilkinson (Minnesota)	Ed Gray, Odessa, Tex., Jerry Tubbs, Breckenridge, Tex.
1957	10	1	0	.909	333	89	Bud Wilkinson (Minnesota)	Don Stiller, Shawnee; Clendon Thomas, Oklahoma City
1958	10	1	0	.909	300	55	Bud Wilkinson (Minnesota)	Joe Rector, Muskogee; Bob Harrison, Stamford, Tex.
1959	7	3	0	.700	234	146	Bud Wilkinson (Minnesota)	Gilmer Lewis, Wichita Falls, Tex.; Bobby Boyd, Garland, Tex.
1960	3	6	1	.350	136	158	Bud Wilkinson (Minnesota)	Ronnie Hartline, Lawton; Marshall York, Amarillo, Tex.
1961	5	5	0	.500	122	141	Bud Wilkinson (Minnesota)	Billy White, Amarillo, Tex.
1962	8	3	0	.727	267	61	Bud Wilkinson (Minnesota)	Wayne Lee, Ada; Leon Cross, Hobbs, N.M.
1963	8	2	0	.800	236	137	Bud Wilkinson (Minnesota)	John Garrett, Stilwell; Larry Vermillion, Chickasha
1964	6	4	1	.600	207	170	Gomer Jones (Ohio State)	Newt Burton, Springfield, Mo.; John Garrett, Stilwell
1965	3	7	0	.300	106	150	Gomer Jones (Ohio State)	Mike Ringer, Pauls Valley; and Carl McAdams, White Deer, Tex.
1966	6	4	0	.600	192	122	Jim Mackenzie (Kentucky)	Ed Hall, Eden, Tex.; Jim Riley, Enid
1967	10	1	0	.909	290	92	Chuck Fairbanks (Mich. St.)	Bob Kalsu, Del City
1968	7	4	0	.636	343	225	Chuck Fairbanks (Mich. St.)	Bob Warmack, Ada; John Titsworth, Heavener; Steve Barrett, Artesia, N.M.
1969	6	4	0	.600	285	289	Chuck Fairbanks (Mich. St.)	Steve Zabel, Thornton, Colo.; Steve Owens, Miami, Okla.; Jim Files, Ft. Smith, Ark.; Ken Mendenhall, Enid.
1970	7	4	1	.636	305	239	Chuck Fairbanks (Mich. St.)	Monty Johnson, Amarillo, Tex. Steve Casteel, Garland, Tex.
1971	11	1	0	.917	534	217	Chuck Fairbanks (Mich. St.)	Jack Mildren, Abilene, Tex.; Glenn King, Jacksboro, Tex.; Steve Aycock, Midland, Tex.
1972	11	1	0	.917	385	74	Chuck Fairbanks (Mich. St.)	Tom Brahaney, Midland, Tex. Greg Pruitt, Houston, Tex.
1973	10	0	1	.955	400	133	Barry Switzer (Ark.)	Gary Baccus, Brownfield, Tex. Eddie Foster, Monahans, Tex. Lucious Selmon, Eufaula Tim Welch, Bowie, Tex.

Oklahoma Coaching Records, 1895-1973

Period	Name and School	Years Coached	W	L	T	Pct.	Pts.	Opp. Pts.	Avg.	Opp. Avg.
1895	Jack Harts (Winfield, Kans. Tchrs.)	1	0	1	0	.000	0	34	0.0	34.0
1897-1900	Vernon Parrington (Harvard)	4	9	2	1	.818	241	64	20.0	5.3
1901	Fred Roberts (Oklahoma)	1	3	2	0	.600	93	29	18.6	5.8
1902-3	Mark McMahan (Texas)	2	11	7	3	.555	301	145	14.3	6.9
1904	Fred Ewing (Knox)	1	4	3	1	.571	204	90	25.5	11.2
1905-26	Bennie Owen (Kansas)	22	122	54	16	.693	5132	1426	26.5	7.3
1927-31	Adrian Lindsey (Kansas)	5	19	19	6	.500	511	435	12.1	10.3
1932-34	Lewie Hardage (Vanderbilt)	3	11	12	4	.478	237	194	8.7	7.1
1935-36	Lawrence "Biff" Jones (Army)	2	9	6	3	.600	183	111	10.1	6.1
1937-40	Tom Stidham (Haskell)	4	27	8	3	.771	590	218	15.5	5.8
1941-45	Dewey "Snorter" Luster (Okla.)	5	27	18	3	.600	936	552	19.5	11.5
1946	Jim Tatum (North Carolina)	1	8	3	0	.727	309	120	28.0	10.9
1947-63	Bud Wilkinson (Minnesota)	17	145	29	4	.833	4954	1730	29.1	10.1
1964-65	Gomer Jones (Ohio State)	2	9	11	1	.473	294	284	14.7	14.2
1966	Jim Mackenzie (Kentucky)	1	6	4	0	.600	192	122	19.2	12.2
1967-72	Chuck Fairbanks (Michigan State)	6	52	15	1	.772	2142	1136	31.5	16.7
1973	Barry Switzer (Arkansas)	1	10	0	1	.955	400	133	36.4	12.1

OU SCORES YEAR BY YEAR

1895
COACH JOHN A. HARTS
Won 0, Lost 1

0, Oklahoma City	34

1896
(No Coach)

12, Norman High	0
16, Norman High	4

1897
COACH V. L. PARRINGTON
Won 9, Lost 2, Tied 1

16, Oklahoma City	0
17, Kingfisher college	8

1898

5, Arkansas City	0
24, Fort Worth U.	0

1899

39, Kingfisher college	6
11, Arkansas U.	5
11, Arkansas City	17

1900

2, Texas	28
27, Chilocco Indians	0
79, Fort Reno	0
0, Kingfisher college	0
10, Arkansas City	0

1901
COACH FRED ROBERTS
Won 3, Lost 2

6, Texas	12
17, Baylor	0
42, Fairmont	0
28, Kingfisher college	6
0, Texas	11

1902
COACH MARK McMAHAN
Won 11, Lost 7, Tied 3

62, Guthrie	0
6, Texas	22
6, Dallas Ath. Club	11
28, Arkansas	0
30, Oklahoma City	0
15, Kingfisher college	0
5, Missouri	22
6, Emporia Normal	5
17, Kingfisher college	0

1903

38, Chilocco Indians	5
0, Kingfisher college	0
6, Texas	6
6, Texas Aggies	0
11, Fairmont	5
6, Emporia Normal	6
5, Kansas	17
5, Texas	11
0, Arkansas	12
12, Missouri Mines	6
10, Bethany	12
27, Lawton	5

1904

COACH FRED EWING
Won 4, Lost 3, Tied 1

0, Kingfisher college	0
33, Pauls Valley	0
0, Kansas	16
6, Lawton	0
75, Oklahoma Aggies	0
10, Texas	40
71, O. C. Military Institute	4
9, Bethany	36

1905

COACH BENNIE OWEN
Won 122, Lost 54, Tied 16

28, Central Normal	0
18, Haskell Indians	12
0, Kansas	34
33, Kansas City Medics	0
6, Washburn	9
2, Texas	0
55, Kingfisher college	0
58, Central Normal	0
29, Bethany	0

1906

12, Central Normal	0
11, Kingfisher college	6
23, Oklahoma Aggies	0
4, Kansas	20
9, Texas	10
17, Central Normal	0
0, Pawhuska	0
48, Sulphur	0
0, Washburn	0

1907

32, Kingfisher college	0
43, Chilocco Indians	0
0, Kansas	15
29, Epworth U.	0
67, Oklahoma Aggies	0
0, Texas Aggies	19
10, Texas	29
0, Washburn	12

1908

51, Central Normal	5
18, Oklahoma Aggies	0
51, Kingfisher college	0
0, Kansas	11
33, Kansas Aggies	4
27, Arkansas	5
24, Epworth U.	0
50, Texas	0
12, Fairmont	4
6, Washburn	6

1909

55, Central Normal	0
46, Kingfisher college	5
0, Kansas	11
23, Alva Normal	2
5, Arkansas	21
42, Washburn	8
11, St. Louis U.	5
8, Texas Aggies	14
0, Texas	30
12, Epworth U.	11

1910

66, Kingfisher College	0
79, Central Normal	0
12, Oklahoma Aggies	0
0, Missouri	26
0, Kansas	2
3, Texas	0
3, Epworth U.	3

1911

104, Kingfisher college	0
62, Oklahoma Christian U.	0
22, Oklahoma Aggies	0
37, Washburn	0
14, Missouri	6
3, Kansas	0
34, Alva Normal	6
6, Texas	3

1912

40, Kingfisher college	0
87, Central Normal	0
21, Texas	6
0, Missouri	14
6, Kansas	5
6, Texas Aggies	28
16, Oklahoma Aggies	0
9, Nebraska	13
12, Colorado	14

1913

74, Kingfisher college	0
83, Central Normal	0
101, Alva Normal	0
17, Missouri	20
21, Kansas	7
6, Texas	14
7, Oklahoma Aggies	0
14, Colorado	3

1914

67, Central Normal	0
67, Kingfisher college	0
96, Ada Normal	6
13, Missouri	0
7, Texas	32
16, Kansas	16
28, Oklahoma Aggies	6
52, Kansas Aggies	10
35, Arkansas	7
33, Haskell Indians	12
26, Henry Kendall	7

1915

67, Kingfisher college	0
55, Weatherford Normal	0
102, Alva Normal	0
24, Missouri	0
14, Texas	13
23, Kansas	14
14, Henry Kendall	13
24, Arkansas	0
21, Kansas Aggies	7
26, Oklahoma Aggies	7

1916

27, Central Normal	0
107, Shawnee Normal	0
140, Weatherford Normal	0
0, Henry Kendall	16
7, Texas	21
14, Missouri	23
13, Kansas	21
96, Kingfisher college	0
13, Kansas Aggies	14
14, Arkansas	13
41, Oklahoma Aggies	7

1917

99, Central Normal	0
179, Kingfisher college	0

52, Phillips U.   9
0, Illinois   44
14, Texas   0
14, Missouri   7
6, Kansas   13
0, Arkansas   0
80, Henry Kendall   0
0, Oklahoma Aggies   9
7, Camp Doniphan   21

1918

44, Central Normal   0
58, Post Field   0
33, Kansas   0
103, Arkansas   0
13, Phillips U.   7
27, Oklahoma Aggies   0

1919

40, Central Normal   0
157, Kingfisher college   0
0, Henry Kendall   27
12, Texas   7
7, Nebraska   7
6, Missouri   6
0, Kansas   0
6, Arkansas   7
14, Kansas Aggies   3
33, Oklahoma Aggies   6

1920

16, Central Normal   7
24, Washington   14
28, Missouri   7
21, Kansas   9
26, Oklahoma Aggies   0
7, Kansas Aggies   7
44, Drake   7

1921

21, Central Normal   0
6, Oklahoma Aggies   0
28, Washington   13
0, Nebraska   44
24, Kansas   7
14, Missouri   24
7, Kansas Aggies   14
27, Rice   0

1922

19, Central Normal   0
7, Kansas Aggies   7
7, Nebraska   39
3, Kansas   19
18, Missouri   14
7, Texas   32
3, Oklahoma Aggies   3
0, Washington   0

1923

0, Nebraska   24
62, Washington   7
12, Oklahoma Aggies   0
3, Kansas   7
13, Missouri   0
14, Texas   26
20, Kansas Aggies   21
20, Drake   26

1924

0, Central Normal   2
14, Nebraska   7

0, Drake   28
0, Oklahoma Aggies   6
0, Missouri   10
0, Kansas   20
7, Washington   0
7, Kansas Aggies   7

1925

0, Kansas Aggies   16
7, Drake   0
9, Southern Methodist   0
0, Nebraska   12
0, Kansas   0
14, Missouri   16
23, Washington   0
35, Oklahoma Aggies   0

1926

13, Arkansas   6
11, Drake   0
12, Kansas Aggies   15
21, Washington   0
10, Missouri   7
9, Kansas   10
47, St. Louis   0
14, Oklahoma Aggies   14

1927

COACH ADRIAN LINDSEY
Won 19, Lost 19, Tied 6

13, Chicago   7
13, Creighton   13
14, Kansas Aggies   20
14, Central Normal   14
23, Washington   7
26, Kansas   7
7, Oklahoma Aggies   13
7, Missouri   20

1928

7, Indiana   10
7, Creighton   0
33, Kansas Aggies   21
0, Iowa State   13
6, Nebraska   44
7, Kansas   0
46, Oklahoma Aggies   0
14, Missouri   0

1929

26, Creighton   0
0, Texas   21
14, Kansas Aggies   13
21, Iowa State   7
0, Kansas   7
13, Nebraska   13
7, Oklahoma Aggies   7
0, Missouri   13

1930

47, New Mexico   0
20, Nebraska   7
7, Texas   17
7, Kansas Aggies   0
19, Iowa State   13
0, Kansas   13
0, Oklahoma Aggies   7
0, Missouri   0

1931

19, Rice   6
0, Nebraska   13
0, Texas   3

0, Kansas Aggies	14
12, Iowa State	13
10, Kansas	0
0, Missouri	7
0, Oklahoma Aggies	0
0, Oklahoma City U.	6
20, Tulsa U.	7
20, Honolulu Town Team	39
7, Hawaii U.	0

1932

COACH LEWIE HARDAGE
Won 11, Lost 12, Tied 4

7, Tulsa	0
21, Kansas	6
10, Texas	17
20, Kansas State	13
0, Oklahoma Aggies	7
6, Missouri	14
19, Iowa State	12
0, Nebraska	5
7, George Washington	7

1933

0, Vanderbilt	0
6, Tulsa	20
9, Texas	0
19, Iowa State	7
7, Nebraska	16
20, Kansas	0
21, Missouri	0
0, Kansas State	14
0, Oklahoma Aggies	13

1934

7, Centenary	0
0, Texas	19
0, Nebraska	6
7, Kansas	7
31, Missouri	0
12, Iowa State	0
7, Kansas State	8
0, Oklahoma Aggies	0
0, George Washington	3

1935

COACH LAWRENCE "BIFF" JONES
Won 9, Lost 6, Tied 3

3, Colorado	0
25, New Mexico	0
7, Texas	12
16, Iowa State	0
0, Nebraska	19
0, Kansas	7
20, Missouri	6
3, Kansas State	0
25, Oklahoma Aggies	0

1936

0, Tulsa	0
8, Colorado	0
0, Texas	6
14, Kansas	0
0, Nebraska	14
7, Iowa State	7
6, Kansas State	6
14, Missouri	21
35, Oklahoma Aggies	13

1937

COACH TOM STIDHAM
Won 27, Lost 8, Tied 3

7, Tulsa	19
6, Rice	0
7, Texas	7
0, Nebraska	0
3, Kansas	6

19, Kansas State	0
33, Iowa State	7
7, Missouri	0
16, Oklahoma Aggies	0

1938

7, Rice	6
13, Texas	0
19, Kansas	0
14, Nebraska	0
28, Tulsa	6
26, Kansas State	0
21, Missouri	0
10, Iowa State	0
19, Oklahoma Aggies	0
28, Washington State	0

Orange Bowl

| 0, Tennessee | 17 |

1939

7, Southern Methodist	7
23, Northwestern	0
24, Texas	12
27, Kansas	7
41, Oklahoma Aggies	0
38, Iowa State	6
13, Kansas State	10
6, Missouri	7
7, Nebraska	13

1940

29, Oklahoma Aggies	27
16, Texas	19
14, Kansas State	0
20, Iowa State	7
0, Nebraska	13
13, Kansas	0
7, Missouri	0
9, Temple	6
13, Santa Clara	33

1941

COACH DEWEY "SNORTER" LUSTER
Won 27, Lost 18, Tied 3

19, Oklahoma Aggies	0
7, Texas	40
16, Kansas State	0
16, Santa Clara	6
38, Kansas	0
55, Iowa State	0
0, Missouri	28
61, Marquette	14
6, Nebraska	7

1942

0, Oklahoma Aggies	0
0, Tulsa	23
0, Texas	7
25, Kansas	0
0, Nebraska	7
14, Iowa State	7
76, Kansas State	0
6, Missouri	6
7, Temple	14
7, William & Mary	14

1943

22, Norman NAS	6
22, Oklahoma Aggies	13
7, Texas	13
6, Tulsa	20

37, Kansas State | 0
21, Iowa State | 7
26, Kansas | 13
20, Missouri | 13
26, Nebraska | 7

1944

14, Norman NAS | 28
21, Texas Aggies | 14
0, Texas | 20
68, Kansas State | 0
34, Texas Christian | 19
12, Iowa State | 7
21, Missouri | 21
20, Kansas | 0
6, Oklahoma Aggies | 28
31, Nebraska | 12

1945

21, Hondo, Tex. AAF | 6
20, Nebraska | 0
14, Texas Aggies | 19
7, Texas | 12
39, Kansas | 7
41, Kansas State | 13
7, Texas Christian | 13
14, Iowa State | 7
6, Missouri | 14
0, Oklahoma A&M | 47

1946

COACH JIM TATUM
Won 8, Lost 3

7, Army | 21
10, Texas Aggies | 7
13, Texas | 20
28, Kansas State | 7
63, Iowa State | 0
14, Texas Christian | 12
13, Kansas | 16
27, Missouri | 6
27, Nebraska | 6
73, Oklahoma Aggies | 12
Gator Bowl
34, North Carolina State | 13

1947

COACH BUD WILKINSON
Won 145, Lost 29, Tied 4

24, Detroit | 20
26, Texas Aggies | 14
14, Texas | 34
13, Kansas | 13
7, Texas Christian | 20
27, Iowa State | 9
27, Kansas State | 13
21, Missouri | 12
14, Nebraska | 13
21, Oklahoma Aggies | 13

1948

17, Santa Clara | 20
42, Texas Aggies | 14
20, Texas | 14
42, Kansas State | 0
21, Texas Christian | 18
33, Iowa State | 6
41, Missouri | 7
41, Nebraska | 14
60, Kansas | 7
19, Oklahoma Aggies | 15
Sugar Bowl
14, North Carolina | 6

1949

46, Boston College | 0

33, Texas Aggies | 13
20, Texas | 14
48, Kansas | 26
48, Nebraska | 0
34, Iowa State | 7
39, Kansas State | 0
27, Missouri | 7
28, Santa Clara | 21
41, Oklahoma Aggies | 0
Sugar Bowl
35, Louisiana State | 0

1950

National Collegiate Champions

28, Boston College | 0
34, Texas Aggies | 28
14, Texas | 13
58, Kansas State | 0
20, Iowa State | 7
27, Colorado | 18
33, Kansas | 13
41, Missouri | 7
49, Nebraska | 35
41, Oklahoma Aggies | 14
Sugar Bowl
7, Kentucky | 13

1951

49, William and Mary | 7
7, Texas Aggies | 14
7, Texas | 9
33, Kansas | 21
55, Colorado | 14
33, Kansas State | 0
34, Missouri | 20
35, Iowa State | 6
27, Nebraska | 0
41, Oklahoma Aggies | 6

1952

21, Colorado | 21
49, Pittsburgh | 20
49, Texas | 20
42, Kansas | 20
49, Kansas State | 6
41, Iowa State | 0
21, Notre Dame | 27
47, Missouri | 7
34, Nebraska | 13
54, Oklahoma A&M | 7

1953

21, Notre Dame | 28
7, Pittsburgh | 7
19, Texas | 14
45, Kansas | 0
27, Colorado | 20
34, Kansas State | 0
14, Missouri | 7
47, Iowa State | 0
30, Nebraska | 7
42, Oklahoma Aggies | 7
Orange Bowl
7, Maryland | 0

1954

27, California | 13
21, Texas Christian | 16
14, Texas | 7
65, Kansas | 0
21, Kansas State | 0
13, Colorado | 6
40, Iowa State | 0

1955

National Collegiate Champions

13,	North Carolina	6
26,	Pittsburgh	14
20,	Texas	0
44,	Kansas	6
56,	Colorado	21
40,	Kansas State	7
20,	Missouri	0
52,	Iowa State	0
41,	Nebraska	0
53,	Oklahoma A&M	0

Orange Bowl

20,	Maryland	6

1956

National Collegiate Champions

36,	North Carolina	0
66,	Kansas State	0
45,	Texas	0
34,	Kansas	12
40,	Notre Dame	0
27,	Colorado	19
44,	Iowa State	0
67,	Missouri	14
54,	Nebraska	6
53,	Oklahoma A&M	0

1957

26,	Pittsburgh	0
40,	Iowa State	14
21,	Texas	7
47,	Kansas	0
14,	Colorado	13
13,	Kansas State	0
39,	Missouri	14
0,	Notre Dame	7
32,	Nebraska	7
53,	Oklahoma State	6

Orange Bowl

48,	Duke	21

1958

47,	West Virginia	14
6,	Oregon	0
14,	Texas	15
43,	Kansas	0
40,	Kansas State	6
23,	Colorado	7
20,	Iowa State	0
39,	Missouri	0
40,	Nebraska	7
7,	Oklahoma State	0

Orange Bowl

21,	Syracuse	6

1959

13,	Northwestern	45
42,	Colorado	12
12,	Texas	19
23,	Missouri	0
7,	Kansas	6
21,	Nebraska	25
36,	Kansas State	0
28,	Army	20
35,	Iowa State	12
17,	Oklahoma State	7

1960

3,	Northwestern	19
15,	Pittsburgh	14
0,	Texas	24
13,	Kansas	13
49,	Kansas State	7
0,	Colorado	7
6,	Iowa State	10
19,	Missouri	41
14,	Nebraska	17
17,	Oklahoma State	6

1961

6,	Notre Dame	19
15,	Iowa State	21
7,	Texas	28
0,	Kansas	10
14,	Colorado	22
17,	Kansas State	6
7,	Missouri	0
14,	Army	8
21,	Nebraska	14
21,	Oklahoma State	13

1962

7,	Syracuse	3
7,	Notre Dame	13
6,	Texas	9
13,	Kansas	7
47,	Kansas State	0
62,	Colorado	0
41,	Iowa State	0
13,	Missouri	0
34,	Nebraska	6
37,	Oklahoma State	6

Orange Bowl

0,	Alabama	17

1963

31,	Clemson	14
17,	Southern California	12
7,	Texas	28
21,	Kansas	18
34,	Kansas State	9
35,	Colorado	0
24,	Iowa State	14
13,	Missouri	3
20,	Nebraska	29
34,	Oklahoma State	10

1964

COACH GOMER JONES
Won 9, Lost 11, Tied 1

13,	Maryland	3
14,	Southern California	40
7,	Texas	28
14,	Kansas	15
44,	Kansas State	0
14,	Colorado	11
30,	Iowa State	0
14,	Missouri	14
17,	Nebraska	7
21,	Oklahoma State	16

Gator Bowl

19,	Florida State	36

1965

9,	Pittsburgh	13
0,	Navy	10
0,	Texas	19
21,	Kansas	7
27,	Kansas State	0
0,	Colorado	13
24,	Iowa State	20

0, Missouri   30
9, Nebraska   21
16, Oklahoma State   17

1966

COACH JIM MACKENZIE
Won 6, Lost 4

17, Oregon   0
33, Iowa State   11
18, Texas   9
35, Kansas   0
0, Notre Dame   38
21, Colorado   24
37, Kansas State   6
7, Missouri   10
10, Nebraska   9
14, Oklahoma State   15

1967

COACH CHUCK FAIRBANKS
Won 51, Lost 15, Tied 1

21, Washington State   0
35, Maryland   0
7, Texas   9
46, Kansas State   7
7, Missouri   0
23, Colorado   0
52, Iowa State   14
14, Kansas   10
21, Nebraska   14
38, Oklahoma State   14
Orange Bowl
26, Tennessee   24

1968

21, Notre Dame   45
28, North Carolina State   14
20, Texas   26
42, Iowa State   7
27, Colorado   41
35, Kansas State   20
27, Kansas   23
28, Missouri   14
47, Nebraska   0
41, Oklahoma State   7
Astro-Bluebonnet Bowl
27, Southern Methodist   28

1969

48, Wisconsin   21
37, Pittsburgh   8
17, Texas   27
42, Colorado   30
21, Kansas State   59
37, Iowa State   14
10, Missouri   44
31, Kansas   15
14, Nebraska   44
28, Oklahoma State   27

1970

28, Southern Methodist   11
21, Wisconsin   7
14, Oregon State   23
9, Texas   41
23, Colorado   15
14, Kansas State   19
29, Iowa State   28
28, Missouri   13
28, Kansas   24
21, Nebraska   28
66, Oklahoma State   6
Astro-Bluebonnet Bowl
24, Alabama   24

1971

30, Southern Methodist   0
55, Pittsburgh   29
33, Southern Cal   20
48, Texas   27
45, Colorado   17
75, Kansas State   28
43, Iowa State   12
20, Missouri   3
56, Kansas   10
31, Nebraska   35
58, Oklahoma State   14
Sugar Bowl
40, Auburn   22

1972

49, Utah State   0
68, Oregon   3
52, Clemson   3
27, Texas   0
14, Colorado   20
52, Kansas State   0
20, Iowa State   6
17, Missori   6
31, Kansas   7
17, Nebraska   14
38, Oklahoma State   15
Sugar Bowl
14, Penn State   0

(OU forfeited games against Missouri,
Kansas, and Oklahoma State in 1972
because it was later discovered that
OU used an ineligible player in those
games.)

1973

COACH BARRY SWITZER
Won 10, Lost 0, Tied 1

42, Baylor   14
7, Southern California   7
24, Miami, Fla.   20
52, Texas   13
34, Colorado   7
56, Kansas State   14
34, Iowa State   17
31, Missouri   3
48, Kansas   20
27, Nebraska   0
45, Oklahoma State   18

OU BOWL GAMES

OU NATIONAL RANKINGS
(Associated Press started in 1936 and United
Press International started in 1950)

1938 4th in AP	1958 5th in AP, 5th in UPI
1948 5th in AP	1959 17th in UPI
1949 2nd in AP	1962 8th in AP, 7th in UPI
1950 1st in AP, 1st in UPI	1963 10th in AP, 8th in UPI
1951 10th in AP, 11th in UPI	1967 3rd in AP, 3rd in UPI
1952 4th in AP, 4th in UPI	1968 11th in AP, 10th in UPI
1953 4th in AP, 5th in UPI	1970 20th in AP, 15th in UPI
1954 3rd in AP, 3rd in UPI	1971 2nd in AP, 3rd in UPI
1955 1st in AP, 1st in UPI	1972 2nd in AP, 2nd in UPI
1956 1st in AP, 1st in UPI	1973 3rd in AP, 2nd in UPI
1957 4th in AP, 4th in UPI	

TEAM RECORDS

Most consecutive victories—47 in 1953-1957.
Most consecutive games scoring—123 in 1946-1957.
Most yards rushing one game—711 against Kansas State in 1971.
Highest rushing average per game in one season—472.4 in 1971.
Highest average first downs per game in one season—21.5 in 1971.
Average touchdowns rushing and passing per game in one season—6.4 in 1956 (64 in 10 games).
Most fumbles lost in one season—35 in 1948 (fumbled 45 times)

INDIVIDUAL RECORDS

Most rushes in one game—55 by Steve Owens against Oklahoma State in 1969.
Most rushes in one season—358 by Steve Owens in 1969.
Most rushes in career—905 by Steve Owens in 1967-1969.
Most rushing yards in career—3,867 by Steve Owens in 1967-1969.
Most consecutive games rushing for 100 yards or more—17 by Steve Owens in 1968-1969.
Most touchdowns by rushing in one season—23 by Steve Owens in 1969.
Most touchdowns by rushing in career—56 by Steve Owens in 1967-1969.
Most yards per pass completion in one game (minimum of 5 completions)—49.2 by Monte Deere against Colorado in 1962 (246 yards in 5 passes).
Lowest percentage of passes intercepted in career—(minimum of 100 passes) 0.9 percent by Claude Arnold in 1950 (1 interception in 114 passes).
Highest average gain per punt return in career—23.6 by Jack Mitchell in 1946-1948.
Most touchdowns on punt returns in career—7 by Jack Mitchell in 1946-1948.
Highest average per kickoff and punt return in career—23.3 by Jack Mitchell in 1946-1948.
Most touchdowns on kickoff and punt returns in career—7 by Jack Mitchell in 1946-1948.

OU NATIONAL STATISTICS LEADERS
(Compiled since organization of National
Collegiate Athletic Bureau in 1937)
TEAM LEADERS

TOTAL OFFENSE

1955—Average of 410.7 yards a game rushing and passing.
1956—Average of 481.7 yards a game rushing and passing.
1971—Average of 566.5 yards a game rushing and passing.

RUSHING

1953—Average of 306.9 yards a game.
1955—Average of 328.9 yards a game.
1956—Average of 391 yards a game.
1971—Average of 472.4 yards a game.
1972—Average of 368.8 yards a game.

RUSHING DEFENSE

1938—Average of 43.3 yards a game by opponents.
1946—Average of 58 yards a game by opponents.
1949—Average of 55.6 yards a game by opponents.

SCORING
(National records compiled only since 1957)

1971—Averaged 44.9 points a game.

INTERCEPTION AVOIDANCE

1950—.021 of passes attempted intercepted.

INDIVIDUAL LEADERS

RUSHING

1969—1,523 yards by Steve Owens.

SCORING

1949—117 points by George Thomas.
1956—108 points by Clendon Thomas.
1969—138 points by Steve Owens.

PUNTING

1962—Average of 43.4 yards a punt by Joe Don Looney

SCORING BY KICKING

1971—80 points by John Carroll.

OU ALL-AMERICA SELECTIONS
CONSENSUS ALL-AMERICA SELECTIONS
(Selected on a majority of the teams recognized by the NCAA)

1938—End Roland "Waddy" Young, Ponca City.
1948—Guard Paul "Buddy" Burris, Muskogee.
1950—Tackle Jim Weatherall, White Deer, Texas, and back Leon Heath, Hollis.
1951—Tackle Jim Weatherall, White Deer, Texas.
1952—Back Billy Vessels, Miami.
1953—Guard J. D. Roberts, Dallas, Texas.
1954—End Max Boydston, Muskogee, and center Kurt Burris, Muskogee.
1955—Guard Bo Bolinger, Muskogee.
1956—Center Jerry Tubbs, Breckenridge, Texas, and back Tommy McDonald, Albuquerque, New Mexico.
1957—Guard Bill Krisher, Midwest City, and back Clendon Thomas, Oklahoma City.
1958—Center Bob Harrison, Stamford, Texas.
1963—Back Jim Grisham, Olney, Texas.
1964—Tackle Ralph Neely, Farmington, New Mexico.
1965—Linebacker Carl McAdams, White Deer, Texas.
1967—Middle guard Granville Liggins, Tulsa.
1969—Back Steve Owens, Miami.
1971—Center Tom Brahaney, Midland, Texas, and back Greg Pruitt, Houston, Texas.
1972—Center Tom Brahaney, Midland, Texas, and back Greg Pruitt, Houston, Texas.
1973—Middle guard Lucious Selmon, Eufaula, and linebacker Rod Shoate, Spiro.

OTHER ALL-AMERICA SELECTIONS

1913—Back Claude Reeds, Norman.
1915—Back Forest "Spot" Geyer, Norman.
1920—Tackle Roy "Soupy" Smoot, Lawton, and back Phil White,

Oklahoma City.

1927—Tackle Granville Norris, Laverne.

1934—Tackle Cash Gentry, Lawton.

1935—Tackle J. W. "Dub" Wheeler, Davis.

1937—End Pete Smith, Muskogee.

1939—End Frank "Pop" Ivy, Skiatook, and tackle Gilford "Cactus Face" Duggan, Benton, Arkansas.

1946—Guard Paul "Buddy" Burris, Muskogee, guard Plato Andros, Oklahoma City, and center John Rapacz, Kalamazoo, Michigan.

1947—Guard Paul "Buddy" Burris, Muskogee.

1948—Back Jack Mitchell, Arkansas City, Kansas.

1949—End Jim Owens, Oklahoma City, tackle Wade Walker, Gastonia, North Carolina, guard Stan West, Enid, back Darrell Royal, Hollis, and back George Thomas, Fairland.

1950—End Frankie Anderson, Oklahoma City, and safety Buddy Jones, Holdenville.

1951—Center Tom Catlin, Ponca City.

1952—Center Tom Catlin, Ponca City, back Eddie Crowder, Muskogee, and back Buck McPhail, Oklahoma City.

1956—Tackle Ed Gray, Odessa, Texas, and guard Bill Krisher, Midwest City.

1959—Guard Jerry Thompson, Ada.

1962—Guard Leon Cross, Hobbs, New Mexico, center Wayne Lee, Ada, and back Joe Don Looney, Fort Worth, Texas.

1963—Tackle Ralph Neely, Farmington, New Mexico.

1964—Linebacker Carl McAdams, White Deer, Texas.

1966—Middle guard Granville Liggins, Tulsa.

1967—Tackle Bob Kalsu, Del City.

1968—Back Steve Owens, Miami.

1969—End Steve Zabel, Thornton, Colorado, and center Ken Mendenhall, Enid.

1971—Back Jack Mildren, Abilene, Texas.

1972—Tackle Derland Moore, Poplar Bluff, Missouri.

1973—Tackle Eddie Foster, Monahans, Texas.

Oklahoma Rank in Conference Play

(1915-1973)

SOUTHWEST CONFERENCE

Year	W	L	T	Pct.	Pts.	Opp. Pts.	Rank	Coach
1915	3	0	0	1.000	64	20	1st	Bennie Owen
1916	2	1	0	.667	62	41	3rd(T)	Bennie Owen
1917	1	1	1	.500	14	9	3rd	Bennie Owen

Year	W	L	T	Pct.	Pts.	Opp. Pts.	Rank	Coach
1918	2	0	0	1.000	130	0	1st(T)	Bennie Owen
1919	2	1	0	.667	51	20	3rd	Bennie Owen
Total	10	3	1	.769	321	40		

OLD MISSOURI VALLEY CONFERENCE

Year	W	L	T	Pct.	Pts.	Opp. Pts.	Rank	Coach
1920	4	0	1	1.000	124	44	1st	Bennie Owen
1921	2	3	0	.400	63	102	7th(T)	Bennie Owen
1922	1	2	2	.333	25	79	7th	Bennie Owen
1923	2	4	0	.333	118	85	6th	Bennie Owen
1924	2	3	1	.400	28	72	6th	Bennie Owen
1925	2	3	1	.400	49	44	5th(T)	Bennie Owen
1926	3	2	1	.600	77	46	5th	Bennie Owen
1927	2	3	0	.400	82	67	7th	Ad Lindsey
Total	18	20	6		566	539		

BIG SIX CONFERENCE

Year	W	L	T	Pct.	Pts.	Opp. Pts.	Rank	Coach
1928	3	2	0	.600	60	78	2nd(T)	Ad Lindsey
1929	2	2	1	.500	48	53	4th	Ad Lindsey
*1930	3	1	1	.700	46	33	2nd	Ad Lindsey
1931	1	4	0	.200	24	47	5th(T)	Ad Lindsey
1932	3	2	0	.600	66	50	2nd(T)	Lewie Hardage
1933	3	2	0	.600	67	37	3rd	Lewie Hardage
1934	2	2	1	.500	57	21	3rd	Lewie Hardage
1935	3	2	0	.600	39	32	2nd	Biff Jones
1936	1	2	2	.400	41	48	4th	Biff Jones
1937	3	1	1	.700	62	13	2nd	Tom Stidham
1938	5	0	0	1.000	90	0	1st	Tom Stidham
1939	3	2	0	.600	91	43	3rd	Tom Stidham
1940	4	1	0	.800	54	20	2nd	Tom Stidham
1941	3	2	0	.600	115	35	2nd(T)	Snorter Luster
1942	3	1	1	.700	121	20	2nd	Snorter Luster
1943	5	0	0	1.000	130	40	1st	Snorter Luster
1944	4	0	1	.900	152	40	1st	Snorter Luster
1945	4	1	0	.800	120	41	2nd	Snorter Luster
1946	4	1	0	.800	158	35	1st(T)	Jim Tatum
1947	4	0	1	.900	102	60	1st(T)	Bud Wilkinson

BIG SEVEN CONFERENCE

Year	W	L	T	Pct.	Pts.	Opp. Pts.	Rank	Coach
1948	5	0	0	1.000	217	34	1st	Bud Wilkinson
1949	5	0	0	1.000	196	40	1st	Bud Wilkinson
1950	6	0	0	1.000	228	80	1st	Bud Wilkinson
1951	6	0	0	1.000	217	61	1st	Bud Wilkinson
1952	5	0	1	.916	234	67	1st	Bud Wilkinson
1953	6	0	0	1.000	197	34	1st	Bud Wilkinson
1954	6	0	0	1.000	228	26	1st	Bud Wilkinson
1955	6	0	0	1.000	253	34	1st	Bud Wilkinson
1956	6	0	0	1.000	292	51	1st	Bud Wilkinson
1957	6	0	0	1.000	185	48	1st	Bud Wilkinson
1958	6	0	0	1.000	205	20	1st	Bud Wilkinson
1959	5	1	0	.833	164	55	1st	Bud Wilkinson

BIG EIGHT CONFERENCE

Year	W	L	T	Pct.	Pts.	Opp. Pts.	Rank	Coach
1960	2	4	1	.355	118	111	5th	Bud Wilkinson
1961	4	3	0	.571	95	86	4th	Bud Wilkinson
1962	7	0	0	1.000	247	19	1st	Bud Wilkinson
1963	6	1	0	.857	181	83	2nd	Bud Wilkinson
1964	5	1	1	.785	164	63	2nd	Gomer Jones
1965	3	4	0	.429	97	108	5th	Gomer Jones
1966	4	3	0	.571	157	75	5th	Jim Mackenzie
1967	7	0	0	1.000	201	59	1st	Chuck Fairbanks
1968	6	1	0	.857	247	112	1st(T)	Chuck Fairbanks
1969	4	3	0	.571	183	233	4th	Chuck Fairbanks
1970	5	2	0	.714	209	133	2nd(T)	Chuck Fairbanks
1971	6	1	0	.857	328	119	2nd	Chuck Fairbanks
1972	6	1	0	.857	109	68	1st	Chuck Fairbanks
1973	7	0	0	1.000	275	79	1st	Barry Switzer
Total	203	53	12	.779	6868	2444		
Grand Total	231	76	19	.792	7755	3273		

(1972 does not reflect three forfeits in Big Eight Conference play)

BIG EIGHT CONFERENCE RECORDS HELD BY OU
(According to conference yearbook)

TEAM RECORDS

Most yards rushing in one game—711 against Kansas State in 1971.

Most yards rushing in one season—5,196 in 1971.

Most points in one season—494 in 1971.

Most first downs in one game—36 against Kansas State in 1971.

Most first downs in one season—279 in 1972 in one game.

Most total offense (rushing and passing combined)—785 against Kansas State in 1971.

Most total offense in one season—6,232 in 1971.

Fewest rushing yards yielded in one season—638 in 1938.

Fewest pass completions yielded in one game—0 against Missouri in 1966 (shared with others).

Lowest pass completion percentage in one season—32.6 in 1937.

Most fumbles in one game—12 against Northwestern in 1959 (shared with others).

Most fumbles lost in one season—35 in 1948.

Most yards punts returned in one game—227 against Kansas State in 1948.

Most yards punts returned in one season—936 in 1948.

Fewest penalties in one game—0 against Nebraska in 1971 (shared with others).

Most penalties in one game—17 against Nebraska in 1949.

Most penalties in one season—82 in 1955.

Most yards penalized in one game—153 against Nebraska in 1949.

Most yards penalized in one season—862 in 1955.

Most consecutive victories—47 straight in 1953-1957.
Most consecutive conference victories—44 in 1952-1959.
Most consecutive conference games without defeat—74 in 1946-1959.
Most consecutive games scored—123 in 1946-1959.

INDIVIDUAL RECORDS

Most yards rushing in one season—1,665 by Greg Pruitt in 1971.
Most rushes in one game—55 by Steve Owens against Oklahoma State in 1969.
Most rushes in one season—358 by Steve Owens in 1969.
Most rushes in career—958 by Steve Owens in 1967-1969.
Best pass completion percentage in career—54.5 by Bob Warmack in 1966-1968.
Most consecutive pass completions in season—11 by Tommy McDonald in 1956.
Most consecutive pass completions in career—11 by Tommy McDonald in 1956.
Longest pass interception return—100 yards by Al Needs against Kansas State in 1945 (shared with others).
Most pass interceptions in one game—5 by Bill Pansze against Tulsa in 1931.
Most pass interceptions in career—17 by Darrell Royal in 1946-1949.
Most points in one game—30 by Steve Owens against Nebraska in 1968.
Most points in career—342 by Steve Owens in 1967-1969.
Most touchdowns in one season—23 by Steve Owens in 1969.
Most touchdowns in career—57 by Steve Owens in 1967-1969.
Most field goals in one game—4 by Mike Vachon against Texas in 1966 (Shared with others).

OU SCHOOL RECORDS

TEAM RECORDS

SCORING

One game—179 points against Kingfisher College in 1917.
One season—534 points in 1971.
Highest average per game—46.6 points in 1956.

MOST YARDS RUSHING AND PASSING

One game—785 against Kansas State in 1971 (711 rushing and 74 passing).
One season—6,232 in 1971 (5,196 rushing and 1,036 passing).

MOST YARDS RUSHING

One game—711 against Kansas State in 1971.
One season—average of 472.4 per game in 1971.

MOST YARDS PASSING

One game—289 against Colorado in 1962.
One season—average of 157.3 in 1968.

MOST FIRST DOWNS

One game—36 against Kansas State in 1971.
One season—average of 21.5 per game in 1971.

FEWEST POINTS BY OPPONENTS

One season (10 or more games)—29 in 1938.
Most shut outs in one season—8 in 1938.

CONSECUTIVE STREAKS

Most victories—47 straight in 1953-1957.
Most defeats—5 straight in 1961.
Most shut outs—5 straight in 1938.
Most games in which OU scored—123 straight in 1946-1957.
Most conference wins—44 straight in 1952-1959.
Most conference games without defeat—75 straight in 1946-1959.
Most victories at Norman—25 straight in 1947-1953.
Most victories away from Norman—23 in 1953-1956.

INDIVIDUAL RECORDS

MOST POINTS

One game—30 by Steve Owens against Nebraska in 1968.
One season—138 by Steve Owens in 1969.
Career—336 by Steve Owens in 1967-1969.

MOST TOUCHDOWNS

One game—5 by Steve Owens against Nebraska in 1968.
One season—23 by Steve Owens in 1969.

Career—56 by Steve Owens in 1967-1969.

MOST CONVERSIONS

One game—9 by Dave Wallace against Oklahoma A&M in 1946 and Bruce
Derr against Oklahoma State in 1970.
One season—53 by John Carroll in 1971.
Career—103 by Bruce Derr in 1968-1970.
Most consecutive—57 by Rick Fulcher in 1972-1973.

HIGHEST CONVERSION PERCENTAGE

One season—100.0 by George Jarman in 1961 (14 of 14).
Career—90.3 by Bruce Derr in 1968-1970 (103 of 114).

MOST FIELD GOALS

One game—4 by Mike Vachon against Texas in 1966.
One season—9 by Mike Vachon in 1966, John Carroll in 1971, and Rick
Fulcher in 1972.
Career—12 by Mike Vachon in 1966-1967.
Longest field goal—60 yards by Tony DiRienzo against Kansas in 1973.

MOST POINTS BY KICKING

One season—80 by John Carroll in 1971.
Career—132 by Rick Fulcher in 1972-1973.

TOTAL OFFENSE
(Rushing and Passing Combined)

One game—323 by Jack Mildren against Iowa State in 1971 (148 rushing
and 175 passing).
One season—2,818 by Jack Mildren in 1971 (1,140 rushing and 878
passing).
Career—4,818 by Jack Mildren in 1969-1971 (1,803 rushing and 3,015
passing).

MOST YARDS RUSHING

One game—294 by Greg Pruitt against Kansas State in 1971.
One season—1,665 by Greg Pruitt in 1971.
Career—3,867 by Steve Owens in 1967-1969.

BEST AVERAGE PER RUSH

One game—23.4 by Joe Golding against Kansas State in 1946 (164 yards in
7 carries).
One season—9.41 by Greg Pruitt in 1971 (1,665 yards in 178 carries).
Career—7.69 by Greg Pruitt in 1970-1972 (2,844 yards in 375 carries).

MOST RUSHES

One game—55 by Steve Owens against Oklahoma State in 1969.
One season—358 by Steve Owens in 1969.
Career—905 by Steve Owens in 1967-1969.
Longest rush—96 yards by Buck McPhail against Kansas State in 1951.

MOST PASS COMPLETIONS

One game—15 by Jack Mildren against Nebraska in 1969.
One season—106 by Bob Warmack in 1968.
Career—243 by Bob Warmack in 1966-1968.

MOST YARDS PASSING

One game—246 by Monte Deere against Colorado in 1962.
One season—1,548 by Bob Warmack in 1968.
Career—3,527 by Bob Warmack in 1966-1968.

MOST TOUCHDOWN PASSES THROWN

One game—4 by Claude Arnold against Kansas in 1950 and against
Oklahoma A&M in 1950 and by Eddie Crowder against Colorado in
1951.
One season—13 by Claude Arnold in 1950.
Career—25 by Jack Mildren in 1969-1971.

BEST COMPLETION PERCENTAGE

One game—100.0 by Jack Jacobs against Kansas in 1941 (9 of 9).
One season—63.1 by Hugh McCullough in 1938 (70 of 111).
Career—63.6 by Tommy McDonald in 1954-1956 (28 of 44).

MOST PASSING ATTEMPTS

One game—Record not available

One season—189 by Bob Warmack in 1968.
Career—443 by Bob Warmack in 1966-1968.

MOST PASS RECEPTIONS

One game—10 by Gordon Brown against Oklahoma State in 1965 and by
Eddie Hinton against Oklahoma State in 1968.
One season—60 by Eddie Hinton in 1968.
Career—114 by Eddie Hinton in 1966-1968.

MOST YARDS BY RECEPTION

One game—165 by Ben Hart against Florida State in 1964.
One season—967 by Eddie Hinton in 1968.
Career—1,735 by Eddie Hinton in 1966-1968.

MOST TOUCHDOWNS BY RECEPTIONS

One game—3 by Jack Lockett against Oklahoma A&M in 1950.
One season—6 by Eddie Hinton in 1968.
Career—11 by Eddie Hinton in 1966-1968.
Longest reception—95 yards by Ben Hart against Florida State in 1964
(Passed by Ron Fletcher).

MOST PASS INTERCEPTIONS

One game—5 by Dale Arbuckle against Southern Methodist in 1925 and by
Bill Pansze against Tulsa in 1931.
One season—7 by Huel Hamm in 1942, by Darrell Royal in 1947 and by
Steve Barrett in 1967.
Career—17 by Darrell Royal in 1946-1949.

MOST YARDS INTERCEPTIONS RETURNED

One season—177 yards by Joe Golding in 1946 (3 interceptions).
Career—232 by Ed Lisak in 1948-1950.
Longest pass interception return—100 yards by Al Needs against Kansas
State in 1945.

PUNTING AVERAGES

One game—50.6 yards per punt by Jack Jacobs against Missouri in 1941.
One season—47.8 by Jack Jacobs in 1940.

Career—Record not available.

Longest punt—91 yards by Wahoo McDaniel against Iowa State in 1958.

MOST YARDS RETURNED PUNTS

One game—Record not available.

One season—517 yards by Jack Mitchell in 1948.

Career—927 yards by Jack Mitchell in 1946-1948.

Longest punt return—95 yards by Darrell Royal against Kansas State in 1948.

Most touchdowns on punt returns in career—7 by Jack Mitchell in 1946-1948.

BEST AVERAGE ON KICKOFF RETURNS

One game—Record not available.

One season—43.8 yards by Orville Mathews in 1940.

Career—39.1 yards by Orville Mathews in 1939-1941 (274 yards on 7 returns).

Longest kickoff return—95 yards by George Thomas against Boston College in 1949.

OU CONFERENCE STATISTICS LEADERS

INDIVIDUAL LEADERS

TOTAL OFFENSE
Big Six

1937—Jack Baer 660 yards in 9 games.

1943—Derald Lebow 497 yards in 10 games.

1944—Derald Lebow 875 yards in 10 games.

1946—Joe Golding 923 yards in 10 games.

Big Seven

1952—Billy Vessels 1,281 yards in 10 games.

1953—Larry Grigg 819 yards in 10 games.

1955—Tommy McDonald 967 yards in 10 games.

1956—Tommy McDonald 1,036 yards in 10 games.

PASSING
Big Six

1937—Jack Baer 430 yards in 9 games.
1944—Derald Lebow 385 yards in 10 games.
1945—John West 229 yards in 10 games.

RECEIVING
Big Six

1939—Bill Jennings 21 catches for 244 yards.
1940—Bill Jennings 26 catches for 292 yards.
1941—Joe Golding 20 catches for 214 yards.

Big Eight

1968—Eddie Hinton 60 catches for 967 yards.

RUSHING
Big Six

1943—Bob Brumley 566 yards in 9 games.
1944—Derald Lebow 489 yards in 10 games.
1945—Jack Venable 316 yards in 10 games.
1946—Joe Golding 902 yards in 10 games.
1947—Jack Mitchell 537 yards in 10 games.

Big Seven

1948—George Thomas 835 yards in 10 games.
1949—George Thomas 859 yards in 10 games.
1951—Buck McPhail 865 yards in 10 games.
1952—Billy Vessels 1,072 yards in 10 games.
1953—Larry Grigg 792 yards in 10 games.
1955—Tommy McDonald 702 yards in 10 games.
1956—Tommy McDonald 853 yards in 10 games.

Big Eight

1967—Steve Owens 808 yards in 10 games.
1968—Steve Owens 1,536 yards in 10 games.
1969—Steve Owens 1,523 yards in 10 games.
1971—Greg Pruitt 1,665 yards in 10 games.

1973—Joe Washington 1,173 yards in 11 games.

SCORING
Big Six

1939—Beryl Clark 50 points.
1940—John Martin 60 points.
1943—Bob Brumley 79 points.
1944—Derald Lebow 66 points (shared with another).
1945—Jack Venable 48 points.
1946—Joe Golding 78 points.

Big Seven

1948—Jack Mitchell and George Thomas 60 points each.
1949—George Thomas 117 points.
1951—Buddy Leake 78 points (shared with another).
1952—Billy Vessels 108 points.
1953—Larry Grigg 87 points.
1954—Buddy Leake 79 points.
1955—Tommy McDonald 96 points.
1956—Clendon Thomas 108 points.

Big Eight

1967—Steve Owens 72 points.
1968—Steve Owens 126 points.
1969—Steve Owens 138 points.
1971—Jack Mildren 106 points.
1973—Steve Davis 108 points.

PUNTING
Big Six

1940—Jack Jacobs 47.8 average.
1941—Jack Jacobs 40.0 average.
1942—Huel Hamm 37.1 average.
1943—Derald Lebow 37.4 average.
1946—Darrell Royal 36.1 average.

Big Eight

1962—Joe Don Looney 43.4 average.

FIELD GOALS
(Statistics compiled since 1955)

1966—Mike Vachon 9.
1971—John Carroll 9.

INTERCEPTION RETURNS
(Statistics compiled since 1959)

1963—Larry Shields 6 for 66 yards.

SCORING BY KICKING
(Statistics compiled since 1958)

1959—Jim Davis 25 points.
1963—George Jarman 38 points.
1966—Mike Vachon 66 points.
1971—John Carroll 80 points.

PUNT RETURNS
(Statistics compiled since 1949)

1953—Merrill Green 45-yard average.
1954—Buddy Leake 13.5-yard average.
1955—Tommy McDonald 18.8-yard average.
1956—Tommy McDonald 11.5-yard average.
1957—Jakie Sandefer 14.6-yard average.
1959—Jackie Holt 10.3-yard average.
1962—Paul Lea 14.9-yard average.
1964—Larry Shields 16.3-yard average.

RECORDS BY OU OPPONENTS

MOST POINTS

Team in one game—59 by Kansas State in 1969.
Individual in one game—24 by Fred Biletnikoff of Florida State in 1964, by Bill Butler of Kansas State in 1971, and by Jeff Kinney of Nebraska in 1971.
Individual in career—42 by Jeff Kinney of Nebraska in 1969-1971.

MOST YARDS IN TOTAL OFFENSE

Team in one game—571 by Notre Dame in 1968.
Individual in one game—365 by Lynn Dickey of Kansas State in 1969
(minus 15 rushing and 380 passing).
Individual career—851 by Lynn Dickey of Kansas State in 1968-1970
(minus 93 rushing and 944 passing).

MOST YARDS RUSHING

Team in one game—370 by Colorado in 1968.
Individual in one game—220 by Alan Thompson of Wisconsin in 1969.
Individual in career—353 by Jack Crain of Texas in 1939-1941.

MOST YARDS PASSING

Team in one game—406 by Missouri in 1951.
Individual in one game—380 by Lynn Dickey of Kansas State in 1969.
Individual in career—944 by Lynn Dickey of Kansas State in 1968-1970.

MOST PASSES COMPLETED

One game—29 by Dennis Morrison of Kansas State in 1971.
Career—73 by Lynn Dickey of Kansas State in 1968-1970.

MOST PASS RECEPTIONS

One game—13 by Fred Beletnikoff of Florida State in 1964.
Career—21 by Hermann Eben of Oklahoma State in 1968-1970.

MOST YARDS ON PASS RECEPTIONS

One game—203 by Jim Doran of Iowa State in 1949.
Career—378 by Hermann Eben of Oklahoma State in 1968-1970.

MOST TOUCHDOWNS IN CAREER

Rushing—7 by Jeff Kinney of Nebraska in 1969-1971.

Passing—5 by Steve Tensi of Florida State in 1964 and by Lynn Dickey of Kansas State in 1969-1970.

MOST FIELD GOALS

One game—3 by Charles Durkee of Oklahoma State in 1964 and by Happy Feller of Texas in 1969.
Career—5 by Happy Feller of Texas in 1968-1970.

OU ALL-CONFERENCE SELECTIONS

MISSOURI VALLEY

1907—Back Owen Acton.
1920—End Howard Marsh, tackle Roy Smoot, guard Bill McKinley, back Harry Hill and back Sol Swatek.
1921—End Howard Marsh and back Harry Hill.
1922—End Howard Marsh.
1923—End King Price.
1924—Back Obie Bristow.
1926—End Roy LeCrone, center Pollack Wallace and back Frank Potts.
1927—End Roy LeCrone.

BIG SIX

1928—End Tom Churchill.
1929—End Tom Churchill and back Frank Crider.
1930—Guard Hilary Lee and back Buster Mills.
1931—Guard Charles Teel.
1932—Guard Ellis Bashara and back Bob Dunlap.
1933—Tackle Cassius Gentry, guard Ellis Bashara, guard James Stacy, and back Bob Dunlap.
1934—Tackle Dub Wheeler, tackle Cassius Gentry, guard James Stacy, and back Ben Poynor.
1935—Tackle Dub Wheeler, tackle Ralph Brown, back Nick Robertson, and back Bill Breeden.
1936—Tackle Ralph Brown and center Red Conkright.
1937—End Pete Smith, end Roland Young, center Mickey Parks, and back Jack Baer.
1938—End Roland Young, tackle Gilford Duggan, back Hugh McCullough, and back Earl Crowder.
1939—End Frank Ivy, tackle Gilford Duggan, tackle Justin Bowers, back Beryl Clark, and back Robert Seymour.

1940—End Bill Jennings, tackle Roger Eason, guard Harold Lahr, and back John Martin.

1941—Tackle Roger Eason and back Jack Jacobs.

1942—End W. G. Lamb, tackle Homer Simmons, guard Clare Morford, center Jack Marsee, back William Campbell, and back Huel Hamm.

1943—End W. G. Wooten, tackle Lee Kennon, guard Gale Fulghum, center Bob Mayfield, back Bob Brumley, and back Derald Lebow.

1944—End W. G. Wooten, tackle John Harley, center Bob Mayfield, and back Derald Lebow.

1945—End Omer Burgert, tackle Tommy Tallchief, guard Lester Jensen, back John West, and back Jack Venable.

1946—End Warren Geise, tackle Homer Paine, tackle Wade Walker, guard Buddy Burris, guard Plato Andros, center John Rapacz, and back Joe Golding.

1947—End Jim Tyree, tackle Wade Walker, guard Buddy Burris, center John Rapacz, and back Jack Mitchell.

BIG SEVEN

1948—End Jim Owens, tackle Wade Walker, guard Buddy Burris, guard Clair Mayes, and back Jack Mitchell.

1949—End Jim Owens, tackle Wade Walker, guard Stan West, back Darrell Royal, and back George Thomas.

1950—End Frankie Anderson, tackle Jim Weatherall, guard Norman McNabb, center Harry Moore, center Tom Catlin, back Claude Arnold, back Leon Heath, and back Billy Vessels.

1951—Tackle Art Janes, tackle Jim Weatherall, guard Roger Nelson, guard Bert Clark, guard Fred Smith, center Tom Catlin, back Eddie Crowder, back Larry Grigg, and back Buck McPhail.

1952—End Max Boydston, tackle Ed Rowland, tackle Jim Davis, guard J. D. Roberts, center Tom Catlin, back Eddie Crowder, back Billy Vessels, and back Buck McPhail.

1953—End Max Boydston, tackle Roger Nelson, guard J. D. Roberts, center Kurt Burris, back Gene Calame, and back Larry Grigg.

1954—End Max Boydston, end Carl Allison, guard Bo Bolinger, center Kurt Burris, back Buddy Leake, and back Gene Calame.

1955—Tackle Ed Gray, tackle Cal Woodward, guard Bo Bolinger, guard Cecil Morris, center Jerry Tubbs, back Jimmy Harris, back Bob Burris, and back Tommy McDonald.

1956—Tackle Ed Gray, tackle Tom Emerson, guard Bill Krisher, center Jerry Tubbs, back Tommy McDonald, and back Clendon Thomas.

1957—End Don Stiller, end Ross Coyle, guard Bill Krisher, center Bob Harrison, and back Clendon Thomas.

1958—End Ross Coyle, tackle Steve Jennings, tackle Gilmer Lewis, guard Dick Corbitt, center Bob Harrison, and back Prentice Gautt.

1959—Tackle Jerry Thompson, back Bobby Boyd, and back Prentice Gautt.

1960—Tackle Billy White.

1961—Tackle Billy White.

1962—Tackle Dennis Ward, guard Leon Cross, center Wayne Lee, back Jim Grisham, and back Joe Don Looney.

1963—End John Flynn, tackle Ralph Neely, guard Newt Burton, and back Jim Grisham.

1964—Offense: tackle Ralph Neely, guard Newt Burton, and back Jim Grisham. Defense: linebacker Carl McAdams.

1965—Defense: linebacker Carl McAdams.

1966—Offense: end Ben Hart and tackle Ed Hall. Defense: linebacker Eugene Ross.

1967—Offense: tackle Bob Kalsu, halfback Steve Owens, and halfback Bob Warmack. Defense: end John Kollar and tackle Granville Liggins.

1968—Offense: end Steve Zabel, guard Ken Mendenhall, back Eddie Hinton, and back Steve Owens. Defense: back Steve Barrett.

1969—Offense: end Steve Zabel, guard Bill Elfstrom, guard Ken Mendenhall, and back Steve Owens.

1970—Offense: back Joe Wylie. Defense: linebacker Steve Aycock, and back Monty Johnson.

1971—Offense: end Albert Chandler, guard Ken Jones, center Tom Brahaney, back Jack Mildren, and back Greg Pruitt. Defense: end Raymond Hamilton, tackle Derland Moore, linebacker Steve Aycock, and back John Shelley.

1972—Offense: tackle Dean Unruh, guard Ken Jones, center Tom Brahaney, back Greg Pruitt, and back Leon Crosswhite. Defense: tackle Derland Moore, tackle Lucious Selmon, tackle Raymond Hamilton, and linebacker Rod Shoate.

1973—Offense: tackle Eddie Foster, guard John Roush, and back Joe Washington. Defense: end Gary Baccus, guard Lucious Selmon, linebacker Rod Shoate, and back Randy Hughes.

OU INDIVIDUAL BESTS

MOST POINTS IN CAREER

	Tds.	PAT.	Pts.
Steve Owens, '67-'69	56	0-0	336
Buddy Leake, '51-'54	28	74-84	241
Greg Pruitt, '70-'72	38	2	232
Clendon Thomas, '55-'57	36	0-0	216
George Thomas, '46-'49	35	4-6	214
Billy Vessels, '50-'52	35	0-0	210
Tom McDonald, '54-'56	35	0-0	210
Jack Mildren, '69-'71	29	4	182
Jack Mitchell, '46-'48	24	0-0	144

MOST POINTS IN SEASON

	Tds.	PAT.	Pts.
Steve Owens, '69	23	0-0	138
Steve Owens, '68	21	0-0	126
George Thomas, '49	19	3-5	117
Billy Vessels, '52	18	0-0	108
Clendon Thomas, '56	18	0-0	108
Steve Davis, '73	18	0-0	108
Jack Mildren, '71	17	2	106
Greg Pruitt, '71	17	0-0	102
Tommy McDonald, '56	17	0-0	102
Tommy McDonald, '55	16	0-0	96
Billy Vessels, '50	15	0-0	90

MOST YARDS TOTAL OFFENSE IN CAREER

	Rushing	Passsing	Total
Jack Mildren, '69-'71	1,803	3,015	4,818
Bob Warmack, '66-'68	810	3,527	4,337
Steve Owens, '67-'69	3,867	58	3,925
Greg Pruitt, '70-'72	2,844	0	2,844
Billy Vessels, '50-'52	2,085	249	2,334
Jim Grisham, '62-'64	2,297	0	2,297
Tommy McDonald, '54-'56	1,683	571	2,254
Clendon Thomas, '55-'57	2,120	115	2,235
George Thomas, '46-'49	2,106	0	2,106
Buck McPhail, '50-'52	1,985	0	1,985

<h1 style="text-align:center">MOST YARDS TOTAL OFFENSE IN SEASON</h1>

	Yds. Rush	Yds. Pass	Total Yds.	TDs. RFor*
Jack Mildren, 1971	1140	878	2018	27
Steve Davis, 1973	887	934	1821	27
Bob Warmack, 1968	266	1548	1814	15
Greg Pruitt, 1971	1665	0	1665	17
Jack Mildren, 1969	345	1319	1664	15
Steve Owens, 1968	1536	33	1569	23
Steve Owens, 1969	1523	25	1548	23
Claude Arnold, 1950	291	1048	1339	17
Dave Robertson, 1972	278	1054	1332	15
Billy Vessels, 1952	1072	209	1281	19
Joe Washington, 1973	1173	40	1213	10
Jack Mildren, 1970	318	818	1136	12
Tommy McDonald, 1956	853	183	1036	16
Hugh McCullough, 1938	383	637	1020	9
Buck McPhail, 1952	1018	0	1018	8
Waymon Clark, 1973	1014	0	1014	6
Joe Wylie, 1970	984	10	994	14
Monte Deere, 1962	157	789	946	12
Eddie Crowder, 1952	226	704	930	8
Jack Jacobs, 1940	361	567	928	10

*Touchdowns responsible for rushing, throwing, and receiving.

<h1 style="text-align:center">MOST YARDS RUSHING IN CAREER</h1>

3,867 Steve Owens, 1967-69 (3 yrs.)
2,844 Gregg Pruitt, 1970-72 (3 yrs.)
2,297 Jim Grisham, 1962-64 (3 yrs.)
2,120 Clendon Thomas, 1955-57 (3 yrs.)
2,106 George Thomas, 1946-49 (4 yrs.)
2,085 Billy Vessels, 1950-52 (24 games)
1,985 Buck McPhail, 1950-52 (3 yrs.)
1,848 Leon Crosswhite, 1970-72 (3 yrs.)
1,803 Jack Mildren, 1969-71 (3 yrs.)
1,803 Joe Washington, 1972-73 (2 yrs.)
1,683 Tom McDonald, 1954-56 (3 yrs.)
1,669 Leon Heath, 1948-50 (3 yrs.)

275

MOST YARDS RUSHING IN SEASON

1,665	Greg Pruitt, 1971
1,536	Steve Owens, 1968
1,523	Steve Owens, 1969
1,173	Joe Washington, 1973
1,140	Jack Mildren, 1971
1,072	Billy Vessels, 1952
1,018	Buck McPhail, 1952
1,014	Waymon Clark, 1973
984	Joe Wylie, 1970
938	Greg Pruitt, 1972
902	Joe Golding, 1946
887	Steve Davis, 1973
861	Jim Grisham, 1963
859	George Thomas, 1949
853	Tommy McDonald, 1956
852	Joe Don Looney, 1962

MOST YARDS PASSING IN CAREER

	Att.	Comp.	Intc.	Yds.	Tds.	Pct.
Bob Warmack, 1966-68	443	243	16	3527	22	52.5
Jack Mildren, 1969-71	346	164	25	2984	25	47.4
Claude Arnold, 1948-50	155	81	6	1572	18	52.2
Jack Jacobs, 1938-41	211	106	21	1379	9	50.2
Dave Robertson, 1970-72	126	64	7	1231	10	50.8
Eddie Crowder, 1950-52	110	61	4	1189	11	55.4
Darrell Royal, 1946-49	163	73	16	1086	16	44.7
Steve Davis, 1973	91	38	6	934	9	41.8
Buddy Leake, 1951-54	80	35	11	841	8	43.7
Monte Deere, 1960-62	74	41	1	825	9	55.3
Jimmy Harris, 1954-56	75	36	4	711	10	48.0
Bobby Boyd, 1957-59	110	47	9	653	6	42.7

MOST YARDS PASSING IN SEASON

	Att.	Comp.	Intc.	Yds.	Tds.	Pct.
Bob Warmack, 1968	189	106	6	1548	10	56.3
Jack Mildren, 1969	172	79	12	1319	8	45.9
Bob Warmack, 1967	151	80	6	1136	6	53.0

Dave Robertson, 1973	110	56	4	1054	9	50.9
Claude Arnold, 1950	114	57	1	1048	13	50.0
Steve Davis, 1973	91	38	6	934	9	41.8
Jack Mildren, 1971	64	31	2	878	10	48.4
Bob Warmack, 1966	103	57	4	843	4	55.3
Jack Mildren, 1970	110	54	11	818	7	49.1
Monte Deere, 1962	65	38	0	789	9	58.4
Eddie Crowder, 1952	52	30	3	704	6	57.6
Jack Jacobs, 1941	82	46	6	647	4	56.0
Hugh McCullough, 1938	109	69	6	637	3	63.3
Darrell Royal, 1949	63	34	1	509	4	53.9

MOST PASS RECEPTIONS IN CAREER

	Rec.	Yds.	Tds.
Eddie Hinton, 1966-68	114	1735	11
Bill Jennings, 1938-40	70	735	6
Steve Zabel, 1967-69	63	773	8
Ben Hart, 1964-66	53	915	6
Gordon Brown, 1963-65	43	573	2
*Jimmy Owens, 1946-49	37	487	4
Tinker Owens, 1972-73	35	770	4
Joe Killingsworth, 1967-69	34	624	5
John Reddell, 1950-52	31	765	8
Al Chandler, 1970-72	31	696	8
Greg Pruitt, 1970-72	30	450	3
Jon Harrison, 1970-71	28	766	6
Max Boydston, 1952-54	28	698	6

*Played four years

MOST PASS RECEPTIONS IN SEASON

	Rec.	Yds.	Tds.
Eddie Hinton, 1968	60	967	6
Gordon Brown, 1965	35	413	1
Ben Hart, 1966	33	565	2
Bill Jennings, 1940	26	292	1
Steve Zabel, 1967	22	333	3
Greg Pruitt, 1970	19	240	2
Lance Rentzel, 1964	18	268	2

Joe Killingsworth, 1967	18	250	1
Tinker Owens, 1973	18	472	3
John Carroll, 1972	17	343	3
Tinker Owens, 1972	17	298	1
Jon Harrison, 1971	17	494	4
Roy Bell, 1969	15	215	1
Jim Owens, 1949	15	207	1
Al Chandler, 1972	14	301	3
John Reddell, 1951	13	363	3
Max Boydston, 1952	13	334	4

BEST PUNTING AVERAGE IN CAREER

	Att.	Avg.
Jack Jacobs, 1939-41	110	42.3
Darrell Royal, 1946-49	149	38.1

BEST PUNTING AVERAGE IN SEASON

	Att.	Avg.
Jack Jacobs, 1940	30	47.84
Joe Don Looney, 1962	34	43.4
Tom Stidham, 1966	48	42.3
Dick Heatly, 1949	41	40.79
Joe Wylie, 1971	12	40.67
Darrell Royal, 1949	18	40.67
Lance Rentzel, 1964	34	40.5
Max Boydston, 1954	14	40.2

EXTRA POINT LEADERS IN SEASON
(Minimum of 14 Attempts)

		Made	Pct.
1961	George Jarman	14 of 14	100.0
1952	Buddy Leake	32 of 33	97.0
1959	Jim Davis	19 of 20	95.0
1972	Rick Fulcher	38 of 40	95.0
1970	Bruce Derr	34 of 36	94.4

1953	Buddy Leake	17 of 18	94.4
1969	Bruce Derr	33 of 35	94.3
1940	Jack Haberlein	13 of 14	92.8
1973	Rick Fulcher	49 of 53	92.5
1964	Butch Metcalf	22 of 24	91.6
1963	George Jarman	29 of 32	90.6
1971	John Carroll	53 of 62	85.5
1966	Mike Vachon	17 of 20	85.0
1952	Buck McPhail	21 of 25	84.0

MOST PASS INTERCEPTIONS IN CAREER

Darrell Royal, 1946-49 (4 yrs.)	17
Darrell Royal, 1946-49 (3 yrs.)	15
Ed Lisak, 1948-50	13
Larry Shields, 1963-64	10
Tommy McDonald, 1954-56	9
Steve Barrett, 1966-67	9
Randy Hughes, 1972-73	9
Bill Jennings, 1938-40	8
Huel Hamm, 1940-42	8
Jack Ging, 1951-53	8

MOST PASS INTERCEPTIONS IN SEASON

	No.	Yds.
Huel Hamm, 1942	7	68
Darrell Royal, 1947	7	38
Steve Barrett, 1967	7	32
Otis Rogers, 1938	6	47
Ed Lisak, 1948	6	63
Jack Jacobs, 1941	6	77
Tommy McDonald, 1956	6	136
Larry Shields, 1963	6	66

LONGEST RUSHING GAINS

Yds.
96   Buck McPhail, K-State, 1951.
91   Jimmy Harris, Kansas 1954.

90   George Thomas, Okla. A&M 1949.
86   Leon Heath, LSU 1950.
85   George Thomas and Ed Kreick, Iowa State 1947.
84   Joe Don Looney, Colo. 1962.
82   George Thomas, Santa Clara 1948.
82   Mike McClellan, K-State 1961.
78   Jack Mildren, Pittsburgh 1969.

LONGEST PASSING GAINS

95   Ben Hart from Ronnie Fletcher, Florida State 1965.
90   Lance Rentzel from John Hammond, Maryland 1964.
87   Max Boydston from Buddy Leake, California 1954.
86   Wahoo McDaniel from Bobby Boyd, West Virginia 1958.
83   Virgil Boll from Monte Deere, Colorado 1962.
80   Larry Grigg from Buddy Leake, Pittsburgh 1953.
79   Ross Coyle from Brewster Hobby, Syracuse 1959.
77   Joe Killingsworth from Jack Mildren, Kansas State 1969.
75   Steve Zabel from Bob Warmack, Iowa State 1967.
75   Willie Franklin from Jack Mildren, Iowa State 1970.

LONGEST INTERCEPTION RETURNS

Yds.
100 Al Needs, K-State 1945.
95   Joe Golding, Texas 1946.
95   Randy Hughes, Colorado 1973.
94   Eddie Johnson, Oklahoma A&M 1923.
94   David Baker, Duke 1958.
90   Obie Bristow, K-State 1923.
82   Johnny West, K-State 1944.
82   Carl Dodds, Maryland 1956.
78   Jerry Tubbs, I—State 1956.

LONGEST PUNT RETURNS

Yds.
96   Darrell Royal, K-State 1948.
93   Eddie Hinton, Colorado 1966.
91   Tommy McDonald, I-State 1955.

83   Buddy Jones, Iowa State 1949.
81   Jakie Sandefer, I-State 1957.
80   Merrill Green, Texas 1953.
80   Joe Washington, Missouri 1973.
77   Orville Mathews, Temple 1940.
77   Bill Pansze, Rice 1931
77   Bill Pansze, I-State 1931.

OU Football Lettermen (1895-1973)

1895
Edwin Barrow, Fred Bean, Jim Brown, Jasper Clapham, Bert Dunn, John P. Evans, John A. Harts, Bert Long, Newt Medlock, Joe Merkle, Fred Perry, Bernard Reuter, R. L. Risinger, Will Short, Horace Summers.

1896
Alfred Att, Edwin Barrow, Homer Burson, Harry Ford, Hugh Haycraft, Gordon Hopping, Ray Hume, Ross Hume, Paul Mackay, John Prickett, Elmo Richey, C. C. Roberts, Harvey Short, Frank Taylor.

1897
Edwin Barrow, Jasper Clapham, Harry Ford, Hugh Haycraft, John Hefley, Clifton Howell, Bill McCutcheon, Paul Mackay, Fred Merkle, Joe Merkle, C. C. Roberts, Harvey Short, Ray Smith.

1898
Edwin Barrow, Jasper Clapham, Harry Ford, Jess Gambill, John Hefley, Bill McCutcheon, Joseph Henry McGraw, Fred Merkle, Joe Merkle, John Ray, C. C. Roberts, Dan Short, Harvey Short, Tom Tribbey.

1899
Clyde Bogle, Jasper Clapham, Milton Jay Ferguson, John Hefley, Delbert Jenkins, Oscar Johnston, Fred Merkle, Joe Merkle, Willard Pool, C. C. Roberts, Fred Roberts, Dan Short, Harvey Short, Ray Smith, Tom Tribbey, Robert Wingate.

1900

Lee Arnold, Clyde Bogle, Wyatt Burch, Jasper Clapham, Alex Clement, Ray Crowe, John Hefley, Delbert Jenkins, Oscar Johnston, John McCartney, Frank McCoy, C. C. Roberts, Dan Short, Harvey Short, Tom Tribbey.

1901

Lee Arnold, Roscoe Aston, Clyde Bogle, John Boory, Wyatt Burch, Alex Clement, Ray Crowe, Fred Green, John Hefley, Oscar Johnston, Frank McCoy, Fred Roberts, Dan Short, Tom Tribbey.

1902

Clyde Bogle, Ed Burch, Wyatt Burch, Alex Clement, George Duncan, Fred Green, Delbert Jenkins, Frank McCoy, Byrom McCreary, Thomas Becker Matthews, Jim Monnett, Chester Reeds, Clarence Reeds, Dan Short, Tom Tribbey, Walter Wright.

1903

Lee Arnold, Hugh Bodine, Clyde Bogle, Otto Brown, Hugh A. Carroll, W. M. Clark, Alex Clement, Harry Hughes, Byrom McCreary, Thomas Becker Matthews, Jim Monnett, C. G. Nesbitt, Chester Reeds, Bob Severin, Dan Short, Wade Terrill, Tom Tribbey, Walter Wright.

1904

Hugh Bodine, Clarence Cook, Edward Cook, William Cross, Harry Hughes, Frank Long, Byrom McCreary, Thomas Becker Matthews, Carl Milam, Jim Monnett, Claud Pickard, Chester Reeds, Clarence Reeds, Hugh Roberts, Bob Severin, Roy Waggoner.

1905

Owen Acton, William Cross, Harry Hughes, Frank Long, Byrom McCreary, Thomas Becker Matthews, Jim Monnett, Claud Pickard, Chester Reeds, Leonard Runbeck, Bob Severin, George Trousdale, Key Wolf.

1906

Owen Acton, Wyatt Burch, William Cross, Willard Douglas,

Harry Hughes, Oliver Irwin, Frank Long, Jim Monnett, Harry
Price, Bob Severin, Cleveland Thompson, George Trousdale,
Roy Waggoner, Vernon Walling, Key Wolf.

1907

Owen Acton, Fred Allen, Charles Armstrong, Howard Browne,
Ralph Campbell, William Cross, Willard Douglas, Clyde Lisman,
Frank Long, Harry Price, Earle Radcliffe, J. W. Rogers, Vernon
Walling, Charles Wantland, Key Wolf.

1908

Charles Armstrong, Ralph Campbell, Roy Campbell, Fred
Capshaw, Willard Douglas, Porter English, Dave Fox, Frank
Long, James Nairn, Claud Pickard, Earle Radcliffe, Hugh
Roberts, Cleveland Thompson, Vernon Walling, Charles Want-
land, Key Wolf.

1909

Charles Armstrong, James M. Buchanan, Fred Capshaw, Glenn
Clark, Willard Douglas, Porter English, Roy Morter, James
Nairn, Artie Reeds, Grady Ross, P. Z. Swartz, Cleveland
Thompson, Otto Wilhite, Key Wolf, Robert Wood, Mort Woods.

1910

Hubert Ambrister, Roger Berry, Sam Burton, Howard Browne,
Fred Capshaw, Glenn Clark, Earl Coots, John Harley, Weaver
Holland, Sabert Hott, Clarence McReynolds, Roy Morter, James
Nairn, Harry Price, Earle Radcliffe, Claude Reeds, James
Rogers, Cleveland Thompson, Robert Wood, Mort Woods.

1911

Hubert Ambrister, Roger Berry, Fred Capshaw, Glenn Clark,
Raymond Courtright, Sabert Hott, Robert Martin, Ed Mea-
cham, William Moss, James Nairn, Claude Reeds, Charles
Rogers, Roy Spears, Henry Weedn.

1912

Hubert Ambrister, Manley Bailey, Roger Berry, Sam Burton,
Elmer Capshaw, Glenn Clark, William Clark, Raymond Courtright, Dortis Holland, Sabert Hott, Tom Lowry, Ed Meacham,

Charles Orr, Claude Reeds, Charles Rogers, Roy Spears, Floyd Tribbey, Henry Weedn.

1913

Hubert Ambrister, Curry Bell, Elmer Capshaw, William Clark, Raymond Courtright, Forest Park (Spot) Geyer, Oliver Hott, Sabert Hott, Willis Hott, Neil Johnson, Tom Lowry, Ed Meacham, Claude Reeds, Charles Rogers, Roy Spears.

1914

George Anderson, Curry Bell, John Bell, Elmer Capshaw, William Clark, Harve Collins, Jess Fields, Malcolm Gentry, Forest Park (Spot) Geyer, Oliver Hott, Willis Hott, Montford Johnson, Neil Johnson, Thomas McCasland, Homer Montgomery.

1915

George Anderson, Curry Bell, Elmer Capshaw, Jess Fields, Rayburn Foster, Forest Park (Spot) Geyer, Oliver Hott, Willis Hott, Montford Johnson, Prentiss Lively, Frank McCain, Howard McCasland, Clifford Meyer, Homer Montgomery, Leon (Red) Phillips, Charles Swatek.

1916

Frank Balcer, Otto Brewer, Albert Briscoe, W. E. Durant, Jess Fields, Floyd Gammill, Thomas Graham, Bennett Griffin, Roy Hancock, Oliver Hott, Willis Hott, Graham Johnson, Montford Johnson, Ross Johnson, Forest Kramer, Frank McCain, Hugh McDermott, George McFerron, Claude McGlothlin, Sam Montgomery, James Tolbert, Claude Tyler, Rudolph Von Tungeln, J. Barney Whisenant, Everett Wilmoth.

1917

Wallace Abbott, Earl Bechtold, Joe Brown, Dorsey Boyle, Arlo (Skivey) Davis, Erl Deacon, A. J. Douglass, W. E. Durant, Thomas Graham, Graham Johnson, Ross Johnson, Earl Light, Dewey (Snorter) Luster, Hugh McDermott, Claude McGlothlin, Clinton Shaw, James Tolbert, Everett Wilmoth.

1918

Page Belcher, Robert M. Bass, Erl Deacon, A. J. Douglass,

Herschel Graham, Dow Hamm, Russell Hardy, Lawrence (Jap) Haskell, Harry Hill, Paul Johnston, Adair Lawrence, Dewey (Snorter) Luster, Howard Marsh, Fred Martin, Roy Smoot, Roy Swatek, Myron Tyler, Phil White.

1919

Earl Bechtold, Dorsey Boyle, Arlo (Skivey) Davis, Erl Deacon, Dow Hamm, Russell Hardy, Harry Hill, Paul Johnston, Ross Johnston, Dewey (Snorter) Luster, Hugh McDermott, William McKinley, Howard Marsh, Roy Smoot, Roy Swatek, Claude Tyler, Myron Tyler, Phil White.

1920

Ronald Cullen, Arlo (Skivey) Davis, Erl Deacon, Van Edmondson, Dow Hamm, Lawrence (Jap) Haskell, Harry Hill, Paul Johnston, Dewey (Snorter) Luster, William McKinley, Howard Marsh, Clarence Morrison, Frank Ogilvie, Dwight Ross, Roy Smoot, Roy Swatek, Myron Tyler, Phil White.

1921

Warren Bailey, Clifford Bowles, Ronald Cullen, Van Edmondson, Dow Hamm, Lawrence (Jap) Haskell, Earl Hendricks, Harry Hill, Alvin Jackson, Harold James, Edward Johnson, William McKinley, Howard Marsh, Clarence Morrison, William Stahl, Roy Swatek, James Thompson, Myron Tyler.

1922

Lloyd Boatright, Clifford Bowles, Gordon Bristow, Ronald Cullen, Van Edmondson, Herschel Graham, Bernard Hammert, Glenn Hartford, Alvin Jackson, Edward Johnson, John R. Lee, Alfred McFadden, Howard Marsh, Don Mathes, Clarence Morrison, James Penick, Charles Pokorny, Herbert Schafer, Clinton Steinberger, Charles Strouvelle, Orville Vogle, Lazelle White.

1923

Dale Arbuckle, Clifford Bowles, Gordon Bristow, Edwin Brockman, Lloyd Fleming, Roy Guffey, Bernard Hammert, Glenn Hartford, Earl Hendricks, Edward Johnson, Roy Lamb, Alfred McFadden, James Penick, King Price, Elmer Slough, Clinton Steinberger, Lazelle White, John Wilcox.

1924

Gordon Bristow, Edwin Brockman, Lawrence Frary, William Haller, Earl Hendricks, Roy Lamb, Charles Mathias, James Penick, King Price, Elmer Slough, P. A. Wallace, Lazelle White, William Wolfe, Loyal Woodall.

1925

Dale Arbuckle, Edwin Brockman, Mart Brown, Roy Guffey, Houston Hill, Roy Lamb, Ray LeCrone, Roy LeCrone, Howard Martin, Hal Muldrow, Granville Norris, Frank Potts, Elmer Slough, Hall Snodgrass, Bob Sumter, P. A. Wallace, William Wolfe.

1926

Dale Arbuckle, Mart Brown, Bob Cooke, William Haller, Bill Hamilton, Bus Haskins, Sumter Kidd, Ray LeCrone, Roy LeCrone, Doc Martin, Prentiss Mooney, Hal Muldrow, Granville Norris, Frank Potts, Bob Sumter, Ben Tayler, P. A. Wallace, Paul Ward.

1927

Harry Berry, Mart Brown, Jack Carmen, Tom Churchill, Sam . Clammer, Frank Crider, Bruce Drake, Bill Hamilton, Bus Haskins, Sumter Kidd, Ray LeCrone, Roy LeCrone, Howard Marsh, Al Mayhew, Prentice Mooney, Hal Muldrow, Granville Norris, T. Ray Phillips, Glaucus Short, Paul Ward.

1928

Curtis Berry, Harry Berry, Tom Churchill, Frank Crider, Bruce Drake, Bob Fields, Earl Flint, Cash Gentry, Bus Haskins, Abe Kitchell, John Lee, Dick Marsh, Al Mayhew, Colonel Mills, Alvin Muldrow, Ellis Orr, Martin Phillips, Clifton Shearer, Iron Singletary, Fenton Taylor, Paul Ward.

1929

Curtis Berry, Tom Churchill, Frank Crider, Bruce Drake, Darrell Ewing, Bob Fields, Earl Flint, Weldon Gentry, Clyde Kirk, Hiliary Lee, John Lee, Victor Marsh, Al Mayhew, Colonel Mills, Roy Nelson, Ellis Orr, Francis Roberts, Raymond Stanley,

<h2 style="text-align:center">1930</h2>

Curtis Berry, Orin Borah, C. C. Buston, Fred Cherry, Darrell Ewing, Bob Fields, Clyde Kirk, Frank Lee, Hiliary Lee, Hardy Lewis, Ernest Massad, Colonel Mills, Harold Roberts, Richard Simms, Ernest Snell, Charles Stogner, Raymond Stanley, Charles Teel, Ab Walker, Guy Warren, Charles Wilson, Paul Young.

<h2 style="text-align:center">1931</h2>

Ellis Bashara, Orin Borah, Evans Chambers, Fred Cherry, Orville Corey, Edsel Curnutt, Robert Dunlap, Marvin Ellstrom, Gordon Graalman, Tom Grimmett, Henry Haag, Grady Jackson, Hardy Lewis, Ernest Massad, Vincent Maloney, William Pansze, Richard Simms, Ernest Snell, Charles Stogner, Joe Swofford, Charles Teel, Ab Walker, Guy Warren, Smith Watkins, Charles Wilson, Claude Whittington, Paul Young.

<h2 style="text-align:center">1932</h2>

Ellis Bashara, Orin Borah, Evans Chambers, Fred Cherry, Edsel Curnutt, Orville Corey, Robert Dunlap, Harold Fleetwood, Henry Haag, Arthur Pansze, William Pansze, T. Ray Phillips, Richard Simms, James Stacey, Dewey Tennyson, Ab Walker, Smith Watkins, Claude Whittington, Paul Young.

<h2 style="text-align:center">1933</h2>

Ellis Bashara, Wesley Beck, Casey Cason, Clay Childs, Jeff Coker, Orville Corey, Robert Dunlap, Harold Fleetwood, Marion Foreman, Raleigh Francis, Karey Fuqua, Cash Gentry, John Harris, Kenneth Little, Beede Long, Morris McDannald, Mutt Miller, John Miskovsky, Arthur Pansze, William Pansze, George Parrish, Ben Poyner, Melbourne Robertson, LeRoy Robison, James Stacey, J. W. Wheeler, Claude Whittington.

<h2 style="text-align:center">1934</h2>

Connie Ahrens, Ralph Brown, Jeff Coker, William Conkright, R. A. Cox, Harry Ellis, Ferd Ellsworth, Raleigh Francis, Karey Fuqua, Cash Gentry, Jack Harris, Elmo Hewes, Cal Hubbard, Kenneth Little, Beede Long, Morris McDannald, Mutt Miller, John Miskovsky, Vivian Nemecek, Pat Page, Arthur Pansze, Mickey Parks, George Parrish, Ben Poyner, Melbourne Robertson, LeRoy Robison, James Stacey, Delmar Steinbock, Dewey Tennyson, J. W. Wheeler.

1935

Connie Ahrens, Fred Ball, Jack Baer, Bill Breeden, Ralph Brown, William Conkright, Albert Corrotto, Dean Cutchall, Harry Ellis, Ferd Ellsworth, Raleigh Francis, Karey Fuqua, Jack Harris, Elmo Hewes, Woodrow Huddleston, Kenneth Little, Morris McDannald, John Miskovsky, Vivian Nemecek, Wesley Peck, Ben Poyner, Melbourne Robertson, Pete Smith, Delmar Steinbock, Dewey Tennyson, Jiggs Walker, J. W. Wheeler.

1936

Connie Ahrens, Fred Ball, Jack Baer, Bill Breeden, Ralph Brown, Clay Casey, William Conkright, Albert Corrotto, Gene Corrotto, Earl Crowder, Ferd Ellsworth, George Grace, Elmo Hewes, Woodrow Huddleston, Norval Locke, Webber Merrill, Otis Rogers, Tom Short, Pete Smith, Jim Thomas, Jiggs Walker, Walter Young.

1937

Fred Ball, Jack Baer, Jerry Bolton, Raphael Boudreau, Alton Coppage, Albert Corrotto, Gene Corrotto, Earl Crowder, Gilford Duggan, George Grace, Woodrow Huddleston, Frank (Pop) Ivy, Howard McCarty, Hugh McCullough, J. R. Manley, Webber Merrill, Mickey Parks, Otis Rogers, Bob Seymour, John Shirk, Tom Short, Pete Smith, Ralph Stevenson, Howard Teeter, Jim Thomas, Jiggs Walker, George Wilhelm, Roland Young.

1938

Jerry Bolton, Raphael Boudreau, Justin Bowers, Beryl Clark, Alton Coppage, Gene Corrotto, Earl Crowder, Gilford Duggan, Harold Edgeman, Dick Favor, Louis Hotchkiss, Frank (Pop) Ivy, Bill Jennings, Gus Kitchens, Harold Lahar, Bill LaRue, Norval Locke, Howard McCarty, Hugh McCullough, J. R. Manley, Johnny Martin, Wright Phebus, Otis Rogers, Bob Seymour, John Shirk, Cliff Speegle, Ed Spottswood, Ralph Stevenson, Jim Thomas, Bob West, George Wilhelm, Novel Wood, Roland Young.

1939

Jerry Bolton, Justin Bowers, Beryl Clark, Alton Coppage, Gilford Duggan, Roger Eason, Dick Favor, L. G. Friedrichs, Ralph Harris, Frank (Pop) Ivy, Bill Jennings, Jack Jacobs, Olin Keith, Gus Kitchens, Harold Lahar, Norval Locke, J. R. Manley, Jack Marsee, Johnny Martin, Orville Mathews, Ray Mullen, J. S. Munsey, Byron Potter, Bob Seymour, Louis Sharpe, John Shirk, Lyle Smith, Cliff Speegle, Ralph Stevenson, Marvin Whited, George Wilhelm, Novel Wood, Paul Woodson.

1940

Joe Allton, Boyd Bibb, Laddie Birge, Bill Campbell, Roger Eason, Jack Haberlein, Huel Hamm, Bill Jennings, Jack Jacobs, Olin Keith, Harold Lahar, W. G. Lamb, Johnny Martin, Orville Mathews, Bill Mattox, Tom Rousey, Mitch Shadid, Louis Sharpe, Homer Simmons, Lyle Smith, Cliff Speegle, Jack Steele, Howard Teeter, Marvin Whited, Novel Wood, Paul Woodson.

1941

Joe Allton, Plato Andros, Bill Bentley, George Boudreau, Carl Brewington, Bill Campbell, Pete Cawthon Jr., Lee Cowling, Eddy Davis, Roger Eason, Max Fischer, John Funk, George Gibbons, Joe Golding, Jack Haberlein, Huel Hamm, Ralph Harris, Jack Jacobs, W. G. Lamb, Don McDonald, Jack Marsee, Orville Mathews, Bill Mattox, Clare Morford, Bill Morris, J. S. Munsey, Clovis Pierce, Mitch Shadid, Pat Shanks, Louis Sharpe, Homer Simmons, Lyle Smith, Jack Steele, Sammy Stephens, Howard Teeter, Jim Tyree, Chad Valance, Marvin Whited, Thurston Wright.

1942

Boone Baker, Bill Campbell, Pete Cawthon Jr., Eddy Davis, Albert Downs, Don Fauble, George Gibbons, Buddie Goodall, Myrle Greathouse, Stanley Green, Huel Hamm, W. G. Lamb, Chris Lambert, Don McDonald, Jack Marsee, Bill Mattox, Clare Morford, Bill Morris, LeRoy Neher, Mitch Shadid, Pat Shanks, Homer Simmons, Jack Steele, Sammy Stephens, Jim Tyree, Thurston Wright, W. G. Wooten.

1943

Joe Breeden, Bob Brunley, Omer Burgert, Merle Dinkins, Bob

Estep, Gale Fulgham, James Gassaway, Bill Geter, John Harley, Charles Heard, Elvin Jackson, Lee Kennon, Derald Lebow, Bob Mayfield, Lloyd Meinert, Homer Sparkman, Thurman Tigart, Donald Tillman, W. G. Wooten.

1944

John Austin, Omer Burgert, Max Culver, Millard Cummings, Merle Dinkins, Louis Dollarhide, Bob Estep, Bob Gambrell, Bill Hallett, John Harley, Charles Heard, Elvin Jackson, Derald Lebow, George Martin, Bob Mayfield, Tom Meason, Dick Peddycoart, Steve Sawyer, Basil Sharp, Harley Smalley, Homer Sparkman, Albert Stover, Bob Stover, Thurman Tigart, Donald Tillman, Al Vogel, Don Weir, John West, W. G. Wooten, John Wright.

1945

Bob Avent, Woody Barkett, Jim Basham, DeRoy Bergman, Bob Bodenhamer, Bob Brindley, Omer Burgert, Elmer Friday, Alan Greenburg, Joe Harrell, Everett Harvell, Howard Hawkins, Jim Hill, Bill Huffman, Lester Jensen, Gerald Lovell, Aubrey McCall, Alfred Needs, Gayl Pair, Gene Preston, Roy Rhodes, Joe Richardson, Carl Schreiner, Henry Schreiner, Basil Sharp, Cliff Stone, Tommy Tallchief, Thurman Tigert, Donald Tillman, Jack Venable, Al Vogel, John West.

1946

John V. Allsup, Dee Andros, Plato Andros, Boyd Bibb, George Brewer, Paul (Buddy) Burris, Eddy Davis, Merle Dinkins, Max Fischer, Warren Giese, Bobby Goad, Joe Golding, Myrle Greathouse, Gene Heape, John Husak, Edward Kreick, Norman McNabb, Jack Mitchell, Bill Morris, LeRoy Neher, Jim Owens, Homer Paine, John Rapacz, Darrell Royal, Charles Sarratt, George Thomas, Pete Tillman, Nute Trotter, Jim Tyree, Wade Walker, David Wallace, Stan West.

1947

John V. Allsup, Dan Anderegg Jr., Frankie Anderson, Dee Andros, Bob Bodenhamer, George Brewer, Paul (Buddy) Burris, Eddy Davis, Merle Dinkins, Charles Dowell, Max Fischer, Bobby Goad, Myrle Greathouse, Earl Hale, Laddie Harp, John Husak,

Wilbur (Buddy) Jones, Edward Kreick, Leon Manley, Jack
Mitchell, William Morris, Jim Owens, Homer Paine, Kenneth
Parker, John Rapacz, Darrell Royal, Charles Sarratt, George
Thomas, Pete Tillman, Kenneth Tipps, Nute Trotter, Jim Tyree,
Wade Walker, David Wallace, Stan West, Curtis Wright.

1948

Frankie Anderson, Dee Andros, Claude Arnold, Bob Boden-
hamer, George Brewer, Paul (Buddy) Burris, Charles Dowell,
Bob Ewbank, Bobby Goad, Tommy Gray, Myrle Greathouse,
Leon Heath, Joe Horkey, Wilbur (Buddy) Jones, Ed Lisak,
Reese McGee, Norman McNabb, Leon Manley, Clair Mayes,
Leslie Ming, Jack Mitchell, Harry Moore, Alfred Needs, Jim
Owens, Homer Paine, Kenneth Parker, Lindell Pearson, Bill
Remy, Darrell Royal, Dean Smith, George Thomas, Pete
Tillman, Kenneth Tipps, Nute Trotter, Wade Walker, Stan West,
Truman Wright.

1949

Frankie Anderson, Dee Andros, Claude Arnold, Bob Boden-
hamer, George Brewer, Bert Clark, J. W. Cole, Charles Dowell,
Bobby Goad, Gene Heape, Leon Heath, Dick Heatly, Joe
Horkey, Wilbur (Buddy) Jones, Nolan Lang, Ed Lisak, Jack
Lockett, Norman McNabb, Leon Manley, Delton Marcum, Clair
Mayes, Harry Moore, Jim Owens, Kenneth Parker, Lindell
Pearson, Bill Price, Darrell Royal, Dean Smith, Fred Smith,
George Thomas, Kenneth Tipps, Wade Walker, Jim Weatherall,
Stan West.

1950

Frankie Anderson, Claude Arnold, Bill Beckman, Melvin Brown,
Sam Carnahan, Tom Catlin, Bert Clark, J. W. Cole, George
Cornelius, Eddie Crowder, Joe Cunningham, Tommy Gray,
Merrill Green, Leon Heath, Dick Heatly, Joe Horkey, Jerry
Ingram, Art Janes, Wilbur (Buddy) Jones, Kay Keller, Ed Lisak,
Jack Lockett, Norman McNabb, Buck McPhail, Clair Mayes,
Harry Moore, Alfred Needs, John Reddell, Ed Rowland, Frank
Silva, Dean Smith, Fred Smith, Billy Vessels, Jim Weatherall.

1951

Sam Allen, Carl Allison, Hugh Ballard, Billy Bookout, Dick

Bowman, Max Boydston, Kurt Burris, Chet Bynum, Gene Calame, Tom Catlin, Bert Clark, George Cornelius, Bill Covin, Eddie Crowder, Jim Davis, Dick Ellis, Bob Gaut, Joe Gaynor, Jack Ging, Larry Grigg, Darlon (Doc) Hearon, Dick Heatly, Jerry Ingram, Art Janes, John (Buddy) Leake, Jack Lockett, Buck McPhail, Roger Nelson, John Reddell, J. D. Roberts, Ed Rowland, Jack Santee, Frank Silva, Fred Smith, Jack Van Pool, Billy Vessels, Jim Weatherall.

1952

Sam Allen, Carl Allison, Dick Bowman, Max Boydston, Don Brown, Melvin Brown, Kurt Burris, Chet Bynum, Gene Calame, Tom Catlin, George Cornelius, Eddie Crowder, Jim Davis, Dick Ellis, Bob Ewbank, Bob Gaut, Jack Ging, Merrill Green, Larry Grigg, Darlon (Doc) Hearon, Auston Ingram, Jerry Ingram, Kay Keller, Lester Lane, John (Buddy) Leake, Buck McPhail, Gene Mears, Roger Nelson, Ray Powell, John Reddell, J. D. Roberts, Ed Rowland, Jack Santee, Billy Vessels.

1953

Carl Allison, Virgilee (Bo) Bolinger, Dick Bowman, Max Boydston, Don Brown, Melvin Brown, Kurt Burris, Robert Burris, Gene Calame, Tom Carroll, Jerry Donaghey, Jack Ging, Duane Goff, Merrill Green, Larry Grigg, Darlon (Doc) Hearon, Bob Herndon, Kay Keller, John (Buddy) Leake, Emery Link, Wray Littlejohn, Bob Loughridge, Gene Mears, Joe Mobra, Cecil Morris, Roger Nelson, Pat O'Neal, J. D. Roberts, Milton Simmons, Jack Van Pool, Calvin Woodworth.

1954

Carl Allison, John Bell, Virgilee (Bo) Bolinger, Max Boydston, Don Brown, Kurt Burris, Robert Burris, Gene Calame, Tom Carroll, Gene (Buddy) Cockrell, Bob Darnell, Robert Derrick, Tom Emerson, Duane Goff, Ed Gray, Wayne Greenlee, Jimmy Harris, Bob Herndon, John (Buddy) Leake, Wray Littlejohn, Delbert Long, Bob Loughridge, Tommy McDonald, Gene Mears, Joe Mobra, Cecil Morris, George Nelson, Ken Northcutt, Jay O'Neal, Pat O'Neal, Tommy Pearson, Bill Pricer, Milton Simmons, Bob Timberlake, Jerry Tubbs, Robert Van Dee, Calvin Woodworth.

1955

Hugh Ballard, John Bell, Virgilee (Bo) Bolinger, Robert Burris, Bill Brown, J. Henry Broyles, Bob Darnell, Robert Derrick, Carl Dodd, Tom Emerson, Duane Goff, Ed Gray, Wayne Greenlee, Ken Hallum, Jimmy Harris, Fred Hood, Doyle Jennings, Bill Krisher, Benton Ladd, Delbert Long, Bob Loughridge, Tommy McDonald, Joe Mobra, Cecil Morris, Dennit Morris, Ken Northcutt, Jay O'Neal, Buddy Oujesky, Bill Pricer, Byron Searcy, Dale Sherrod, Don Stiller, Billy Sturm, Clendon Thomas, Bob Timberlake, Jerry Tubbs, Calvin Woodworth.

1956

David Baker, Hugh Ballard, John Bell, Bill Brown, J. Henry Broyles, Lynn Burris, Ross Coyle, Dale DePue, Robert Derrick, Carl Dodd, Tom Emerson, Ed Gray, Dick Gwinn, Bill Harris, Jimmy Harris, Bob Harrison, Lonnie Holland, Doyle Jennings, Steve Jennings, Bill Krisher, Benton Ladd, Jim Lawrence, Delbert Long, Tommy McDonald, Bob Martin, Dennit Morris, Jay O'Neal, Buddy Oujesky, John Pellow, Roland Powell, Bill Pricer, Joe Rector, David Rolle, Jakie Sandefer, B. W. Scott, Byron Searcy, Dale Sherrod, Don Stiller, Clendon Thomas, Bob Timberlake, Jerry Tubbs.

1957

David Baker, Chuck Bowman, Bobby Boyd, Dick Carpenter, Dick Corbitt, Ross Coyle, Jim Davis, Carl Dodd, Jere Durham, Prentice Gautt, Dick Gwinn, Bob Harrison, Brewster Hobby, Mickey Jackson, Doyle Jennings, Steve Jennings, Bill Krisher, Benton Ladd, Jim Lawrence, G. A. Lewis, Edward (Wahoo) McDaniel, Billy Jack Moore, Dennit Morris, Don Nelson, Ken Northcutt, Buddy Oujesky, Jerry Payne, John Pellow, Joe Rector, David Rolle, Jakie Sandefer, B. W. Scott, Byron Searcy, Dale Sherrod, Cloyd Shilling, Don Stiller, George Talbott, Clendon Thomas, Jerry Thompson, Bennett Watts.

1958

David Baker, Bobby Boyd, Dick Carpenter, Jimmy Carpenter, Dick Corbitt, Bob Cornell, Ross Coyle, Jim Davis, Jere Durham, Richard Evans, Jimmy Feagan, Prentice Gautt, Dick Gwinn, Bob Harrison, Ronnie Hartline, Brewster Hobby, Jackie Holt,

Steve Jennings, Mickey Johnson, Vernon Lang, Jim Lawrence, Gilmer Lewis, Edward (Wahoo) McDaniel, Billy Jack Moore, Max Morris, Benton O'Neal, Jerry Payne, John Pellow, Joe Rector, David Rolle, Jakie Sandefer, Robert Scholl, Cloyd Shilling, Jerry Thompson, Jerry Tillery, Stan Ward, Ben Wells, Marshall York.

1959

Paul Benien, Bobby Boyd, Lester Bradley, Jim Byerly, Dick Carpenter, Bob Cornell, Tom Cox, Glenn Cunningham, Jim Davis, Prentice Gautt, Ronnie Hartline, Brewster Hobby, Jackie Holt, Mickey Jackson, Vernon Lang, Bill Levonitis, Gilmer Lewis, Phil Lohmann, Mike McClellan, Edward (Wahoo) McDaniel, Karl Milstead, Billy Jack Moore, Bob Morford, Bob Page, Jerry Payne, Ronny Payne, Jared Rowe, Robert Scholl, Jerry Thompson, Jerry Tillery, Bill Watts, Bennett Watts, Billy White, Marshall York.

1960

Paul Benien, Jim Byerly, Jimmy Carpenter, Duane Cook, Bob Cornell, Tom Cox, Leon Cross, Monte Deere, Donald Dickey, H. O. Estes, Claude Hamon, Ronnie Hartline, Dale Keadle, Vernon Lang, Wayne Lee, Phil Lohmann, Mike McClellan, Billy Meacham, Karl Milstead, Brent Morford, Max Morris, James Parker, Ronny Payne, Dale Perini, Elton Salmon, Melvin Sandersfeld, John Tatum, Jerry Tillery, Bennett Watts, Billy White, Bill Winblood, Gary Wylie, Marshall York.

1961

Richard Beattie, John Benien, Paul Benien, Virgil Boll, Jimmy Carpenter, Duane Cook, Jackie Cowan, Tom Cox, Leon Cross, Samuel Davis, Monte Deere, Jimmy Gilstrap, Claude Hamon, Richard Inman, George Jarman, Paul Lea, Wayne Lee, Phil Lohmann, Mike McClellan, James McCoy, Karl Milstead, Bob Page, Ronny Payne, Dale Perini, Jerry Pettibone, Bennie Shields, George Stokes, John Tatum, Loyd Geary Taylor, Bill Van Burkleo, Dennis Ward, Billy White, Bobby Wyatt, Gary Wylie.

1962

Virgil Boll, Allen Bumgardner, Newt Burton, Glen Condren,

Duane Cook, Leon Cross, Monte Deere, Bud Dempsey, John
Flynn, John Garrett, Jimmy Gilstrap, Bert Gravitt, Jim Gris-
ham, Ron Harmon, Bill Hill, Paul Lea, Alvin Lear, Wayne Lee,
Joe Don Looney, Charles Mayhue, Rick McCurdy, Ed McQuar-
ters, Butch Metcalf, Ralph Neely, Bobby Page, Bill Pannell,
Larry Pannell, Jim Parker, Jimmy Payne, John Porterfield,
Lance Rentzel, Melvin Sandersfeld, Wes Skidgel, Norman Smith,
George Stokes, John Tatum, Larry Vermillion, David Voiles,
Dennis Ward, Gary Wylie.

1963

Marion Bayles, Virgil Boll, Gordon Brown, Larry Brown, Allen
Bumgardner, Newt Burton, Glen Condren, Jackie Cowan,
Teddy Dodson, John Flynn, John Garrett, Jerry Goldsby, Jim
Grisham, John Hammond, Ron Harmon, Bill Hill, George
Jarman, Carl McAdams, Rick McCurdy, Ed McQuarters, Charles
Mayhue, Butch Metcalf, Ralph Neely, Bobby Page, Tommy
Pannell, John Porterfield, Lance Rentzel, Mike Ringer, Carl
Schreiner, Larry Shields, Wes Skidgel, Norman Smith, George
Stokes, Robert Vardeman, Larry Vermillion, David Voiles.

1964

Mike Base, Gordon Brown, Larry Brown, Allen Bumgardner,
Vernon Burkett, Gregory Burns, Newt Burton, Bill Carlyle,
Glen Condred, Rodney Crosswhite, Ron Fletcher, John Garrett,
Jerry Goldsby, Jim Grisham, Ed Hall, John Hammond, Ben
Hart, Ray Haynes, Alan Henderson, Bill Hill, Jon Kennedy, Carl
McAdams, Rick McCurdy, Ed McQuarters, Charles Mayhue,
Butch Metcalf, Ralph Neely, Bobby Page, Tommy Pannell,
Lance Rentzel, Jim Riley, Mike Ringer, Eugene Ross, Carl
Schreiner, Larry Shields, Norman Smith, Bill Thomas, David
Voiles.

1965

Mike Base, Gordon Brown, Larry Brown, Vernon Burkett, Mike
Burns, Wes Butts, Gene Cagle, Bill Carlyle, Bob Craig, Rodney
Crosswhite, Stan Crowder, Larry Crutchmer, Bob Flanagan,
Rick Goodwin, Ed Hall, John Hammond, Ben Hart, Ray
Haynes, Alan Henderson, Stan Henderson, Bob Kalsu, Jon
Kennedy, Don Kindley, Gene Knight, John Koller, Mark

Kosmos, Granville Liggins, Carl McAdams, Tommy Pannell, Joe
Poslick, Jim Riley, Mike Ringer, Bobby Robinson, Eugene Ross,
Ron Shotts, Bob Stephenson, Robert Vardeman, Phil Wether-
bee, Ron Winfrey.

1966

Boots Bagby, Paul Bagwell, Steve Barrett, Byron Bigby, Jim
Burgar, Rickey Burgess, Vernon Burkett, Gene Cagle, Bob
Craig, Rodney Crosswhite, Stan Crowder, Larry Crutchmer,
Don Davis, Rick Goodwin, Ed Hall, Gary Harper, Ben Hart, Ray
Haynes, Alan Henderson, Ricky Hetherington, Harry Hettmann-
sperger, Eddie Hinton, Jim Jackson, Bob Kalsu, Jon Kennedy,
Don Kindley, John Koller, Mark Kosmos, Granville Liggins,
Fred Malone, Randy Meacham, Dick Paaso, Thurman Pitchlynn,
Joe Poslick, Jim Riley, Bobby Robinson, Eugene Ross, Ron
Shotts, Bob Stephenson, Tom Stidham, John Titsworth, Mike
Vachon, Bob Warmack, Ron Winfrey, Charles Williams.

1967

Rick Baldridge, Steve Barrett, Byron Bigby, Jim Burgar, Wes
Butts, Gene Cagle, Bob Craig, Larry Crutchmer, Bo Denton, Bill
Elfstrom, Jim Files, Rick Goodwin, Joe Grayson, Gary Harper,
Mike Harper, Eddie Hinton, Bob Kalsu, Joe Killingsworth,
David King, John Koller, Ed Lancaster, Granville Liggins,
Randy Meacham, Ken Mendenhall, Wayne Nelson, Steve Owens,
Dick Paaso, Joe Pearce, Don Pfrimmer, Joe Poslick, Ron Shotts,
Bob Stephenson, Bruce Stensrud, John Titsworth, Mike
Vachon, Bob Warmack, Gordon Wheeler, Steve Zabel.

1968

Rick Baldridge, Johnny Barr, Steve Barrett, Byron Bigby, Larry
Bross, Jim Burgar, Steve Casteel, Gary Chrisman, Bo Denton,
Bruce Derr, Bill Elfstrom, Jim Files, David Frazer, Gary Harper,
Mike Harper, Ricky Hetherington, Eddie Hinton, Gary Jamar,
Joe Killingsworth, Joe Kusiak, Ed Lancaster, Jim Linn, Larry
MacDuff, Fred Malone, Randy Meacham, Ken Mendenhall,
Wayne Nelson, Charles Newton, Steve Owens, Dick Paaso, Joe
Pearce, Don Pfrimmer, Forb Phillips, Jack Porter, Mickey
Ripley, Jerry Sims, Bruce Stensrud, Steve Tarlton, Bobby
Thompson, John Titsworth, Bob Warmack, John Watson, Steve
Zabel.

1969

Steve Aycock, Rick Baldridge, Johnny Barr, Roy Bell, Steve Casteel, Gary Chrisman, Lionell Day, Bruce DeLoney, Bruce Derr, Jeep Dewberry, David Dillingham, Bill Elfstrom, Darryl Emmert, Jim Files, Alger Flood, Kevin Grady, Mike Harper, Mike Hawpe, Jerry Hetherington, Ricky Hetherington, Montford T. (Monty) Johnson III, Joe Killingsworth, Glenn King, Bob Klitzman, Joe Kusiak, Vince LaRosa, Larry MacDuff, Edd McGehee, Everett Marshall, Rick Mason, Ken Mendenhall, Jack Mildren, Mike Mullen, Danny Noles, Geoffrey Nordgren, Steve O'Shaughnessy, Steve Owens, Joe Pearce, Forb Phillips, Jack Porter, Albert Qualls, Mickey Ripley, John Shelley, Jerry Sims, Bruce Stensrud, Garry Swanson, Steve Tarlton, Nelson Todd, John Watson, Steve Zabel.

1970

Steve Aycock, Gary Baccus, Roy Bell, Tom Brahaney, Steve Casteel, Albert Chandler, Gary Chrisman, Leon Crosswhite, Lionell Day, Bruce DeLoney, Bruce Derr, Jeep Dewberry, Mark Driscoll, Darryl Emmert, Willie Franklin, Kevin Grady, Pete Halfman, Raymond Hamilton, Jon Harrison, Montford T. (Monty) Johnson III, Ken Jones, Vic Kearney, Glenn King, Vince LaRosa, Everett Marshall, Rick Mason, Jack Mildren, Jon Milstead, Derland Moore, Danny Mullen, John Nicholson, Geoffrey Nordgren, Steve O'Shaughnessy, A. G. Perryman, Forb Phillips, Greg Pruitt, Albert Qualls, Larry Roach, Dan Ruster, Tommy Saunders, John Shelley, Steve Shotts, Jerry Sims, Mike Smith, Ron Stacy, Steve Tarlton, Dean Unruh, John Watson, Joe Wylie.

1971

Steve Aycock, Roy Bell, Tom Brahaney, John Carroll, Albert Chandler, Leon Crosswhite, Lionell Day, Max Dayton, Bruce DeLoney, Jeep Dewberry, Steve Dodd, Mark Driscoll, Darryl Emmert, Eddie Foster, Willie Franklin, David Geren, Raymond Hamilton, Jon Harrison, Robert Jensen, Ken Jones, Phil Jordan, Vic Kearney, Glenn King, John McLaughlin, Mike McLaughlin, Everett Marshall, Jack Mildren, Jon Milstead, Derland Moore, Danny Mullen, Geoffrey Nordgren, Steve O'Shaughnessy, Harold Paul, Kenith Pope, Clyde Powers, Greg Pruitt, Albert

Qualls, Larry Roach, Dave Robertson, Dan Ruster, Tommy Saunders, Lucious Selmon, John Shelley, Ron Stacy, Ricky Stokes, Mike Struck, Nelson Todd, Dean Unruh, Tim Welch, Joe Wylie.

1972

Neil Acker, Jerry Arnold, Gary Baccus, Tom Brahaney, Dennis Buchanan, Paul Bunge, Grant Burget, John Carroll, Gary Carter, Albert Chandler, Leon Crosswhite, Kyle Davis, Steve Dodd, Eddie Foster, Rick Fulcher, Gary Gibbs, Pete Halfman, Raymond Hamilton, Mike Hawpe, Wayne Hoffman, Randy Hughes, Pat Hussey, Kerry Jackson, Robert Jensen, Ken Jones, Vic Kearney, Durwood Keeton, John McLaughlin, Mike McLaughlin, Jon Milstead, Derland Moore, Danny Mullen, Bill Orendorff, Tinker Owens, Kenith Pope, Clyde Powers, Greg Pruitt, Gary Rhynes, Larry Roach, Dave Robertson, John Roush, Kleyn Russell, Dan Ruster, Tommy Saunders, Dewey Selmon, LeRoy Selmon, Lucious Selmon, Rod Shoate, David Smith, Mike Struck, Jim Taylor, Dean Unruh, Joe Washington, Ron Waters, Tim Welch, Joe Wylie.

1973

Drake Andarakes, Jerry Arnold, Gary Baccus, John Barresi, Bob Berg, Bill Brooks, Anthony Bryant, Dennis Buchanan, Grant Burget, Steve Calonkey, Waymon Clark, Glenn Comeaux, Steve Davis, Kyle Davis, Tony DiRienzo, Steve Dodd, Jimbo Elrod, Chez Evans, Eddie Foster, Rick Fulcher, Gary Gibbs, Scott Hill, Wayne Hoffman, Randy Hughes, Pat Hussey, Durwood Keeton, Kirk Killion, Jim Littrell, Jaime Melendez, Richard Mildren, Obie Moore, Tinker Owens, Tony Peters, Kenith Pope, Clyde Powers, John Roush, Clyde Russell, Dewey Selmon, LeRoy Selmon, Lucious Selmon, Rod Shoate, E. N. Simon, David Smith, Ricky Stokes, Mike Struck, Jim Taylor, Jamie Thomas, Eric Van Camp, Joe Washington, Ron Waters, Terry Webb, Tim Welch, Brad White, Gary Young.

ACKNOWLEDGMENTS

I am grateful to the many coaches and players whose co-operation made this book possible.

Special acknowledgment goes to Harold Keith for his book, *Oklahoma Kickoff*; Volney Meece for his book, *Thirteen Years of Winning Oklahoma Football*; John Keith, OU sports publicist; and Mrs. Addie Lee Barker, OU sports information assistant, who provided invaluable assistance in gathering material.

And a special thanks goes to Kolm von Rauenwald (Pica), my 16-year-old miniature schnauzer who spent many an hour sleeping by my desk during the writing of this book.